INSIDE
BASEBALL

TEAMS, TRADITIONS, AND PLAYERS

GREG GARBER

PRINCIPAL PHOTOGRAPHER: BILL HARRINGTON

FRIEDMAN/FAIRFAX
PUBLISHERS

A FRIEDMAN/FAIRFAX BOOK

©1994 by Michael Friedman Publishing Group, Inc.

ISBN 1-56799-062-2

Editor: Sharon Kalman
Designer: Robert W. Kosturko
Photography Researcher: Daniella Jo Nilva

Typeset by BPE Graphics
Color separations by Kwong Ming Graphicprint Co.
Printed and bound in China by Leefung-Asco Printers Ltd.

The publisher wishes to acknowledge that extensive attempts have been made to ensure that this book be as accurate and up to date as possible at press time.

For bulk purchases and special sales, please contact:
Friedman/Fairfax Publishers
15 West 26th Street
New York, NY 10010
212/685-6610   FAX 212/685-1307

Dedication

For Emily and Gerry, who endured an endless summer of baseballese.

Acknowledgments

Many thanks to the baseball men who gave their time to this project, usually without complaint, particularly: Phil Niekro, Tommy John, Don Mattingly, Mookie Wilson, Keith Hernandez, Dwight Gooden, Ozzie Smith, Jose Oquendo, Whitey Herzog, George Brett, Wade Boggs, Rick Cerone, Rich Gedman, Dwight Evans, Mike Schmidt, Don Baylor, Dan Quisenberry, Luke Appling, Eddie Mathews, Nolan Ryan, George Toma, Don Sutton, Larry Bowa, A. Bartlett Giamatti, Willie Wilson, Carl Yastrzemski, and Harvey Greene. And sincerest gratitude to these students of the game: Claire Smith, Bob Sudyk, Steve Buckley, and Jack O'Connell of the *Hartford Courant*; Bruce Lowitt of the *St. Petersburg Times*; John Delery of the *Morristown Record*; and Bill Guilfoile of the Baseball Hall of Fame. Finally, thanks to Bill Harrington for superb photographs and rare persistence, and Michael Friedman Group editor Sharon Kalman for continuing support.

© W. T. Harrington

TABLE OF CONTENTS

CHAPTER 1

THE GAME OF BASEBALL

The hopeless Red Sox fan shifts uneasily in his chair and acknowledges that this year's Boston entry, the team that has failed to win the World Series every season since 1918, may well fall short again. In a strange way, this kind of consistency seems to comfort him. And in an even more strange and wonderful way, it is fitting that Angelo Bartlett Giamatti, the former president of Yale University, the man who once said, "All I ever wanted to be was the president of the American League," was briefly the commissioner of the great American pastime. "Baseball," Giamatti wrote in a 1978 essay for the *Hartford Courant*, "is about going home and how hard it is to get there and how driven is our need. It tells us how good home is. Its wisdom says you can go home again, but that you cannot stay. The journey must always start once more, the bat an oar over the shoulder, until there is an end to all the journeying."

The metaphor, obvious as it is, works. Baseball, the only truly timeless sport among the major leagues of football, basketball, and hockey (the clock never ticks on the diamond), has been with us since the turn of the century. As a result, this peculiar journey has produced more legend and lore, miracle and myth, than any other athletic pursuit. Writers and movie makers have always

been drawn by the game's lyrical grace, its compelling combination of grit and geometry. Baseball's universal appeal isn't just based on its history. Every fan can see himself at the plate, hurling a crackling Nolan Ryan fastball over the hulking Green Monster at Fenway Park in Boston. This is because we can see baseball players for what they are: In most cases, they are mortal-sized men whose emotions are not obscured by high-tech equipment. The sight of Bob Boone—still the best overall catcher in baseball—playing cards in the Royals' clubhouse at the age of forty-one is vaguely reassuring. When former Met Lee Mazzilli, thirty-four, started his day in the clubhouse with a cup of coffee like many frazzled commuters, well, then everything is alright with the world.

"It's a very nice-paying job, considering the hours we put in," says former Yankee pitcher Tommy John, whose twenty-six seasons represent the standard of this century. "This is not exactly sheer hell. Sure, it's a living, but it's always been a game." In 1988, the average baseball player made $438,000 a year, and the major league teams set an overall attendance record of 28,499,636. Even with ticket prices spiraling, America is still buying into the game of baseball. This says a lot about its basic, enduring structure.

It is safe to say that these Philadelphia Athletics made something less than $438,000 per man, per year.

Baseball Hall of Fame

Baseball Hall of Fame

ORIGINS OF THE GAME

The line between invention and appropriation is a fine one indeed. There are references in English literature to "Base ball" as far back as the early eighteenth century, and though baseball clearly resembles "Rounders," a boys' game that flourished in Great Britain early in the nineteenth century, it is distinctly American. It's merely a question of which American was most responsible. Rounders was played with a soft, stuffed ball that was thrown at base-runners to record an out. "Town Ball" in America was played with a harder ball that traveled farther when hit; runners were tagged out by fielders. A distinguished panel of experts (the Mills Commission) was commissioned by sporting goods magnate Albert G. Spalding in 1905 to determine when and where the village green sport began to evolve into twentieth-century baseball. The Mills Commission findings suggested that one Abner Doubleday was responsible.

Doubleday later went on to West Point and eventually served in the Mexican and Civil Wars. As a captain, he fired the first gun for the Union forces at Fort Sumter, South Carolina. It was Abner Graves, a friend of Doubleday's, who convinced the commission that baseball was born in Cooperstown, New York, in 1839. According to Graves, Doubleday modified the game of Town Ball, a contest that involved twenty to forty boys who chased balls hit by a "tosser." Doubleday drew a diamond-shaped field with a stick, then limited the number of players, added bases, and came up with the

idea of a pitcher and catcher. That's the way the Mills Commission saw it.

Seven years later, on June 19, 1846, the first organized game of baseball took place on the Elysian Fields in Hoboken, New Jersey. Alexander Cartwright, a local surveyor, provided a set of slightly different rules for two amateur teams, the New York Nine and the Knickerbockers. There were ninety feet between the bases, nine innings of play, and three outs per inning. And though the New York Nine won a laugher, 23-1, no one was giggling twenty-three years later when Cincinnati, hungry for a winner, put together the first group of baseball professionals. Harry Wright, head of a local amateur team, was paid $1,200 to manage and play center field for the Red Stockings. Wright's brother George played shortstop and the roster was stocked with talented veterans eager to play for pay. The barnstorming Red Stockings were an enormous success, recording fifty-six victories and one tie in fifty-seven games in 1869. Then, on June 14, 1870, the Red Stockings met the Brooklyn Atlantics on the Capitoline Grounds. The Atlantics scored three runs in the bottom of the eleventh inning to win 8-7 and the Red Stocking's dominance had ended. After a series of losses, the franchise folded in a sea of red ink. Yet, Cincinnati had established a new standard of excellence.

One year later, the National Association of Professional Baseball Players was formed by ten men of vision during a meeting at Collier's Cafe at New York's Broad-

In the bucolic setting of the Elysian Fields in Hoboken, New Jersey, baseball was first played in an organized fashion. In 1846, outfield fences and exploding scoreboards were still a few years away.

Baseball Hall of Fame

Above: *The Brooklyn Atlantics (circa 1864) were a part of the early baseball landscape.*

Right: *As a captain in the Union Army, Abner Doubleday fired the first gun at Fort Sumter. His contribution to baseball was equally epic; it was Doubleday who invented the idea of a diamond, the bases, the pitcher, and catcher.*

way and 13th Street on St. Patrick's Day. Franchises were placed in Boston, Massachusetts; Chicago, Illinois; Cleveland, Ohio; Fort Wayne, Indiana; New York, New York; Philadelphia, Pennsylvania; Rockford, Illinois; and two in Washington, D.C. The Philadelphia Athletics ran away with the title, winning twenty-two of twenty-nine games. In 1875, when accusations of gambling and corruption undercut public support, the National Association fell apart. One year later, a businessman named William A. Hulbert formed the National League. He reasoned that with better management,

Baseball Hall of Fame

baseball could flourish. Hulbert lured several important players from the defunct league, such as the aforementioned Albert Spalding and Čap Anson. In 1881, a rival league surfaced when Cincinnati, forced from the National League for playing games on Sunday, joined forces with leaders in Pittsburgh to form the American Association. The two leagues competed bitterly for fans, with the American Association slashing the admission price from 50 to 25 cents. Finally, in 1883, National League President A.G. Mills called a truce and a National Agreement was signed that called for a postseason championship game and other player contract protections.

For twenty years, professional baseball went through more radical changes, with names and places changing almost on a yearly basis. Eventually, the Western Association changed its name to the American League, and in 1903 the National League joined forces with the American out of economic necessity. The first World Series was played after the season and the American League's Boston Red Sox beat the Pittsburgh Pirates of the National League five games to three. That series, which was arranged solely by the two teams, was not repeated in 1904. The Red Sox repeated their American League win that season and issued a challenge to the New York Giants, winners of the National League pennant. The Giants refused on the grounds that formal rules and centralized supervision should govern a series of such importance. New York Giants President John T. Brush outlined a proposal that was adopted starting in 1905.

THE NATIONAL BASEBALL HALL OF FAME

Baseball Hall of Fame

Baseball Hall of Fame

You can find the ragged old baseball that started it all, the Doubleday Baseball, in an appropriate place of honor here. Nearly 100 years after Doubleday outlined the game in Cooperstown, a baseball belonging to his old friend Graves was discovered along with other relics of the game in the attic of a nearby Fly Creek, New York, farmhouse. Stephen Clark, a wealthy Cooperstown resident, purchased the ball for five dollars and displayed it in a room at the Village Club. With the help of National League President Ford Frick, Kenesaw Mountain Landis (baseball's first commissioner), and American League President William Harridge, Clark and other local leaders secured the funding to build the National Baseball Hall of Fame, a permanent shrine to the game. The Hall of Fame was dedicated on June 12, 1939, in a celebration that coincided with Cooperstown's baseball centennial. The first class of inductees selected by the Baseball Writers Association of America consisted of Ty Cobb, Walter Johnson, Christy Mathewson, Babe Ruth, and Honus Wagner. All eleven of the living inductees participated in the dedication ceremonies, and baseball finally had a shrine to house its vast store of tradition.

The treasures on view at Cooperstown are breathtaking. In the portrait gallery are bronze plaques of each of the 201 enshrinees. Babe Ruth and Ted Williams stand bat in hand and eerily lifelike in sculptures by the talented Armand LuMontagne. Turnstiles, dugouts, and grandstand seats from some of the great old parks like Forbes Field, the Polo Grounds, and Ebbets Field capture baseball's past beautifully. There are exhibits for sluggers Babe Ruth and Hank Aaron, a World Series Room, a wide-ranging baseball card display, a terrific collection of uniforms, and a staggering number of baseballs—most of them autographed, of course.

Baseball Hall of Fame

The stuff of legend: The balls, bats, busts, and lifelike wax figures of baseball heroes are on display at the Baseball Hall of Fame in Cooperstown, New York.

THAT'S THE WAY THE BALL...

Here is the beauty and mystery of baseball: At age forty-six, Nolan Ryan couldn't begin to explain why his fastball still smoked in at ninety-two miles an hour, while Phil Niekro still has no idea how the knuckleball that won him 318 major league games actually worked. "I've been doing it practically forever," Niekro says, "and I have no idea."

Baseball is a time-honored sport that lends itself almost too easily to cliches, perhaps because they are simply too true. After a tough 2-1 loss, Joe Morgan used to sit in his manager's office at Fenway Park and painfully recount the slow-rolling grounder that crept through the infield and cost him the game. "That's the way the ball bounces, men," he would say in his folksy New England accent. "Baseball's a game of inches."

It is a game that stays with you, whether you're a fan or a player. After he retired in 1968, the New York Yankees' Mickey Mantle had a recurring nightmare. "The worse one is, I go to the ballpark late, jump out of a cab, and I hear the public address system," he says. "I try and get in, and all the gates are locked.

Then I see a hole under the fence and I can see Casey looking for me, and Yogi and Billy Martin and Whitey Ford. I try to crawl through the hole, and I get stuck at the hips. And that's where I wake up sweating."

Some players are never quite able to escape the game's grip. Niekro is one. Instead of retiring to fishing in the Florida sunshine, Niekro is a roving pitching instructor for the Atlanta Braves franchise he served so well for twenty seasons. "I've been exceptionally lucky, no doubt about it," says Niekro. "Sure I won 300 games, but more importantly, I've made a lot of friends. I've flown the best jets, stayed at the best hotels, eaten good meals. I've made a good living and enjoyed myself. I haven't had an operation in thirty years. The odds are stacked against you. . . . Look at all the kids who play ball in high school, in the American Legion, the colleges. You play a boys' game, then get four months vacation.

"I can ask any man I talk to if he'd like to change jobs, and without batting an eyelash, he'll say yes. What more can you say than that?"

Nolan Ryan (below, left) and Phil Niekro (below, right) can't always explain the subtle mechanics of their pitching. Barry Bonds (opposite page), the best player in baseball in the early 1990s, won the National League's Most Valuable Player award in 1990 and 1992.

© W. T. Harrington

If batters were permitted to hit the cover off the ball as they were in the old days, you could observe the complicated composition of the baseball.

© W. T. Harrington

THE BASEBALL

On the surface, a baseball is merely a simple white sphere bound together with red stitching, five ounces in weight, and nine centimeters in circumference. Truly it is the object of this great game, but it also has been the subject of vast speculation over the years. No baseball official or manufacturer has ever acknowledged what many players and managers believe: that the liveliness of the baseball has been tampered with to meet the needs of the day.

"I don't care if anyone admits it or not," says Mets pitcher Dwight Gooden. "The ball is juiced."

"In 1987, they told us the balls weren't juiced up," says St. Louis manager Whitey Herzog, a slightly less partial observer since he doesn't throw baseballs for a living. "It was a joke."

You could look it up. In 1984, the last season under Commissioner Bowie Kuhn, major leaguers hit 3,258 home runs. In 1987, there were 1,200 more, making it the biggest home run season in history. And the players who hit those home runs seemed to suggest that something else beyond four-baggers was up. A total of 171 players hit 10 or more homers in 1987, and ninety-four of them had their career highs. A year later, the 10-homer club was approximately half as large.

In 1987, Joe Niekro wrote to his brother Phil in their book of correspondences, *The Niekro Files:* "I swear the ball is juiced up. I've seen a lot of home runs, long home runs. You expect the big hitters—Mattingly, Winfield, Murray, Rice—to go deep, but little guys are hitting balls the opposite way and to straightaway center. If they don't watch it, a pitcher is going to get seriously hurt, the way the ball jumps off the bat."

The theory as advanced by pitchers, many who tend toward paranoia, is this: A loaded baseball leads to more home runs, which in turn puts more people in the seats. The argument makes a fair amount of sense, since major league records in homers and attendance were set in 1986. When home runs dramatically increased again, attendance followed, moving from 47

million to 52 million. As it turns out, the baseball has been evolving since the game began.

The so-called dead-ball era ended in 1909, when Ben Shibe invented the cork center. In 1920, Babe Ruth hit 54 home runs in his first season with the Yankees, reopening the debate. By that time, baseballs were made with finer wool that, when wrapped more tightly because of improved production methods, seemed to travel farther. The livelier ball and the outlawing of the spitball combined to lift batting averages by forty-five points from 1915 to 1925. While a total of 384 home runs had been hit in 1915, major leaguers belted 1,565 in 1930.

Then a second dead-ball era became evident in the late 1960s, when pitchers dominated the game. Bob Gibson of the St. Louis Cardinals and Denny McLain of the Detroit Tigers both reached the World Series that year—hardly a coincidence. McLain led the American League with a 31-6 record, an .838 winning percentage, and 28 complete games. McLain was one of seven major league pitchers with an earned-run average under 2.00 Gibson, 22-9, led the entire majors in ERA with a phenomenal 1.12 figure (Luis Tiant of the Cleveland Indians was a distant second with a 1.60). Gibson also led all National Leaguers with 13 shutouts and 268 strikeouts. Boston's Carl Yastrzemski led the American League with a paltry .301 batting average and San Francisco's Willie McCovey led the Nationals with 36 home runs. By 1970, Tom Seaver of the New York Mets was the only pitcher who could produce an ERA of under 3.00—a 2.81 figure. At the same time, Yastrzemski hit .329 and finished second in the American League to Alex Johnson of the California Angels by percentage points. Johnny Bench, who hit 45 home runs that season, was one of six National Leaguers to surpass McCovey's 1968 homer total. Naturally, players were suspicious. They called it the rabbit ball.

Recently, players have used the rabbit ball as a handy excuse for any increase in home runs. "I think the ball started getting juiced up right after the strike of 1981," said pitcher Tommy John. "I thought it was their way of getting rid of the bitter taste, letting the ball jump over the fence."

The Rawlings people, who have supplied baseballs to the major leagues since 1977, deny the accusations, just as Spalding did during its 100-year tenure as supplier. How, exactly, does one liven a baseball? First, a little physics background. The technical term for liveliness is the coefficient of restitution (COR). This is a fancy way of describing a baseball's energy. The scientists measure the COR by aiming a ball at a steel plate at 88 feet per second, the approximate speed of a Mark Langston fastball. The energy retained by the ball as it caroms off the plate is the COR. The official specifications of organized baseball insist that a ball's COR fall between the range of .53 and .57, which simply means the ball should retain between 53 and 57 percent of its energy. Of course, your results may vary at home. Certainly, informal ballpark tests have revealed some inconsistencies.

The recipe for a conventional big-league baseball is as follows: A cushion-cork center is placed in a thin rubber housing. Six-ply gray yarn (80 percent virgin wool) is next wrapped by machine around the cork, followed by four-ply white yarn (75 percent wool), three-ply gray yarn (80 percent wool), five-ply white cotton thread, and a final wrapping of synthetic thread. The leather cover is hand-sewn, requiring precisely eighty-eight stitches. The tighter a ball is wrapped, presumably, the farther it will fly.

"Somebody," says John, "is doing a whole lot of tighter wrapping, I kind of wish I pitched in the old dead-ball days. They played with a ball until the cover came off. Think what that would have done for my ERA."

Luke Appling, the old Chicago White Sox shortstop who hit a total of 45 home runs in 20 seasons, sighs. "Man," he says, shaking his head, "what I could have done with this ball they use today. It's like hitting a rock. They might have called me 'Babe.'"

This five-ounce baseball looks innocent enough, but it is the stuff of which controversies are made. Pitchers are convinced it is juiced up; hitters, strangely enough, beg to differ.

THE BAT

The wooden baseball bat, as we know it today, could soon go the way of the giant redwood trees. Even now, they are fossils of a sort.

As Peter Gammons reported during the 1989 season for *Sports Illustrated*, it is possible the major leagues may replace wooden bats with aluminum by the turn of the century. As Jack Hillerich, the third-generation president of Hillerich & Bradsby, maker of the famed Louisville Slugger, told Gammons. "I certainly see a time in the not-too-distant future when everyone will be using some alternative bat—aluminum, graphite, or some composite. A wood bat is a financially obsolete deal. If we were selling them for $40 apiece instead of $14 or $16.50 [the company's price for minor league and major league bats], then we'd be making a sensible profit. But we aren't. We can't charge that much. The time will come when even the majors will use aluminum or graphite.

"While once we were making seven million wood bats a year for all levels of baseball, now we're making a million-and-a-half, 185,000 of which go to the major leagues. Major leaguers want specific orders, so we make three orders [of one dozen bats each] for one player, then shut down the operation. Then we make three more for another player, and shut it down. That's impractical, and it's highly expensive."

The fact of the matter is that aluminum bats last a lot longer than their wooden counterparts. Recognizing the opportunity to save college athletic programs thousands of dollars, the National Collegiate Athletic Association approved aluminum bats for use in 1974. Generally, a college player can use an aluminum bat over the course of the entire season. The trickle-down can be

Courtesy Hillerich & Bradsby/photo by Lin Caulfield

Above and right: *For a few more seasons, at least, baseball bats will be crafted the old-fashioned way: a piece of flawless white ash turned on a lathe.* **Opposite page:** *The bat is the hitter's tool of the trade; his scalpel, his baton. For that reason, it must be constructed to his exact specifications. Unfortunately, the cost involved may lead to the extinction of the wooden bat.*

Courtesy Hillerich & Bradsby/photo by Lin Caulfield

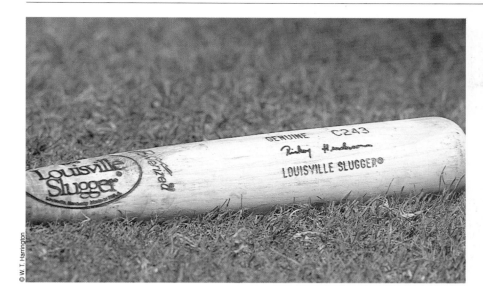

seen on the high school and Little League levels. Because of its status, the major leagues have always had leverage on the bat companies, including Hillerich & Bradsby, Worth, Rawlings-Adirondack, and Cooper. That seems to be changing. Companies have difficulty filling annual orders that can approach thirty- and forty-dozen bats per player made of white ash.

Like the baseball, bats have undergone some changes over the years. Generally speaking, the old-timers swung heavier bats. Babe Ruth, the "Sultan of Swat," used a stick worthy of the game's all-time leading slugger. He never used a bat lighter than forty ounces and reportedly experimented with bats weighing up to fifty-two ounces, probably the heaviest used by any major leaguer. Hank Greenberg, Jimmie Foxx, and Hack Wilson wielded thirty-eight to forty-two-ounce bats in their day. As the game evolved, hitters learned that bat speed had just as much to do with distance as bat weight . . . maybe more. Ted Williams used a thirty-five-inch bat that weighed between thirty-two and thirty-three ounces. Frank Howard, the old Washington Senators slugger who stood six-foot-seven and weighed 260 pounds, used to start the season with a thirty-four-ounce bat, then adjust to the fatigue of the season with a thirty-three-ounce. He finished with a bat that weighed an even two pounds.

"The first rule in picking out a bat," says Hall of Famer Carl Yastrzemski, "is comfort. When you stand at the plate facing a pitcher who can throw anything from a fastball to a breaking ball over any part of the plate, you won't hit him if you can't get comfortable." The bat Yaz used most often, interestingly enough, was named for another Red Sox fielder—a thirty-four-inch Ted Williams Louisville Slugger model.

Today's hitters, even the celebrated home run hitters, usually favor a thirty-one- or thirty-two-ounce stick. "You want something that you can get around on the ball with," says Mets third baseman Howard Johnson, a notorious fastball hitter. "Sure, you want the bat to be big enough to get the job done, but you have to be able to control it through the strike zone. I've swung some of those heavy bats, and I don't know how those old guys did it."

Purists worry that the more powerful aluminum bats and their increased sweet spots will make it impossible to compare eras. Others, like Boston's Wade Boggs, see them as another step in baseball's logical evolution. Boggs, for instance, thinks aluminum bats will allow another hitter to follow Williams with a .400 season. Unfortunately for Boggs, he probably won't be that hitter. Aluminum bats on the major league level are probably at least a decade away.

THE BASEBALL CARD

The card-carrying public is less concerned with the market value of, say, a Kent Hrbek or a David Cone, than with who it will bring in a trade.

The nine-year-old boy opens his thick baseball card book and shows off the cards his father collected thirty-five years before him. There is a Mickey Mantle, circa 1960, a Carl Yastrzemski, with bat poised menacingly. The boy knows all the names and numbers of these players before his time, and though he ticks off the value of each card, money is not the issue here. No, this book is about baseball and its rich tradition; it is about fathers and sons and daughters. The boy moves toward the back of the book and points proudly to his cards. Here is Jose Canseco of the Oakland A's, a member of the forty-forty club (homers and stolen bases) in 1988. There is the Baltimore Orioles' Cal Ripkin (six cards of smiling Ripken faces, in fact), a personal favorite. Even Don Mattingly of the hated New York Yankees is enshrined in this personal Hall of Fame.

Baseball cards (and the stale gum that comes with them) have been an integral part of the game for the better part of a century. While Mantle and Canseco now command some $15,000 for signing autographs at a baseball card show, you can still get a pack of cards for around fifty cents. With a little foresight and a lot of luck you can parlay that into a small fortune. If you scoffed up a Mickey Mantle rookie card by Bowman in 1951 and it is in mint condition today, you are sitting on a $5,500 property. The 1952 Mantle is a $13,000 prop-

"I would say the large majority of collectors are fans. Probably 20 percent couldn't care less about baseball, but they recognize that somewhere in all this cardboard is something that's going to appreciate. This thing has exploded. On a Sunday you can go to six or seven card shows within a short drive of Hartford."

Indeed, the cards produced by Topps, Fleer, and Bowman, among others, make for a $250 million industry. Cards picture the players in fairly typical poses and provide career information on the back. A new entry in the market, Score baseball cards, are already acknowledged as the best. The players are seen in riveting color action shots and a former *Sports Illustrated* writer writes the flip-side notes.

McQueen, a genial, moustachioed man, is asked if he thinks the collecting craze will continue. "Yes," he says. "Forever. Every year kids get introduced to baseball—Little League, Babe Ruth, peewees, juniors, midgets. And there's generally somebody that makes them want to model after a ballplayer, and that gets them interested in cards. There's a new crop every year. Plus, parents are closet collectors. They love to play with cards. They love to help put them in numerical order and make up the want lists. We have them standing in here by the hour going through our boxes, filling out their sets. And that's one of the better parts of this, because you could stay in here all day and spend $2.50. Saturdays and Sundays, especially during the summer, this place hops. It's wall-to-wall people."

The fervor that collectors bring to the table—such as this fan of Ty Cobb (left)—is staggering.

osition. Most fans collect cards for the pure enjoyment, but Chic McQueen of BCD Cards in East Hartford, Connecticut, says investment is also a factor.

"A lot of times those dovetail, but not necessarily," he says at the counter of his store, surrounded by nearly three-quarters of a million cards. "I mean, there's not really a lot of enjoyment in plunking down $400 for a baseball card, but I'm sure in the back of everybody's mind is 'This card is going to appreciate.' If it isn't, why would people buy cardboard for that kind of money?

THE EVOLUTION OF THE UNIFORM AND EQUIPMENT

No sector of the economy is safe from foreign intervention. Like the automobile market, standard American manufacturers are being threatened by Japanese imports. In baseball, equipment makes the man. Here are some moderately low-cut stirrups (opposite page, above left), completely appropriate for a conservative, middle-America Kansas City Royals infielder.

Opposite page, below: *More so than any other player, the catcher's equipment is his lifeline.*

Baseball Hall of Fame

he socks are the clue. Look at a major leaguer's socks and you can see into his personality, his voting record, his past. "The more conservative the look, the better," says New York Mets pitcher Ron Darling, a Yale man. "That's why I wear my socks so low. Me and [Yankee third baseman Mike] Pagliarulo like our socks real low. We're both from Massachusetts and we believe in the hard-working, nothing-fancy work ethic. I like to think of myself as a Puritan, or maybe a Calvinist in a baseball uniform." Players who wear their socks high tend to lean a little more to the left. Or maybe it just seems that way.

Baseball fans tend to take the entire baseball uniform for granted—but then, they don't have to go to work in it. Players seem to take it quite seriously, even down to the science of the wearing of accessories. Outfielder Fred Lynn made a public stink one season when he discovered the Baltimore Orioles' uniforms were without belts. Eventually, the Birds brought belts back. "Historically, the best uniforms are the Yankees', Dodgers', and Cardinals'," says pitcher Tommy John, who wore both pinstripes in New York and Dodger Blue in his long big league career. "But the greatest of all time may have been those old baggy Milwaukee Braves uniforms with the tomahawk across the front. What a wonderful uniform."

Commercial artist Marc Okkonen discovered in a five-year project that the last eighty-nine years of major

Baseball Hall of Fame

league baseball have produced nearly 3,000 different uniforms. The Chicago White Sox, he noted, have worn fifty-six significantly different uniforms since the turn of the century. There have been some truly bad ideas over the years in the continuing evolution of the uniform. A. G. Spalding dressed his White Stockings in a different colored cap for each position, an idea that one observer suggested made the team look like "a Dutch bed of tulips." For nearly a decade in the fifties and sixties, the Cincinnati Reds wore sleeveless shirts. The Pittsburgh Pirates and Cleveland Indians jumped on the bandwagon temporarily before the fashion trend died an abrupt death. And then there was the unfortunate psychedelic period when the Oakland Athletics wore a gruesome gold and kelly green combination in the 1970s. The Houston Astros took the field in a hideous orange conflagration and the San Diego Padres developed a uniform whose primary color was brown.

Generally speaking, the uniform has become more streamlined over the years. Long and baggy flannel shorts and trousers have given way to aerodynamic double-knit polyester. At the same time, the equipment has become more and more high-tech. The catchers masks on display at Cooperstown show that the mask hasn't changed much; Fred Thayer's padded cage circa 1876 looks very much like Carlton Fisk's 1988 version.

The glove has undergone the greatest change. "When I played, we had a little thing that was only a couple of inches beyond my fingers," remembers Hall of Fame shortstop Luke Appling. "The things they got today are huge. It's a wonder they drop anything." In truth, today's gloves are relatively massive. In the late nineteenth century, players sometimes wore two light gloves that resembled skiing mitts. By the turn of the century a padded heel and a webbed thumb were added. First-baseman's mitts came in around the 1920s, the three-fingered mitt rose to prominence in the 1950s before giving way to today's conventional four-fingered mitt. Luckily, equipment has escaped much of the fickle change brought on uniforms.

The emergence of the Orioles in 1989 after their disastrous season the year before was linked to a minor league system that provided a wealth of young talent. Actually, it was probably the critical uniform decision the team made regarding its mascot, the Baltimore Oriole. For years, a cartoon version of the Oriole—a sort of smug yet compelling caricature in orange and black—adorned the players' caps. In 1989, the Birds unveiled an ornithologically correct version of the Baltimore Oriole and their fortunes soared. There's no accounting for taste.

HISTORY'S CHANGEUPS

Count George Toma (right), the legendary groundskeeper, as a fan of real grass. He made his reputation cultivating the green stuff, but he scrubs and vacuums the artificial turf without too many complaints.

There was a time when baseball was always played on a field of dreams. To this day, there are lush, green pastures in places like Anaheim, California, Chicago, and New York. Yet recently, grass has given way to a series of insidious artificial surfaces. Blame the folks in Houston and the research chemists at Monsanto. On April 12, 1965, the Houston Astrodome was unveiled as the Eighth Wonder of the World. Purists quietly suggested that the more accurate phrase was Eighth Blunder of the World. Since there was a roof on the place, grass didn't have a chance. AstroTurf, management reasoned, was the logical answer.

Presently, artificial turf can be found in ten of the major leagues' twenty-eight ballparks; the average is a distressing .428 (6 for 14). "Players hate artificial turf," says legendary groundskeeper George Toma, who grooms the faux grass at Royals Stadium in Kansas City. "It's hard, it doesn't drain well at all and the tobacco and gum get stuck in it all the time. We scrub it, wash it, and vacuum it, but it doesn't always come clean. And the bounces. . . . The ball just zooms off the stuff like a trampoline. George Brett worries about his family jewels on the turf. That's never a problem on grass."

Since there are rarely bad bounces on artificial turf, fielding averages generally have improved; however, the baseball does pick up unnatural speed when it skips off

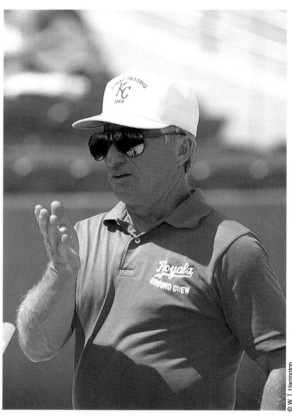

the surface. Consequently, balls that can be reached (barely) in natural grass by infielders slip through for singles. Outfielders have to play deeper to cut off hits to the gaps that might otherwise be doubles and triples. And then there is the wear and tear artificial turf inflicts on players' muscles and joints. "As I get older, I notice the body aches you get with artificial grass," says St. Louis reliever Dan Quisenberry. "It changes the game subtly. For one thing, it takes away some of the aggressiveness you see on grass; guys don't seem to dive as much on the turf because you get rug burns. And you have to be a better bunter on turf because of the speed. It takes a great bunt to move the runner over. From a pitcher's standpoint, the turf sets up more double-play balls because the ball gets to the infielder faster."

Cardinals teammate Willie McGee is typical of the team manager Whitey Herzog has fielded to take advantage of the carpet at Busch Stadium. McGee is a swift, wide-ranging outfielder with a mediocre arm at best. At the plate, he is a slashing hitter with a career average of .295. It is instructive that he has more career triples (69) than home runs (46). "Every manager has his style of play," McGee says. "And Whitey's is speed. It's because of the artificial turf. Speed is a good asset here. Since I'm fast, I guess I like it."

Of course, many purists object to artificial turf because it fundamentally changes the way the game is played, thus making it difficult to compare different eras in baseball. Would McGee have led the National League in hitting in 1985 with a .353 mark (and 18 triples) if he'd been playing on grass? "I don't know," McGee says at length. "I'd like to think so, but I don't know."

Baseball has changed physically, beyond the new, slick surfaces, the advent of the designated hitter, and the increasing specialization of pitchers. Players are, in fact, bigger, stronger, and generally in better shape than their predecessors. "You used to go home after the season and not pick up a baseball for a few months. You just relaxed," says 300-game winner Phil Niekro. "It used to take an organization six weeks to get guys in shape. Now they're doing it in three weeks at the outside because they're working too hard at home. You come to spring training and they're checking your weight, your body fat, and prescribing special diets."

The old-timers will tell you that money is the big difference in the game today. This may be because they didn't earn much when they were playing. "The owners have changed things," says Niekro. "They're giving in to the players by giving them the big money. And that's changed players' attitudes. There's so much at stake now, guys won't play hurt like they used to. There are more guys on the disabled list than ever before. When I played, you were always afraid of guys behind you. You couldn't afford to be on the disabled list for two, three, five weeks. Maybe the whole work ethic in America has changed; the day's work for the dollar just isn't the same." It could be argued, however, that the dollar isn't the same, either.

"Most starting pitchers today feel they only have to get into the sixth inning," says Larry Bowa, longtime shortstop, briefly the manager of the San Diego Padres and now the third-base coach for the Philadelphia Phillies. "They think they've done their job. They're saying, 'The reliever's getting paid a million dollars, that's his job to finish up.'"

Luke Appling, a Hall of Fame shortstop with a .310 career average, says, "I hit .388 [in 1936], and I held out two weeks the next season to get $20,000. But the money is only part of it. They're greedy today, they all want to hit home runs. Every guy up is trying to hit the 400-foot sign. I could have hit twenty-five homers a

year, too, but my average would have been .220. Instead of stroking the ball, hitters are jumping and lunging at the ball. That's no way to hit."

Eddie Mathews, a Hall of Fame third baseman with 512 lifetime home runs, adds, "They've taken the instinct from the players now. The finer points aren't learned anymore. Coaches have to yell at guys, tell the cutoff man where to stand, which base to throw to. These are things you should already know."

Indeed, the game's subtler side has gone largely unmined by today's marquee ballplayers, who can command more than $5 million for a season of work. "No one knows enough about this game that they can't bust their butt," Niekro says. "When you think you know a lot about this game, you've got problems. We used to sit around the clubhouse and hash plays out, talk about what we did in certain situations. Organizations were more close-knit then. That was the best thing about baseball: the clubhouse atmosphere. Now, players don't get together in the clubhouse, they don't sit around and drink beer and fool around. How many guys do you see in the clubhouse after a game?"

Many of the complaints voiced by veterans are merely reflections of general changes in society. "I think the area that's most different is the respect for veteran players and management," says Bowa. "You used to earn your stripes, but now kids come up and expect everything. I had a rookie come up to me—he was wearing something like number 65 and wasn't necessarily going to make the team. Right in the middle of spring training, he asks about taking his girlfriend on road trips. Do you believe that?"

Blessedly, some things never change. At the turn of the century most batters were right-handed, which discouraged the use of left-handed catchers. It was simply easier for righties to maneuver behind the plate and throw runners out on the bases. Well, now that left-handers have gradually closed the gap on righties, there is still a dearth of left-handed catchers. On May 14, 1989—Mother's Day—Benny Distefano of the Pittsburgh Pirates became only the third lefty catcher in the major leagues since 1902. He caught the ninth inning of a 5-2 loss to the Atlanta Braves and joined the Chicago Cubs' Dale Long (1958) and Mike Squires of the 1980 Chicago White Sox. Why are southpaw catchers so rare? "I couldn't tell you," says Pirates manager Jim Leyland. "Baseball's always been conservative, slow to change. There must be something to it, but I haven't figured out what."

At the Kansas City Royals' spring training complex, Toma gets the best (and worst) of both worlds with an artificial infield and a grass outfield.

VERSATILITY KNOWS NO (BO)UNDS

Ah, to be Bo Jackson (below, right and opposite page, above), a star in both baseball and football. Even the majestic flight of a high foul ball he hits bears watching. Deion Sanders (below, left) has raised two-sport participation to a new level. In one day in 1992, he played for the Atlanta Braves and the Atlanta Falcons.

Baseball has always welcomed players with varied skills. An athlete with a pair of soft hands and weak bat can make it as a utility infielder. In the American League, those who can hit but field with the grace of the original Tin Man come under the heading of designated hitter. And then there are gifted players like Bo Jackson and Jose Oquendo.

Mostly because people said he wouldn't, Jackson wasted the Tampa Bay Buccaneers' first overall draft choice in 1986 by opting instead to play baseball for the Memphis Chicks. Jackson, a six-foot-one, 225-pound world-class sprinter, had rushed for 4,303 yards at Auburn University and won the 1985 Heisman Trophy. After batting .277 at Memphis and striking out 81 times in 184 at-bats, Jackson came to his senses. He decided he wanted to play big-league baseball *and* football. The Kansas City Royals of the American League and the Los Angeles Raiders of the National Football League couldn't find a good reason to argue. After hitting a Royals record of 22 home runs for a rookie, Jackson joined the Raiders late and made a memorable 91-yard touchdown run against Seattle on Monday Night Football. "There's nothing physical about

sports," Jackson says. "Handle it in the mind and everything else will take care of itself. If I set my mind to doing something, I get it done. I know how my mind works. It's all determination and how big your heart is." Not to mention your biceps and shoulders.

In 1988, Jackson made a number of scintillating catches in left field and threw out eleven runners on the bases. He also became the first Royals player ever to hit 25 home runs and steal at least 25 bases (27) in a single season. In a 1989 spring training game, Jackson turned around a pitch by Boston's Dennis "Oil Can" Boyd and it traveled over the massive scoreboard at Boardwalk and Baseball in Baseball City, Florida. The ball landed in a pile of sand some 518 feet away from home plate. A few days later, Jackson hit a more routine home run off the scoreboard. It went only 410 feet. And though he has struck out nearly 40 percent of the time in his brief career, Jackson is nothing if not exciting to watch.

Deion Sanders of the Atlanta Braves and Atlanta Falcons made a splash in the early 1990s when he played with great success for both teams. On one memorable day in 1992, Sanders returned kicks and

played cornerback for the Falcons against the Miami Dolphins at Joe Robbie Stadium, then flew to Pittsburgh to play in the National League Championship Series against the Pirates.

Jose Oquendo, on the other hand, is a fairly unspectacular player. All he does is play every position a manager could want—literally. In 1987, the St. Louis Cardinal infielder (more often than not) started at seven positions, with the exception of pitcher and catcher. Still, he made relief pitching appearances both seasons, and in 1988 caught the first inning of his career. The last National Leaguer to play all nine positions in a season was another Cardinals player, Gene Paulette, in 1918. "I have four different gloves," Oquendo says. "Every time I called Rawlings, they didn't want to talk to me."

A shortstop/second baseman by trade, Oquendo took the mound on May 14, 1988, and became the first non-pitcher in twenty years to record a decision, since New York Yankees outfielder Rocky Colavito got eight Detroit Tiger batters out. Oquendo worked the last four innings of the Cardinals' nineteen-inning loss to the Atlanta Braves, going three scoreless frames before allowing two runs in the top of the nineteenth. On September 24 of that year, he caught the seventh inning of a 14-1 loss to the New York Mets. "I had a good time," he said after the game. "Gary Carter was talking to me and I was trying to distract him for a change. I was telling Tim Teufel to be ready because I didn't know what was coming. It was weird because you're so low. Everybody looks like a giant.

"Pitching is different. I throw a fastball, and I might be able to throw a couple of split-fingers. And I don't know if you can call it a slider, but it does something. Atlanta was struggling, which is probably why I lasted so long. Dale Murphy grounded to second base, and I struck out Rick Mahler with a split-finger. I had a real good time pitching, but I hope it doesn't happen again. If it does, it means we're losing or out of players."

Left: *The Cardinals' Jose Oquendo is less spectacular; he only plays one sport, but all nine positions.*

SCREWBALLS AND ASSORTED OFF-SPEED DELIVERIES

Maybe it's all that free time, or the endless stream of bad clubhouse food, or the fact that baseball is a game for kids. For whatever reason, baseball has always attracted more than its share of skewed personalities. Take Luke Appling, the Hall of Fame shortstop for the Chicago White Sox. "One day, Luke asked the White Sox for a bunch of baseballs and they wouldn't give them to him," relates Boston Red Sox manager Joe Morgan. "That day in the game, he fouls off thirty-three pitches into the stands, and then he says, 'There, that will show them.'"

Today's champion of the bizarre is Dave LaPoint, the lefthander (naturally) who has pitched in Milwaukee, St. Louis, San Francisco, Detroit, San Diego, Chicago, Pittsburgh, and New York. When he lined up for the Yankees on Opening Day, 1989, 27 percent of the major leagues' 624 players could claim him as a former current teammate. The only team without an ex-teammate was the Baltimore Orioles, and even they had two players that LaPoint had been traded for—pitcher Mark Thurmond and catcher Bob Melvin. "I definitely lead the league in teammates," LaPoint says. "People ask me what I'm going to do after my career is over, and I tell them I have eight years of old-timers games to attend. I could play in almost every park. My son is five, and he's already been in six father-and-son games. The good thing about it is that I don't have to write a lot of Christmas cards. I've been traded so often that I usually know ten or fifteen guys in every clubhouse." This from the man who told then-Vice President George Bush during a visit to the Pirates' clubhouse, 'Hey, I really like your beer."

Even Roger McDowell, the Philadelphia Phillies' off-center relief pitcher and the man of a thousand masks—from Richard Nixon to King Kong—admits he isn't in LaPoint's league. "I concede," he says. "I wouldn't even try to top some of the stuff he's done." LaPoint's best pranks borrow from baseball's grand tradition, including the classic hotfoot. "My best was against Lance McCullers," LaPoint says. "We were both with the Padres then, and I got him in the dugout between innings, and it was really going when he got up to go to the mound. When it hit him, he flung his shoe right off. It was like a fireball. It shot into the air and fell in front of [manager] Steve Boros. He was a lunatic, screaming and cursing. I stayed in the runway a long time before coming back into the dugout because I knew he knew who did it."

Another LaPoint favorite is the simple (yet delicate) tobacco-spitting gag. "I make it a point to hit the shoes of every one of my teammates at least once each season," La Pointe says. "The only time I got in trouble was when I pulled it on Steve Garvey in San Diego. His face turned red, and the veins in his neck stuck out. He grabbed me and put me in a bear hug that nearly made me pass out. Here was the All-American boy strangling me as he very quietly said, 'I don't like that.'"

Baseball, as Joe Garagiola, among others, has observed, is a funny game. In 1988, California Angels manager Cookie Rojas saw his team grow so frustrated that he installed a punching bag in the dugout runway. It didn't help. The Angels set a club record with twelve consecutive defeats to end the season. The Cardinals' Tom Brunansky has fooled teammates and reporters with a bloody false thumb pierced by a large nail. "I

Right: *Roger McDowell was the incarnation of a living, breathing Japanese horror film when he pitched for the New York Mets.* **Far right:** *Former Los Angeles Dodgers pitcher Don Sutton was one of baseball's legendary practical jokers. Here, he attempts to relieve fellow pitcher Mike Garman of his bat.*

© W. T. Harrington

© AP/Wide World Photos

realize that baseball should be played for fun," says the outfielder. "There is a lot of money and some big pressures involved, but things don't go as well if you forget that it's played for fun."

Pitcher Rick Sutcliffe likes to lure unsuspecting teammates onto the field and then signal the groundskeeper to turn on the grass sprinklers. Relief pitcher Jesse Orosco welcomed free agent Kirk Gibson to the Los Angeles Dodgers during 1988 spring training by smearing his cap band with black shoe polish. Gibson was furious, failing to see the humor.

Andy Van Slyke, the Pittsburgh Pirates' center fielder, can play baseball. In 1988, he hit .288 with 25 home runs and 100 runs batted in, and threw out twelve runners on the bases. . . . Oh, and he also leads the league in good quotes. "The biggest adjustment from the minor leagues to the majors," he says, "is learning how to spend the $45 in meal money a day." Early in his career, Van Slyke played third base, prompting him to critique his glovework, "It was like Teflon. You know, the no-stick surface. They called me Brooks. Mel Brooks."

In some ways the essence of baseball is knowing how to have a ball.

© W. T. Harrington

THE THINKING MAN'S GAME

A few years ago, Mookie Wilson, then a thirty-four-year-old center fielder for the Toronto Blue Jays, was talking about the impertinence of his youth. "When I was twenty-five, I used to go up to the plate just hacking," he said, smiling. "I didn't care what the count was, who was on base, what the pitcher's strengths and weaknesses were. I just hacked. Now, it's 'What's he throwing today? Will the baserunner force him to throw the fastball? Was he just showing me the slider, or will he come back with it?' I've learned to conserve my energy; I used to stand out there and shag every fly I could get to. Now, I just chase the balls I have to. When you're young, you think you know the game, but you really don't. If I knew then what I know now . . ."

Wilson grimaced as he pulled on his spikes; his back was a little tender. Yet, even with ten seasons of mileage on his trim body, he was arguably a better ballplayer than he was in his first or second year, essentially because after all that time he became an appreciably smarter player. Baseball is an exercise in mental gymnastics, which explains why Phil Simms, quarterback of the National Football League's New York Giants, is described as venerable and, well, old at the age of thirty-three, while Wilson, at the age of thirty-four, was still viewed as a relative youngster by the game's considerable over-forty population.

Certainly the relaxed pace of the game is more conducive to older players. Instead of football's sixteen absolutely critical games, the eighty-two-game schedule of basketball or the eighty-game hockey season, major leaguers play some thirty spring training games, then another 162 over the course of regular season. That reduces the sense of urgency on a daily basis.

"If we had to get up for every baseball game like we did for football, we'd barely last two years," says former Red Sox right fielder Dwight Evans, a high school flanker. "The intensity is radically different."

Aside from an occasional close play at the plate, rolling slides at second base, outfield collisions, and the routine pain endured by catchers behind the plate, baseball is not exactly a contact sport. Players last longer, and as they persevere, their experience and intelligence can sometimes compensate for the deterioration of physical skills.

This explains how Tommy John survived in the big leagues past his forty-sixth birthday, how Phillies' third baseman Mike Schmidt pushed past forty, how George Kenneth Griffey, Sr., age thirty-nine, could play for the Cincinnati Reds in 1989 while his son, Ken Jr., broke in with the Seattle Mariners the same year. Just don't call Ken Sr. "Pops." "Yeah, I get that stuff all the time now," the elder Griffey says. "No, I don't give Kenny too many tips. He never listens to anything I say."

Ken Griffey, Jr., and Ken Griffey, Sr. (opposite page), became the first father-and-son teammates in the major leagues when they both played for Seattle. These days, Ken Jr. is a Mariners star and his father is a coach for that team. Griffey Sr. (below, left) and Tommy John (below, right) both learned to survive on guile when time began to erode their talents.

CHAPTER 2

THE CONFRONTATION

© W. T. Harrington

Nolan Ryan (left) *and Tommy John* (opposite page) *represent the wide spectrum of pitching philosophies. Ryan throws one of history's greatest heaters; John, whose fastball was slower than Ryan's, changed speeds with precision.*

THE PITCHER

Tommy John, who was the oldest player in the major leagues, is leaning back on a stool in the New York Yankees' Fort Lauderdale, Florida, spring training clubhouse. The left-hander, who turned forty-six on May 22, 1989, was still pushing men half his age for a job. He survived more than a dozen managers, a ruptured ligament in his throwing elbow that required ground-breaking surgery (a tendon from his right forearm was used in the successful reconstruction), and the inexorable gravity of time itself. This is because he understands intimately the delicate craft of pitching.

"Speed," he muses at length, "is not necessary for the way I pitch. Changing speeds is what's important; it's the essence of pitching.

"That's why they have all these old-timers to teach the young studs who throw the ball ninety miles an hour how to change speeds. Sooner or later, every pitcher, if he's going to hang around, has to learn how to really pitch. Pitching is ninety-five percent thinking and five percent talent. Most guys out there are just throwing the ball. You say to yourself, 'I'll throw this one hard and in, this one slow and away, run this one back in again. Believe it or not, I have more quality pitches now than I did when I won twenty games for the Dodgers in 1977. I was getting by on a sinker and a curve then. Now I've got a slider, a little forkball and a changeup to go with them.

"You hear the guys up in the [broadcast] booth saying, 'Geez, he got the guy swinging on a curveball that was fifty-two miles an hour.' Well, it was fifty-two because it was supposed to be. If the fastball was only seventy-six, it was for a reason. My fastball gets clocked around eighty-four now, but there are still people in baseball who think I can play. And I happen to be one of them. I won't know when it's time to go, but the hitters will. As long as the ball still sinks and the curve breaks, you've got a chance to get them out."

As he says this, John is enthusiastically popping his throwing hand into his Wilson A2002 glove like a rookie. This was to be his twenty-sixth and final major league season, tying him with Deacon McGuire, who played catcher for twelve teams in three different leagues around the turn of the century, for the most major league seasons played. In 1988, John won nine of seventeen games and struck out 81 batters, his highest total since 1979. With 287 career victories and 46 shutouts, John was the winningest active pitcher in the majors, ahead of Nolan Ryan and Bert Blyleven. Though Yankees manager Dallas Green opposed owner George Steinbrenner's training camp invitation to John, he eventually rewarded him with the 1989 Opening Day start against Minnesota—a game he would win with an assortment of well placed off-speed pitches. John became the oldest pitcher ever to win an opening-game assignment. "I still think I'm right, that forty-five-year-

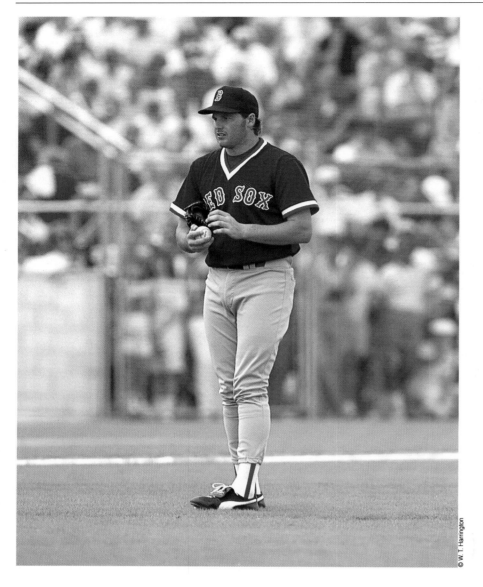

© W. T. Harrington

The Boston Red Sox'
Roger Clemens, who once
struck out twenty Seattle
Mariners in a single
game, is the only pitcher
to win the Most Valuable
Player Award, the
Cy Young Award, and
the All-Star MVP in the
same season.

nine fielders placed strategically to discourage base hits. Aside from that ninety-mile-an-hour fastball, fielders are a pitcher's best friend.

"Sometimes," says New York Mets pitcher Frank Viola, "good pitching is not about striking guys out. It sounds weird, but good pitching is really making them hit the ball . . . where you want them to hit it."

Or, as Phil Niekro says, "Pitching is trying to get them to hit the ball where they don't want to." As Niekro explains it, each at-bat is a project in itself, a mental challenge that can be solved with an infinite variety of pitch combinations, taking into account respect to speed and location.

"Setting up is the whole key," says Niekro. "You start backwards. You know the guy has problems with the curveball, but how can you get to the point that he's not expecting to see it? How do you keep him off balance? Well, you go right at him with an inside fastball, then a couple of sliders away to get him leaning out over the plate. Bing. There's the curve, tight and over the inside part of the plate. He's frozen, he can't pull the trigger. He's out."

Don Sutton, another 300-game winner who endured for years on intellect (and some say an ability to doctor the ball illegally without detection), says, "There are two ways to get hitters out: You can overpower them, or you can try to throw their timing off. Most pitchers aren't blessed with guns like Dwight Gooden and Roger Clemens, so you have to mix it up all the time."

It takes time to learn the subtle patterns that work consistently, but as Tommy John points out, sooner or later the pitchers who make it begin to understand. Mark Gubicza, a six-foot-five righthander, idled along as a .500 pitcher for three years in Kansas City when the nightmare of 1987 left him looking for an alternative to his ninety-three-mile-an-hour fastball. Gubicza lost eighteen games and allowed 120 walks, the American League's third-highest total. With one month left in the season, Gubicza took some advice from the late Hall of Fame pitcher Don Drysdale. "He was trying to force it," Drysdale said. "I told him to stay back, relax, and have loose, supple wrists. I told him, 'You've got to remember to think. I can see a lot of me in you.'"

"I can't understand why it took me so long to realize it," says Gubicza, who won four of his last six starts in 1987. "But I think when I had that kind of record and

olds shouldn't be pitching in the big leagues," Green said. "How many guys can crank it up at that age? Most are lucky they can get out of bed." John's ability to succeed at the highest level, despite his relatively advanced age, was living proof that pitching is and always will be essentially mind over batter.

Pitchers like to complain about all the obstacles they have faced over the years, like the lowering of the pitcher's mound, the alleged livening of the baseball, an ever-shrinking strike zone, pulled-in outfield fences, and the disappearance of the brushback pitch as a tool of intimidation. "Over the years, everything that has come along is designed not to help the pitcher," says Rick Rhoden, who pitched for the Dodgers, Pirates, and Yankees. "It's been to hurt him."

Still, the pitcher is firmly in control of this game. He, after all, stands a mere sixty feet from the batter and knows what kind of pitch he will throw and (more often than not) where it will go. The law of averages is definitely on his side; if a hitter manages to reach base safely three times out of ten, he is considered to be a success.

What are a hitter's options when the ball comes toward him in a blur, rising, sinking, darting out of reach? He must protect the plate at all costs; any pitch that falls between the knees and the uniform letters and crosses the five-sided slab of white rubber is a strike, and the maximum allowable quota is two. The pitcher has seventeen inches of plate to work with, maybe eighteen or nineteen, depending on his reputation. Foul balls hit in the air are fair game. That leaves a ninety-degree slice of territory, guarded zealously by

300 PITCHING VICTORIES (or more)	
Cy Young	511
Walter Johnson	416
Christy Mathewson	373
Grover Alexander	373
Warren Spahn	363
Pud Galvin	361
Kid Nichols	361
Tim Keefe	342
Steve Carlton	329
John Clarkson	327
Nolan Ryan	324
Don Sutton	321
Phil Niekro	318
Gaylord Perry	314
Tom Seaver	311
Old Hoss Radbourne	308
Mickey Welch	307
Eddie Plank	305
Lefty Grove	300
Early Wynn	300

© C. Bernhardt/Allsport

I was having all kinds of trouble out there, that I realized I had to try something different. I felt I had enough talent and knew enough that I could basically do it my way. But when you're not successful, you've got to look for other alternatives."

Gubicza took Drysdale's words to heart and sliced two or three miles an hour off his fastball. As a result, the ball began to sink slightly and Gubicza started getting people out; the ball moves most when it hovers around a batter's knees. Gubicza was 20-8 with an earned run average of 2.70 in 1988 and grew into one of baseball's best young pitchers.

The operative cliche in baseball is "good pitching will beat good hitting." This is generally true. History is strewn with examples of solid pitching clubs that prevailed over teams with power at the plate. The Boston Red Sox, for instance, have traditionally been one of the major league's best-hitting teams. Question: How many World Series titles has Boston won since 1918? Answer: None. With the advent of night baseball and the uneven lighting that goes with it, pitchers have an added advantage. Even when the bats aren't firing for a team, good pitching can keep it in the game.

In the span of a week before the 1989 season, Boston's Roger Clemens, the Mets' Dwight Gooden, and the Dodgers' Orel Hershiser signed contracts that brought them more than $2.5 million a year. Today's pitching aces are at the top of the salary scale because they have the ability to dominate a game in a way that no other position can rival. Consider: A pitcher who goes the nine-inning distance records 27 outs, while the opposing cleanup hitter has only four or five opportunities. Obviously, the player on the mound is in a position to exert more influence, more often.

There is something about a good pitcher that inspires teammates. When the Mets, for instance, know that Gooden is on the mound, they feel good about their chances of winning. Statistically, they score more runs for Gooden than, say, Ron Darling or Sid Fernandez. "It's ironic," says Rick Cerone, the well-traveled catcher, "but the good pitchers get better support even though they need it less."

Former catcher Tim McCarver has a simple approach to pitching. "Concentrate on little things and don't look at everything from the hitter's standpoint," he says. "The first pitch is the biggest of any sequence. Just think about it: Hitters make their money on 1-0, 2-0, 3-1 pitches. Pitchers make their money on 1-2, 0-2 pitches. Concentrate on your strengths. Good pitching is going to get good hitting out."

As Bert Blyleven says, "You can't go out there thinking the world is against you. God gave us the ability to throw a baseball and make it to the big leagues. Just go out and do your job. Pitchers will come out ahead at the end. We always will."

Even if your name is Ty Cobb or Wade Boggs, standing in at the plate while a six-foot-four, 200-pound athlete prepares to unleash a wicked pitch in the general direction of your midsection can leave you weak. Left-handed pitchers tend to have better success with left-handed batters because their throwing arm is on the same side as the hitter. Since the hitter has a split-

The beauty of Ron Guidry, beyond his marvelous slider of course, was his consistency: He finished his career with a 170-91 record, a winning percentage of 65.

second to pick up the ball and guess what it will be doing when it crosses the plate, this is an enormous advantage for the pitcher. And when lefty meets lefty or righty meets righty, the curveball starts at the body and breaks away—if it breaks at all. Even the most disciplined hitters are not always prepared to lean into that curve on faith alone.

Gooden, whose fastball was regularly clocked at ninety-six miles an hour in 1988, says speed is not his greatest asset. He subscribes to the three rules of real estate: location, location, location. "You can throw it ninety-six miles an hour and, eventually, someone's going to hit you," says Gooden, who in his first five big league seasons produced a 91-35 record, an earned run average of 2.62, and 1,067 strikeouts. "I try to get some movement on the ball by gripping it a little different. If I can get it to sail a little, in or out, it's going to be that much harder to hit. It could be the difference between a base hit to left and a pop-up to the shortstop. I'll take a fastball with movement at ninety-four every time, as long as it goes where I want it to."

Like many pitchers, Gooden attributes much of his velocity to powerful legs. As a pitcher hurls himself off the mound and toward the plate, a strong leg drive is just as important as a live arm. Being tall doesn't hurt. The laws of physics suggest that long arms and long legs make it easier to develop speed behind a baseball. In 1989, the Montreal Expos were excited about the prospects of six-foot-ten, 225-pound rookie Randy Johnson, the tallest player in major league history, nudging Johnny Gee (who pitched for Pittsburgh and San Francisco in the 1940s) by an inch for the honor. "He doesn't look that big up there," says teammate Tim Raines. "Just about nine feet tall."

"To me, good pitching is going out every fourth or fifth day and giving it everything you have, even when you don't have your best stuff," Rick Cerone says. "Ron Guidry is the best example of that. Maybe sixty-five, seventy percent of the time not everything was working, and he still found ways to win. When the slider wasn't moving, he'd go to the curve or fastball until it came around . . . if it ever did. You don't win seventy percent of your games on stuff alone."

Actually, the number is 65 percent, based on a lifetime record of 170-91, but "Louisiana Lightning" extended his career appreciably on pure guile. He was only the second unanimous selection for the Cy Young Award in 1978, when he was 25-3 with 248 strikeouts for the New York Yankees. The hard-throwing Guidry established a major league record for winning percentage with 20 wins or more (.893). Then, seven years later, on the heels of a disastrous 10-11 season, Guidry stunned the baseball establishment with a 22-6 mark in 1985. Though Guidry, who by then was no longer a power pitcher, struck out only 143 batters that year, no American League pitcher won more games.

As former major leaguer Jim Kaat says, "Pitching is not so much a game of strength as it is a skill."

Hershiser typifies the thoughtful approach of the modern pitcher. He carries a portable computer on the road that stores information on batters' tendencies and a record of the pitches that have worked for him. In Game Two of the 1988 World Series, Hershiser carried notes about the Oakland Athletics in his back pocket. "Every inning I pitch, I get better," he says. "Every Hall of Famer, every ex-player, especially pitchers, says, 'I wish I knew then what I know now. Then I would have been so much better.' So the theory behind my whole career has been one of just being a sponge and absorbing everything I can."

And so, as long as pitching is a thinking man's enterprise, there will be craftsmen like Tommy John and

© W. T. Harrington

Tom Seaver on the mound. "Now, Seaver is a guy who knew how to pitch," says John of the man who won 311 games and struck out 200 batters or more in nine consecutive seasons, a major league record. "I remember this one game when he was pitching for the White Sox. He had really lost his good stuff by then, but he was so smart. Jose Canseco of the A's had just come up and here was this young slugger against the old veteran. The first time up, with nobody on, Canseco fisted a slow fastball over the second baseman for a hit. Next time up, he rips a curveball on a line to left for another hit. But they didn't do any damage.

"Canseco came up again in the seventh inning with two guys on base. I was standing next to Wes Stock in the bullpen and said, 'Watch this.' The first pitch really had something on it, it was a knee-high fastball. Boom. Canseco sees three straight fastballs on the outside corner, right up the ladder. The last one was in his eyes and he missed it. Seaver showed him a pitch he hadn't seen before. That, to me, is why Tom Seaver was a great pitcher. Sure, he had the great fastball, but even later in his career he got guys out by using his head."

TOP TEN CAREER FIELDING PERCENTAGE FOR PITCHER

1.	Don Mossi	.990
	Gary Nolan	.990
3.	Rick Rhoden	.989
4.	Lon Warneke	.988
	Jim Wilson	.988
	Woodie Fryman	.988
7.	Larry Gura	.986
8.	Grover Alexander	.985
9.	General Crowder	.984
	Bill Monbouquette	.984

Opposite page:

Orel Hershiser, of the Los Angeles Dodgers, never met an experience that didn't make him a better pitcher. He religiously punches notes into a portable computer he carries with him on the road. **Above:** *Like Hershiser and Roger Clemens, the New York Mets' Dwight Gooden is one of the game's highest paid pitchers. He earns better than $75,000 an outing.*

© W. T. Harrington

Above: Roger McDowell is a classic relief pitcher. His sinker is tough to hit, but his off-the-wall attitude is what gets him through the up-and-down business of wins and losses. Both Goose Gossage (opposite page, above) and Dan Quisenberry (opposite page, below) carried their respective teams.

The Relief Pitcher

From 1982 to 1985, there was no better relief pitcher in the major leagues than Dan Quisenberry. He led the American League in saves for four consecutive seasons, running up numbers of 35, 45, 44, and 37. During that time, Quisenberry appeared in 46 percent of the Kansas City Royals' games, almost always at the end of close contests.

"It's an insatiable thing," says Quisenberry, who recently retired from baseball. "You want the ball every game. The good relief pitcher says, 'Jump on my back, I'll carry you.' That's the state of mind you're in; you want the team to depend on you. When you're pitching those last two, three innings, everything's on the line.

"That's what makes us flaky. . . . That's what the buck-stops-here mentality does to you. You are the man, you're the only guy out there with the ball."

Pitchers are generally a twitching bundle of nerve endings to begin with, but relievers are truly in a different league. Remember Al Hrabosky, the Mad Hungarian? Like Quisenberry, he pitched mostly for St. Louis and Kansas City. He led the National League with 22 saves in 1975 and compiled a 13-3 record and an earned run average of 1.67. Before a particularly important pitch, Hrabosky would stroll behind the mound and scream at himself. This arresting habit did as much to psyche out the batter as it did to psych up Hrabosky. Roger McDowell, who earned his reputation as an off-center reliever with the New York Mets before joining the Philadelphia Phillies, says, "If you think about the situation you're in too much, you'll crack up. You try to relieve the stress any way you can."

In this age of growing specialization, the stopper carries the greatest burden. A manager spends most of the game maneuvering to get his bullpen ace into a close game in the eighth or ninth inning. Not only is the game usually tight, but there are often men on base. Says Lee Smith, the hulking fireballer for the St. Louis Cardinals, "The margin for error is very, very small. You have to throw strikes, and usually you can't even let them have a fly ball. Over the course of a season, that kind of pressure can eat at you."

Blame New York Giants manager John McGraw for all this heartache. The man who first brought you pure pinch hitters also began the practice of saving an arm or two for relief situations. In 1903, McGraw's first full season as manager, Roscoe Miller led the National League with all of three saves. The next year, Joe "Iron Man" McGinnity led the league with a 35-8 record and an amazing 408 innings pitched. Yet, McGraw also used his starting ace in tense late-inning situations. McGinnity was 2-0 in relief that year and recorded five saves, though the save statistic was not formalized until 1973.

More often than not, however, relievers were mop-up men who had fallen out of the starting rotation or out of favor with the manager. It wasn't until Hoyt Wilhelm reached the big leagues in 1952 that the modern reliever was born. The right-hander posted a 15-3 record for the New York Giants that season—a winning percentage of .833 that led the National League. Wilhelm also pitched in a league-high seventy-one games, none of them as a starter. After twenty-one seasons with nine different teams, Wilhelm had pitched in more games (1,070) and recorded more relief victories (123) than any pitcher in major league history. Interestingly, he started only fifty-two games over his career. Ron Perranoski made his debut with the Los Angeles Dodgers in 1961, appearing in fifty-three games, only one as a starter. Over his thirteen-year career, Perranoski appeared in 684 more games, all of them as a reliever. Three times Perranoski led the league in games and twice in saves.

As the game grew more sophisticated, managers refined their use of relievers. They used their most effective man in the final two innings and preceded him with set-up men, who would attempt to hold the fort in the middle innings if a starter faded early. From 1968 to 1985, Rollie Fingers saved more games than any man in history—some 341 for the Oakland A's, San

© John McDonough

© W. T. Harrington

TOP TEN CAREER SAVES

1. Lee Smith 398
2. Jeff Reardon 365
3. Rollie Fingers. 341
4. Goose Gossage 309
5. Bruce Sutter 305
6. Dennis Eckersley 275
7. Tom Henke. 260
8. Sparky Lyle 238
9. John Franco 236
10. Hoyt Wilhelm. 227

THE SAVE DEFINED

Qualifications for a save—the pitcher is credited with a save when he meets all three of the following conditions:
(1) he is the finishing pitcher in a game won by his club;
(2) he is not the winning pitcher;
(3) he qualifies under one of the following conditions—
    (a) he enters the game with a lead of no more than three runs and pitches for at least one inning, or
    (b) he enters the game with the potential tying run either on base, at bat, or on deck, or
    (c) he pitches effectively for at least three innings.

© AP/Wide World Photos

Diego Padres, and Milwaukee Brewers. Then came Goose Gossage and Bruce Sutter to dominate the late 1970s and early 1980s. Gossage threw pure heat while Sutter used a nasty split-finger fastball. They would finish their careers fourth and fifth, respectively, on the all-time save list behind Fingers. And then Jeff Reardon (357 saves) and Lee Smith (355 saves) blazed onto the scene in the late 1980s. You'll find Quisenberry seventh with 244 lifetime saves.

According to Quisenberry, the secret of his success was simply ignoring it. "The important thing when I was doing it was not to become captivated by it," he says. "I would try to distract myself with almost anything. You couldn't afford to focus on the game until it was about halfway over. I'd do crossword puzzles, listen to guys telling stories. There were times when I knew that if I started thinking about pitching too soon, I'd leave it in the bullpen."

The debate over where a pitcher is more valuable, as a starter or a closer, has raged for years. Some managers argue that a solid pitcher who starts 35 games and averages 200 to 300 innings a season has more impact than a reliever, even one who appears in 60 or 70 games. Others argue that quality time, specifically late innings in a close game, tips the balance to the closer. The New York Yankees moved Righetti to the bullpen in 1984 after an impressive 14-8 season that included a July 4th no-hitter over the Boston Red Sox. Righetti responded with 162 saves in the next five seasons, including an American League-high 46 in 1986. "At first I didn't like the move," Righetti says. "I liked the idea of being a starter every fifth day. Now, I think I can influence more games as a reliever. One way or another, you always have the last word out there."

TOP TEN CAREER WINS PLUS SAVES

1.	Lee Smith	.465
2.	Rollie Fingers	.448
3.	Jeff Reardon	.437
4.	Goose Gossage	.421
5.	Bruce Sutter	.373
6.	Hoyt Wilhelm	.350
7.	Sparky Lyle	.337
8.	Gene Garber	.314
9.	Dennis Eckersley	.309
10.	John Franco	.298

TOP TEN CAREER RELIEF WINNING PERCENTAGES

1.	Hugh Casey	.718
2.	Guy Bush	.683
3.	Doug Bird	.672
4.	Eddie Rommel	.662
5.	Grant Jackson	.653
6.	Mace Brown	.651
	Pedro Borbon	.651
8.	Al Hrabosky	.646
9.	Al Brazle	.641
10.	Hooks Dauss	.635

Above: *Rollie Fingers, who pitched for the Oakland A's, leads all pitchers with a total of 448 wins plus saves. He helped make it fashionable for managers to save their ace for the end of the game.*

Opposite page: *Bruce Sutter's split-finger fastball is the model for the modern game. His success was based largely on the pitch that most hitters couldn't solve.*

The Brushback Pitch

Perhaps the pitcher's biggest weapon is the very real possibility of bodily harm by a ninety-five-mile-an-hour piece of mayhem. Oh, neither pitchers nor hitters like to talk about it much, but the implied threat usually keeps hitters a respectable distance from the plate, where it is harder to be aggressive and, therefore, more successful.

In 1918, pitcher Carl Mays of the Boston Red Sox, the man with a wicked right underhand, slingshot delivery, wrote in *Baseball Magazine,* "A left-hander not infrequently shoots the ball over on the inside so that the batter has to jump back to get out of the way. But let a right-hander do the same thing and he immediately becomes branded with the reputation of being a beanball pitcher. A twirler has a perfect right to put the ball on either side of the plate. But sometimes the pitcher who is trying to nick the corner of the plate will miss it altogether. Consequently, if the batter is hugging the plate he is likely to get hit. If the left-hander is guilty, all well and good. But if the right-hander is the offender, he is lucky if someone doesn't start the fairy story of beanball pitching.

"I merely wish to say that I am not a murderer, nor do I aim to take unfair advantage of anyone. I have perfected a peculiar delivery. Due either to the freak breaks of this delivery or my desire to take the corners of the plate, I have been unfortunate enough to hit a number of batters, though very seldom in the head."

On August 16, 1920, Mays, pitching for the New York Yankees, hit Ray Chapman, the Cleveland Indians' shortstop, in the head. "Chappie made an effort to get up and charge at Mays," remembered Cleveland manager Tris Speaker, "but it appeared his body was para-

lyzed. Most always he was able to get out of the way of pitches thrown close to his head, but on this occasion he just stood still at the plate as if in a trance and made no effort to pull away from the pitch." Chapman died at 4:50 a.m. the next day and remains the only man ever killed in a major league playing accident.

Seven days after the beaning, Mays took the mound against the Detroit Tigers and blanked them, 10-0. "I didn't mean to hit him," said Mays, who finished his fifteen-year career with a record of 208-126, the fourth-best winning percentage (.623) in history, and an earned run average of 2.92. "But I had to pitch in the strike zone. That's what I was paid to do. I don't like the idea of batters digging in, right on top of the plate and almost defying the pitcher to throw on the inside corner of the plate. Any batter who does that bears equal responsibility."

To this day, pitchers and batters battle over the territorial rights at home plate.

"If you're not going to throw inside, you're not going to be a winning pitcher," says Don Baylor, who holds the major league record for being hit by a pitch with 267 career nicks. "Being hit was a part of the game, as long as they're not throwing at your head. In the old days, if you hit 40 home runs, you'd better be ready to go down sometimes. Now, hitters go crazy if the ball comes near them. Young hitters are terrified of the inside pitch."

Time was when the Los Angeles Dodgers' Don Drysdale, Bob Gibson of the St. Louis Cardinals, and the Philadelphia Phillies' Steve Carlton made their living on the inside of the plate. Now, umpires have a hair-trigger when it comes to potential beanballs, and hitters charge the mound at even the mere suggestion of an inside pitch.

Below: *As Glenn Davis of the Houston Astros will tell you, a little chin music makes for a more honest hitter. It also makes for an unhappy hitter and a dirtier uniform.*

© John McDonough

As Hall of Fame shortstop Luke Appling says, "Now, it's against the rules to throw inside."

Tim McCarver, who caught both Gibson and Carlton in their prime, agrees. "Pitchers have overreacted along with umpires and hitters," he says. "You have to give hitters credit. Their lobbying efforts to push the ball out over the plate has worked. Steve used to get ready for starts by visualizing the inside and outside lanes. Gibby used to say that the middle thirteen inches of the plate belonged to the hitters, and the inside two inches and outside two inches were his."

Not only is the brushback pitch an offensive weapon for a pitcher, it is a means of retaliation. Drysdale explains. "It doesn't take a Rhodes Scholar to figure it out," says the right-hander, who was 209-166 over his career. "If one of my guys got hit, two of theirs got hit. If two of my guys got hit, four of theirs got it. I hit a lot of guys, but never in the head."

Gibson laughs. "Now, Drysdale threw at guys," he says. "He was nasty. I would never throw at guys."

It is not as though pitchers don't have consciences. Ask fireballer Nolan Ryan what he remembers most about pitching in Fenway Park and he'll say, "Hitting Doug Griffin with that pitch. Nothing else is even close. I remember how he sort of froze when the pitch rode in on him. He had squared to bunt. I remember it like it was yesterday."

That was fifteen years after the fact. In May 1974, Ryan hit Griffin in the cheekbone with a pitch that helped to end his career. Griffin suffered a severe concussion, but returned to the Boston lineup in August and actually had two hits in his return, against Ryan. Still, the second baseman was never the same player. "My career ended because of a bad back more than anything," Griffin says. "But that pitch was part of it. I know he wasn't trying to throw at me, but he was definitely trying to back me off the plate. A guy like him, who doesn't have the control, shouldn't even be thinking of doing that. He could kill somebody."

Seven years earlier in August 1967, another Red Sox player, Tony Conigliaro, was felled by a Jack Hamilton fastball at Fenway. The ball hit him in the temple and shattered his cheekbone. The Red Sox were finishing the brushstrokes on their Impossible Dream season, but Conigliaro's nightmare was only just beginning at the age of twenty-two. Headaches and blurred vision persisted, and Conigliaro missed the rest of the 1967 season and all of 1968. He hit twenty home runs in 1969 and was voted Comeback Player of the Year. His vision deteriorated, however, and after hitting only four homers for the California Angels in 1971, he retired. Though he started the 1975 season as the Red Sox' designated hitter and pumped two more home runs out of the park, Conigliaro's career was over.

Above: *No, Lee Mazzilli is not attempting a Pete Rosesque bellyflop slide into third base. No, he is not capitalizing on the new Lambada dance craze. Actually, Mazzilli is gracefully avoiding a pitch in the dirt intended for his toes.*

Baseball Hall Of Fame

Above: *Don Larsen, watched intently by Billy Martin, follows through on his perfect game in the 1956 World Series. It was one of fourteen perfect games in the history of baseball.* **Opposite page:** *Mike Witt, the six-foot-seven, 185-pound righthander for the California Angels, joined such notable pitchers as Jim Bunning, Sandy Koufax, and Catfish Hunter with a no-hit, no-walk gem against the Texas Rangers in 1984.*

The Perfect Game

Consider that there are more than 2,000 games played each regular season. When a pitcher goes the distance he makes his manager very happy, for the bullpen has been spared. When the pitcher throws a shutout, he defies the odds. No-hitters are rare, but usually once a year a Jack Morris or a Dave Righetti makes headlines when he shuts down the opposition without a hit. And then there is the perfect game, the perfectly unnatural outing when a pitcher has everything working. No hits, no walks, no kidding.

There have been only fourteen pitched in the big leagues, the most famous belonging to the New York Yankees' Don Larsen, who threw a perfect game at the Brooklyn Dodgers in the 1956 World Series. On May 26, 1959, left-hander Harvey Haddix of the Pittsburgh Pirates retired all thirty-six Milwaukee Braves batters he faced and, incredibly, lost 1-0 in a 13-inning game. Never before had a perfect nine-inning game been thrown without the win going to the successful pitcher.

A perfect game is an event that grows more awesome with time. Though Jim Bunning pitched for 17 years in the majors and won 224 games, he is best known for the perfect game he pitched against the New York Mets on June 21, 1964. "Yes," says Bunning, now a congressman from Kentucky, "people never forget. I knew what I had done at the time, but not necessarily the historical significance."

Bunning turned thirty-two the day he faced the Mets in the first game of a doubleheader at Shea Stadium. The Philadelphia Phillies' right-hander drove with his wife, Mary, and twelve-year-old daughter, Barbara,

from his Cherry Hill, New Jersey, home. He sailed along until the fifth inning, when Mets catcher Jesse Gonder smashed a line drive to the left of second baseman Tony Taylor. Taylor dove, knocked the ball down, and threw to first baseman Johnny Herrnstein barely in time for the out.

By the time the ninth inning arrived, Bunning began to grow nervous. "He was really silly," said catcher Gus Triandos. "He was jabbering like a magpie. He called me out in the ninth inning and said I should tell him a joke, just to get a breather. I couldn't think of anything. I just laughed at him."

As Charlie Smith stepped to the plate, the 32,904 Mets fans began cheering for Bunning. Bobby Wine ran down Smith's foul pop behind third base, then Bunning struck out pinch hitter George Altman. New York manager Casey Stengel sent John Stephenson, destined to be the answer of a trivia question, to the plate as a pinch hitter. Five curveballs later (two of them missed the plate), Bunning had his tenth strikeout of the game and his perfect game.

It was the National League's first perfect game since 1880, when John Ward of Providence, Rhode Island, threw one at Buffalo. Since Bunning's achievement, Sandy Koufax (1965), Catfish Hunter (1968), Len Barker (1981), Mike Witt (1984), and Tom Browning (1988) have managed the feat.

Browning's turn on the hill was almost washed out. Rain at Cincinnati's Riverfront Stadium delayed the start of the September 16, 1988 game with the Los Angeles Dodgers, but the tarp was pulled back and

Browning threw the first pitch at 10:02 p.m. The Reds' twenty-eight-year-old lefthander needed only one hour and fifty-one minutes to complete his twenty-seven-out perfect game. He threw 102 pitches, 72 of them for strikes, and never went to a three-ball count. Browning was in such command that he needed no spectacular plays from his teammates to bail him out.

"I didn't think I'd be the guy to pitch a no-hitter here," said Browning, who had come within two outs of a no-hitter on June 6, 1988. "I had a one-hitter before, but I had also walked some guys in that game. This one was a lot better."

When it was over, Browning had been congratulated by Reds owner Marge Schott, Baseball Commissioner Peter Ueberroth, and the Hall of Fame. President Ronald Reagan, however, did not even leave a message. "He's from the West Coast," Browning said. "I guess he's a Dodger fan."

Cy Young, who won more games than any other pitcher, threw three no-hitters in his twenty-three-year career. One of them was a perfect game. It happened on May 5, 1904, when the Boston Red Sox right-hander set down twenty-seven Athletics batters without allowing one of them to reach base. It was the first perfect game in twenty-four years and only the second no-hitter in American League history.

"Of all the 879 games I pitched in the big leagues, that one stands clearest in my mind," he once said. "I was real fast in those days, but what very few batters knew was that I had two curves. One of them sailed in there as hard as my fastball and broke in reverse. It was a narrow curve that broke away from the batter and went in just like a fastball. And the other was a wide break. I never said much about them until after I was through with the game. I was pitching against Rube Waddell . . . I never saw many who were better pitchers.

"I'll tell you, a pitcher's got to be awfully lucky to get a perfect game. I don't think I ever had more stuff; I fanned eight. The closest the Athletics came to a hit was in the third, when Monte Cross hit a pop fly that was dropping just back of the infield between first and second. [Buck] Freeman came tearing in from right like a deer and barely caught the ball. Ollie Pickering gave me two bad scares. Once he hit a fly back of second that Chick Stahl caught around his knees after a long run from center. The other time, Ollie hit a slow roller to short and [Freddie] Parent just got him by a step.

"Patsy Dougherty helped me in the seventh when he crashed into the left field fence to get Danny Hoffman's long foul; and I recall that [Lou] Criger almost went into the Boston bench to get a foul by Davis Cross."

"Most of the other batters were pretty easy, but all told there were ten flies hit, six to the outfield. The infielders had seven assists and I had two, and eighteen of the putouts were divided by Criger and [first baseman Candy] La Chance. Well sir, when I had two outs in the ninth and it was Waddell's time to bat, some of the fans began to yell for Connie Mack to send up a pinch hitter. They wanted me to finish what looked like a perfect game against a stronger hitter. But Mr. Mack let Rube take his turn. He took a couple of strikes and then hit a fly ball that [Chick] Stahl caught going away from the infield. You can realize how perfect we all were that day when I tell you the game only took one hour and twenty-three minutes.

"We got three runs off Waddell, and when the game was finished it looked like all the fans came down on the field and tried to shake my hand. One gray-haired fellow jumped the fence back of third and shoved a bill into my hand. It was five dollars."

TOP TEN CAREER COMPLETE GAMES	
1. Cy Young	751
2. Pud Galvin	639
3. Tim Keefe	558
4. Kid Nichols	533
5. Walter Johnson	531
6. Mickey Welch	525
7. Old Hoss Radbourn	489
8. John Clarkson	485
9. Tony Mullane	469
10. Jim McCormick	466

© John McDonough

Steve Carlton (above) and

Tom Seaver (opposite

page, right) are next in

line behind Ryan in

strikeouts. Carlton did it

with a nasty slider, while

Seaver had a terrific

fastball and the cunning

to match.

The No-Hitter

Since perfect games are nearly as rare as an unassisted triple play, most pitchers don't find themselves dwelling on the possibility. No-hitters are a more realistic goal because since July 28, 1875, when Joe Borden of Philadelphia no-hit Chicago in a 4-0 National Association victory, major leaguers have been tossing roughly two no-hitters a season. Like any reasonably successful pitcher, the Toronto Blue Jays' Dave Stieb lusted after a no-hitter. He nearly had one in 1988. Two, actually, in a startling span of a week.

On September 24, Stieb came within one out of a no-hitter against the Cleveland Indians. Julio Franco ran the count to 2-2 before delivering a bad-hop single. In his next start, on September 29 against the Baltimore Orioles, it happened again. In virtually the same scenario, the talented right-hander recorded twenty-six outs before disaster—in the form of Jim Traber—struck again. This time, Traber's 2-2 single left Stieb slapping his thigh with his Wilson glove in frustration. He was in good company. Earlier that season, on May 2, Cincinnati's Ron Robinson was one out from a perfect game. Robinson's teammate, Tom Browning, had a no-hitter going on June 6 when Tony Gwynn's one-out single in the ninth ended those dreams. Though Browning would later throw a perfect game against the Los Angeles Dodgers, four other hurlers would fall just short of a perfect game in 1988: the Houston Astros' Nolan Ryan and Mike Scott, Doug Drabek of the Pittsburgh Pi-

rates, and the Milwaukee Brewers' Odell Jones.

Stieb took the disappointment in stride. After all, he had won both games with shutouts and his 16-8 record was the Blue Jays' best. Then, on August 4, 1989, came a numbing case of *déjà vu*. In the New York Yankees' first visit to the Toronto SkyDome, Stieb was picture-perfect through eight innings: no walks, no hits, no near-misses. In the ninth, Stieb dispatched pinch hitter Hal Morris on a 1-2 count with a high fastball. Next, infielder Ken Phelps swung through another 1-2 fastball for Stieb's eleventh strikeout, and the record crowd of 48,789 at the SkyDome went berserk. At this point, Stieb could be forgiven for thinking negative thoughts. Tentatively, Stieb missed the plate with his first two pitches to outfielder Roberto Kelly. And then Kelly, twice a previous strikeout victim, lined Stieb's eighty-fourth pitch of the game into the left field corner. The shutout was lost moments later when second baseman Steve Sax lined a single into right field. When Stieb finally retired outfielder Luis Poloñia with a ground ball, he was mobbed by teammates at the mound. It was another dominant victory, but Stieb had fallen just short again.

And then there is Nolan Ryan, who has now pitched a staggering seven no-hitters. Cy Young once stood alone with his three no-hitters in many more game opportunities, but along came Ryan, who pitched five no-hit games through 1981, then saved two more for

© W. T. Harrington

TOP TEN CAREER STRIKEOUTS

1. Nolan Ryan 5,714
2. Steve Carlton 4,136
3. Bert Blyleven 3,701
4. Tom Seaver 3,640
5. Gaylord Perry 3,534
6. Don Sutton 3,530
7. Walter Johnson 3,508
8. Phil Niekro 3,342
9. Ferguson Jenkins 3,192
10. Bob Gibson 3,117

© AP/Wide World Photos

the 1990s. Pitching for the Texas Rangers, Ryan no-hit the Oakland Athletics 5-0 on June 11, 1990, then put the record out of sight with a 3-0 victory over Toronto on May 1, 1991.

Rare as the no-hitter is, there are three men in professional baseball history who have managed to produce back-to-back no-hitters. John Samuel "The Dutch Master" Vander Meer joined Cincinnati in 1937 and pitched marginally in nineteen games, hardly exhibiting the promise his sophomore season would reveal. He was a burly left-hander who threw hard but sometimes experienced control problems. In thirteen years in the big leagues, he led the National League in strikeouts three times and bases on balls twice. On June 11, 1938, Vander Meer shut down the Boston Braves without a hit, throwing mostly fastballs in a 3-0 Cincinnati victory. Four days later, he no-hit Brooklyn in a 6-0 victory, the first night game in Ebbets Field history. No major leaguer had ever thrown two straight no-hitters, and to this day no one else has. Though Vander Meer was 15-10 that season, he was erratic to the end, finishing his career with a won-loss record of 119-121.

In 1952, Bill "Ding Dong" Bell of Bristol, Virginia, threw consecutive no-hitters in the Appalachian League. He later appeared in five games for the Pittsburgh Pirates.

Tom Drees, an imposing six-foot-six left-hander, had scuffled along in the White Sox chain with a .500 record

when, inexplicably, everything fell together in the spring of 1989. Drees had undergone shoulder surgery to repair torn cartilage during the off-season, and had struggled early with a 2-3 record. On May 23, he threw a nine-inning no-hitter for Vancouver, the Chicago White Sox AAA franchise. That victory over Calgary was followed on May 28 with a seven-inning no-hitter against Edmonton. That put Drees in a position to become the first triple no-hit pitcher in history. It didn't happen. In the very first inning of his next start, he hung a fastball out over the fat part of the plate and Albuquerque's Tracy Woodson sent it over the fence for a two-run home run. "It would have been nice to at least carry it into the fourth or fifth or sixth inning," Drees said later. "There was all the buildup and all of a sudden, boom, it was over. It was kind of a relief to see it end, but I could think of better ways than a homer."

On May 6, 1953, Alva Lee "Bobo" Holloman pitched St. Louis to a 6-0 victory over Philadelphia. Remarkably, it was Holloman's first major league start (at the age of twenty-nine), and even more incredible, it was a no-hitter. That brilliant game turned out to be a curse, for the six-foot-two, 207-pound right-hander lost seven of his remaining nine decisions that year, his only big-league season. Opposing hitters touched him for 69 hits in just over 56 innings and averaged well over five runs a game, proving that no-hitters are no guarantee of success in the major leagues.

Above, left: *As incredible as Nolan Ryan's five no-hitters are, consider his nine one-hitters and eighteen two-hitters. No wonder Ryan is at the top of the all-time strikeout list, with 5,076.*

The Greatest Pitchers of All Time

Denton True Young wasn't much to look at off the mound. He was a roughly cut man from Gilmore, Ohio, who stood six-foot-two and weighed 210 pounds. But when he toed the slab, something amazing happened. The gaunt, ungainly body seemed perfectly built for the purpose of hurling a baseball sixty feet. The right-hander's career began modestly enough in 1890, when he won nine of sixteen games for Cleveland of the National League. And then Cy Young found himself; he won twenty or more games for fourteen consecutive seasons. Over his twenty-two year career, Young would win 511 games and lose 313. Both figures are first on the all-time list. Certainly, Young pitched in a time when starters went the distance. Young finished 751 of the 815 games he started, piling up a total of 7,356 innings pitched.

To put his accomplishment in perspective, Walter Johnson is second on the victory list, ninety-five behind Young. Young was a strong pitcher whose fastball seemed to pick up speed as the innings went on. He put together some amazing seasons. In 1892, he was 36-11 with a 1.93 earned run average and nine shutouts. Pitching for the Boston Red Sox from 1901 to 1903, Young led the American League three straight years in victories, averaging thirty-one a season.

Critics view Young's feats with skepticism, pointing to the uneven nature of play in the old days. By the time baseball evolved into its present form in 1903, Young was al-

ready a relic at the age of thirty-six. Still, he won twenty-two games in 1907 and twenty-one the following year, at the age of forty-one. Young believed that, like poets, pitchers are born, not made. One thing seems certain: Under baseball's present format, there may never be another pitcher who will match Young's victory total.

Walter Perry Johnson was one man who was ahead of his time. Light-years, in fact. Back when the twentieth century was in its formative stages, strikeouts were not a big part of the game. Yet, Johnson threw a blinding sidearm fastball for the Washington Senators, a heater that was once clocked at 99.7 miles an hour. It might have been faster. Consult the record book and you will find his name among the best strikeout pitchers of all time. Johnson, who pitched from 1907 to 1927, is the only hurler listed who didn't pitch at least into the 1970s.

Johnson was saddled with a sometimes woeful Washington team, yet managed to record a 416-279 career mark and a mind-boggling 110 shutouts, first on the all-time list. Beginning in 1910, Johnson led the American League in strikeouts twelve times in fifteen seasons, including eight times in a row. Johnson won at least twenty games ten years in a row, and was regularly the league leader in earned run average, complete games, and innings pitched.

Christy Mathewson overlapped the careers of both Young and Johnson and was very nearly their equal on the mound. He was blessed with a good team—the New York Giants—and a live right arm that could throw a darting fastball and a sweeping curve with equal skill. His "out" pitch was the famous fadeaway, a pitch known today as a screwball. What made the pitch so effective was Mathewson's ability to disguise it with his usual overhand motion.

Mathewson was a sparkling 373-188 in seventeen seasons, produced an earned run average of 2.13 and pitched eighty shutouts. Perhaps his greatest achievement was his performance in the 1905 World Series. In three games against Philadelphia, Mathewson pitched 27 innings, struck out 18 batters, walked only one, and did not allow a single run to score. The three shutouts led the Giants to victory over Philadelphia, four games to one, and made him a legend in New York at the age of twenty-five.

Grover Cleveland Alexander, a contemporary of Johnson's, had his supporters. Some argued that his sidearm curveball, consistency, and control made him a better pitcher than Johnson, though his 373 victories tie him with Mathewson, forty-three behind Johnson. He was a workhorse for both Philadelphia and Chicago of the National League and led his circuit in victories five of his first seven seasons in the big leagues. Alexander wasted no time on the mound. Generally, his games required only ninety minutes. He was gifted with physical skill, but

▲ **Cy Young**

old-timers say Alexander's pitching mix was unmatched; he always seemed to have hitters off balance.

Sandy Koufax's name cannot be found anywhere near the top of history's top ten lists for victories, games pitched, strikeouts, or shutouts. Koufax pitched only thirteen seasons for the Dodgers of Brooklyn and Los Angeles, but he left a legacy of quality over quantity; for a stretch of six seasons, from 1961 to 1966 when he retired with arthritis wracking his left arm, he was baseball's dominant pitcher. He threw a rising fastball that exploded through the strike zone and a celebrated curveball that behaved like a sinker, breaking straight down, usually out of reach.

Koufax, who spent the first six years of his major league career trying to master his craft without much minor-league seasoning, won 129 games over that final six-year period and lost only 47. That works out to a winning percentage of .773. Along the way, there were five consecutive earned run average titles that are hard to appreciate in this day of 7-5 scores: 2.54, 1.88, 1.74, 2.04, and 1.73. Koufax led the National League in strikeouts four of those years, including a gargantuan 382-whiff season in 1965. Koufax remains one of only two pitchers (Nolan Ryan is the other) to average more than one strikeout per inning, compiling a 9.28 figure.

Three pitchers who have yet to reach the Hall of Fame are certain to be enshrined at Cooperstown when they become eligible. Nolan Ryan, Steve Carlton, and Tom Seaver are the top three pitchers on the all-time strikeout list and the best of the present generation of pitchers.

Nolan Ryan was still pitching well enough at the age of forty-two to play in the 1989 All-Star game—and it wasn't a token appearance. At the time, Ryan led the major leagues in strikeouts for the Texas Rangers.

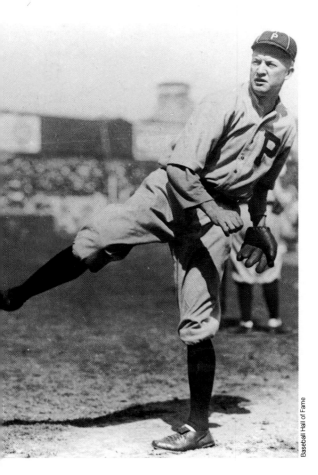

▲ **Grover Cleveland Alexander**

▲ **Sandy Koufax**

Leroy "Satchel" Paige spent fifteen seasons barnstorming in the Negro Leagues by summer and visiting the Latin-American countries by winter. He was finally allowed to pitch in the major leagues at the age of forty-two. Some of the players knew about Paige; Rogers Hornsby had gone down on strikes five times in one game against him, Jimmie Foxx and Charlie Gehringer had struck out three times each. Dizzy Dean, who lost a 1934 exhibition game 1-0 in seventeen innings to Paige, knew all about the lean six-foot-three right-hander. "He is," Dean conceded at the time, "the greatest pitcher in the world."

Carl Hubbell of the New York Giants posted a 253-154 record in sixteen seasons. The left-hander's best pitch was a screwball that was compared favorably with Mathewson's fadeaway pitch. Though he was never a power pitcher, in the 1934 All-Star Game on July 10, Hubbell struck out Babe Ruth, Lou Gehrig, and Jimmie Foxx with two men on base—on a total of twelve pitches.

Mordecai Brown lost half of his index finger as a young farm boy, and as Three-Finger Brown pitched his way to a 239-129 record and a career earned run average of 2.06, third on the all-time list. His best pitch was a nasty curveball, which he basically threw off his thumb.

Whitey Ford, the New York Yankees' left-hander, retired with a 236-106 record in 1967, good for a winning percentage of .690, a figure surpassed only by Bob Caruthers (218-97, .692), who pitched from 1884 to 1892. Ford was 10-8 in World Series games, both all-time records.

▲ **Satchel Paige**

His notorious fastball that July night registered at only ninety-two miles an hour, but his changeup was clocked at eighty-seven. Through 1989, Ryan had amassed 5,076 strikeouts, a total that may not be threatened for a very long time. Ryan, who was never blessed with sharp-hitting teams, might have won 350 games with a powerful offensive squad.

Steve Carlton's career ended in 1989, when his long left arm finally ran out of steam. He had undergone shoulder surgery the previous September, but the arm did not respond to treatment. Carlton's 4,136 career strikeouts are second only to Ryan, and his twenty-two year record of 329-244 placed him ninth on the all-time victory list. Warren Spahn, with 363 wins, is the only left-hander with more victories. Carlton's best pitch was

the slider, a hard- and late-breaking pitch that usually left batters dumbfounded. His National League records included years pitched (22), games started (677), consecutive starts (534), walks (1,717), and strikeouts (4,000).

Tom Seaver's calling card was consistent excellence. Over the nine-year period from 1968 to 1976, he struck out more than 200 batters per year, a major league record. In 1969, Seaver almost single-handedly carried the New York Mets to a World Championship. He was 25-7 that season, with a league-leading winning percentage of .781. Seaver's first fifteen seasons were all winning efforts, and his 311 victories place him in very good company.

There are other pitchers worthy of consideration:

The Balk

Before 1988, the balk was one of those arcane baseball rules that had been on the books for years and rarely enforced. Balks, basically rules for a pitcher's mound etiquette, suddenly came to the forefront. Blame Whitey Herzog. "Before he started bitching about the Twins' pitchers in the 1987 World Series, you never heard the word balk," says one major league manager. "After that, all hell broke loose."

Indeed, the St. Louis manager, perhaps looking for a miniscule psychological edge, complained that Minnesota pitcher Bert Blyleven was not coming to a complete stop in his stretch motion. Herzog, whose light-hitting team depended on stolen bases for offense, did succeed in freezing Blyleven for the slightest moment before he made his offering to the mound, and perhaps the umpires, among others, were slightly intimidated. Certainly, major league officials were impressed. In spring training, pitchers were taken aback when umpires began calling a flurry of balks. The official explanation: The balk rule had been redefined to prevent American Leaguers from quasi-legal moves on the mound, in an effort to shorten the leads of would-be stealers. Umpires were instructed to make sure that pitchers came to a "single, complete, and discernible stop" with runners on base.

"We felt the balk rule needed clarification," said Bill Murray, director of Major League Baseball Operations and a member of the rules committee that subtly changed the balk rule. "There was not a consistency between the two leagues. We wanted to make sure it was a single stop and you could see it."

The umpires made their point early. Texas Rangers knuckleballer Charlie Hough was called for an amazing nine balks in one spring training exhibition game. Twenty balks were called in the first twenty-six games played in the American League, eighteen in the first twenty-one games played in the National League. The season before, there were three balks called in the American League's first twenty-one games and six in the first fifteen National League contests. "Pitchers have to change," explained American League umpire crew chief Larry Barnett, "or we'll have ten million balk calls." Before the season was three weeks old, American League umpires had called 138 balks, more than in any previous season. Oakland's Dave Stewart broke the major league individual record (twelve) in May. National League umpires were more reluctant,

breaking the circuit's record of 219 at the relatively late date of July 4.

"I really hoped it would go away after spring training," said Houston Astros pitcher Rick Rhoden. "How do you expect guys who have been playing for years to adjust overnight? I don't know why they have to be messing with the game all of the time."

Predictably, pitchers saw the move as another assault on their craft. "They believe that, for the betterment of baseball, they must put more offense into the game," says former Yankee pitcher Tommy John. "They believe the average fan would rather see a 9-8 ballgame than a 2-1 game. The intent of the rule is to put more running in the game."

Says pitcher Frank Viola of the New York Mets, "It's a pain in the neck for the game, period. The game is getting slower and slower as it is, and I don't think baseball needs that."

The balk, one of baseball's more esoteric rules, enjoyed a comeback of sorts in 1988 when umpires called them on pitchers in record numbers, thanks largely to the objections of Whitey Herzog (opposite page) in the 1987 World Series. There are thirteen ways to commit this indiscretion, six of them involving the pitching rubber.

THE BALK RULE

It is a balk when the pitcher:
1. Fakes making a pitch.
2. Fails to come to a complete and discernible stop in the set position.
3. While on the rubber, fakes throwing to first.
4. While on the rubber, fails to step toward the base to which he is throwing.
5. While on the rubber, throws or fakes a throw to an unoccupied base except for the purposes of making a play.
6. Makes an illegal pitch.
7. Pitches when he is not facing the batter.
8. Makes any pitching motion while not on the rubber, or makes any pitching motion on the rubber without making the pitch.
9. Unnecessarily delays the game.
10. Stands on or aside the rubber without the ball.
11. When in a pitching position, takes one hand off the ball without throwing.
12. Drops the ball while on the rubber.
13. Pitches when the catcher is not in the catcher's box.

THE PITCHES

The Fastball

The fastball is baseball in its purest sense: nothing fancy, just raw heat forged from an I-can-throw-it-by-you attitude.

It is known in baseball parlance as the Number One, which is how many fingers the catcher uses to signal for the devastating pitch, and this preeminence among all pitches is well-deserved. There may be no greater drama in the game than when a hulking reliever challenges a classic high fastball hitter with the hardest offering he can muster. That potential swing from strikeout to home run is what consistently puts fans in the seats.

In terms of sheer speed, Bob Feller of the Cleveland Indians is the fastest major leaguer on record. In 1946, the year the right-hander won twenty-six games, struck out a ludicrous 348 batters, and recorded ten shutouts, Feller was clocked at 107.9 miles an hour. Second on the list is Nolan Ryan, the Texas Rangers' fireballer, who was caught on the radar gun at 100.8 miles an hour in 1974. Through 1988, Ryan held sixteen major league pitching records, almost all of them attributable to his wicked fastball. Through 1992, Ryan had struck out more batters (5,668) and thrown more no-hitters (seven) than any man in baseball history. At the age of forty-three, the right-hander was still clocking ninety miles an hour with his best pitch. A year earlier, he struck out a National League high of 270

The fastball grip is hardly scientific, but the result, as authored by pitchers like the New York Mets' Dwight Gooden (opposite page), can be pure poetry. Nolan Ryan (below), in his last years with the Texas Rangers, seemed to be getting better even as his fastball showed signs of calming down.

batters, averaging 11.48 per nine innings pitched, breaking Dwight Gooden's mark of 11.39, set in 1984. Gooden was nineteen at the time, while Ryan was forty. How was this possible?

"Twenty years from now, fifteen years from now," Ryan says, "you may be talking to Dwight Gooden, Roger Clemens, one of those guys, asking, 'How do you feel about breaking Nolan Ryan's strikeout record?' There's no reason to say one of them might not be able to. But there's a factor there that none of us can explain. Why was I able to continue to throw that hard and Tom Seaver and Steve Carlton and some of those guys weren't? I don't have the answer. I don't think anyone does.

"I never envisioned being a different type of pitcher than anyone else," he says. "I just assumed I'd be out of the game, like most other power pitchers, by my mid-thirties. Tom and Steve certainly took care of themselves. I can't say I've done anything that made the difference that they didn't do."

Seaver left baseball in October 1986. On April 27, 1988, the day Carlton, forty-three, was released by the Minnesota Twins, Ryan came within two outs of throwing a no-hitter against the Philadelphia Phillies. Ryan's across-the-seams grip is conventional in every way; his smooth delivery is fairly typical, too. The answer is the Texan's live right arm and an understanding of pitching that has grown deeper each season. When Ryan broke in with the New York Mets in 1966, he was so feared that teammate Bud Harrelson refused to face him in batting practice. In 1974, an accidental beaning left the Red Sox's Doug Griffin with a severe concussion and all of baseball wary of Ryan's fastball. In truth, Ryan had a decent command of his out pitch—the ball just moved so quickly in and out of the strike zone. Ryan first led the majors' in strikeouts (329) in 1972, his first season with the California Angels. And though he also led in walked batters (157), Ryan's two-to-one ratio was more than acceptable. In fact, he led the American League in both categories six times over a span of seven seasons.

© W. T. Harrington

Roger Clemens of the Boston Red Sox is one of the premier power pitchers in today's game.

Now, Ryan has the almost unfair benefit of experience with much of the physical talent he had twenty years earlier. "It used to be that his earliest form of intimidation centered around the fact that he threw so hard that at any given time at bat he was apt to hit you and hurt you," says veteran catcher Ted Simmons. "Now, it's different. I find myself profoundly intimidated by a man who throws consistently for strikes three or four different ways. And, frankly, this is worse. Sinkerball . . . Strike . . . Changeup . . . Slow curveball . . . Strike . . . eighty-nine to ninety-mile-an-hour heat . . . Strike. I'm here to get hits and this Ryan intimidates the mess out of me."

Ryan smiles and says he wouldn't change a thing. "I cannot say I have any regrets," says Ryan, "other than naturally wanting to see a better won-loss record and maybe having become more polished at an earlier age."

And though Ryan's career record still hovers just over .500, many of the premier fastballers were more successful in that respect. Feller won 266 games and lost only 162 in eighteen years. Walter Johnson of the Washington Senators, who delivered a fastball estimated at close to one hundred miles an hour with a sidearm motion, struck out 3,508 batters in twenty-one seasons and won a staggering 416 games, second only to Cy Young's 511. Don Drysdale, the strapping Dodgers right-hander, threw a fastball clocked at ninety-five miles an hour and produced a career record of 209-166 and an earned run average of 2.95. Johnson and Drysdale, like Ryan, used the intimidation factor to their advantage.

These days, you find many of the flamethrowers in the bullpen. Goose Gossage threw a rising fastball that surpassed ninety-nine miles an hour. Today's fastball ace is Boston Red Sox reliever Lee Smith. The sight of the six-foot-six, 250-pound Smith on the mound is enough to send hitters back to the dugout without a swing. Though the reliever, whose fastball crackles in the ninety-eight, ninety-nine-mile-an-hour range, has an economical motion from the stretch position, the ball nearly explodes from his hand on a line into the catcher's mitt.

One name that doesn't usually come up when the legendary fastballs are discussed is one Steve Dalkowski. It should. Believe it or not, Dalkowski threw the baseball left-handed at speeds estimated at close to 110 miles an hour. Really.

No less an authority than Ted Williams will tell you that of all the pitchers he ever saw, including Feller, Ryan, and Sandy Koufax, Dalkowski was the fastest. "I could always throw," says Dalkowski, now fifty and living in Oildale, California. "It was amazing. I just got faster and faster as the years went by. I don't know where the speed came from. It was God-given."

It is hard to separate the fact from fiction. There was the time his fastball broke a batter's arm, the time he sent an umpire to the hospital with a concussion (the pitch smashing his mask and knocking him fifteen feet backward), the splintered batting helmets, the time he tore off a batter's ear lobe. Dalkowski threw so many pitches through the screen, fans in many parks refused to sit behind home plate. Once, as a junior in high school, Dalkowski threw a fastball through the webbing of his father's glove that bounced off a stone wall twelve feet behind him and knocked him out.

Pitching for New Britain High School in Connecticut, the five-foot-ten, 185-pound Dalkowski struck out twenty-four New London batters one day in May 1956. In 154 innings at New Britain, he fanned 313 batters, walked 180, allowed forty-six hits and thirty-five runs for a 13-6 record. Dalkowski accepted a $16,000 bonus, plus a car, from the Baltimore Orioles in 1957 and set off on a nine-year adventure through the minor leagues with stops at Kingsport, Wilson, Kennewick, and Aberdeen. The price Dalkowski paid for his unsurpassed speed was wildness. In one game in Kingsport, Tennessee, that summed up his career, he struck out twenty-four batters, walked seventeen, hit four batters, threw six wild pitches in a row, and lost 9-8.

In 1963, the Orioles invited Dalkowski to spring training in Miami. He had pitched seven scoreless innings when his arm came unhinged against the New York Yankees. He struck out Roger Maris on three pitches, then got two strikes on Bobby Richardson when a rising fastball landed on the screen behind home plate. "Something let go in the elbow," Dalkowski says. "I never had arm trouble in my life. The elbow swelled up and I had to leave the game. They tried everything the next few years, but the arm was gone."

FASTEST PITCHERS

Bob Feller, Cleveland Indians, 107.9 mph, 1946
Nolan Ryan, California Angels, 100.8 mph, 1974
J.R. Richard, Houston Astros, 100.0 mph, 1978
Walter Johnson, Washington Senators, 99.7 mph, 1914
Jim Maloney, Cincinnati Reds, 99.5 mph, 1965
Goose Gossage, New York Yankees, 99.4 mph, 1984
Lee Smith, Chicago Cubs, 99.0 mph, 1984
Steve Barber, Baltimore Orioles, 95.5 mph, 1960
Don Drysdale, Los Angeles Dodgers, 95.0 mph, 1960
Mike Scott, Houston Astros, 95.0 mph, 1986
Roger Clemens, Boston Red Sox, 95.0 mph, 1986

© John Swart/Allsport

A live arm and leverage were an unbeatable combination for Goose Gossage. While pitching for the New York Yankees, he nearly broke the 100 mile-an-hour barrier.

The Curveball

As far back as everyone can remember, Dwight Eugene Gooden always had the tools to throw a major league fastball. Trouble was, it wasn't enough when he finally got to the majors.

At Hillsborough High School in Tampa, Florida, Gooden struck out 130 batters in seventy-four innings and compiled a 14-4 record. All he threw, all he had to throw, were fastballs. "I could kill them in high school with the heat," Gooden says. "At that level you're not too sophisticated, so you just go with your best. When I went to the minors, I found out I needed more. You can throw BBs out there, but if that's all you've got, they're going to figure out a way to hit it."

Specifically, Gooden needed a curveball to complement his blazing fastball that has been clocked as high as ninety-six miles an hour. Gooden signed with the New York Mets right out of high school and played the 1982 season for Kingsport and Little Falls, Class A teams in the Mets' chain. The right-hander split ten decisions, and when he arrived at Lynchburg of the Carolina League the next year, pitching instructor John Cumberland was waiting for him. Cumberland convinced Gooden to experiment with the curveball—though at first, the results were weak at best.

"It was different and it took time to adjust," Gooden says. "I'd say at the beginning that maybe one in thirty

The curveball curves because of the positioning of the fingers on the seams and the bend in the wrist. A loose wrist and a good release are the keys to this pitch. Dwight Gooden, of the New York Mets, demonstrates the pitch that took him years to perfect (opposite page). Now, major leaguers refer to his curve as "Lord Charles."

curves performed the way I wanted. They would hang and I'd get hit an awful lot, but eventually, I got it down. I put my index and middle finger on the seam, and when you throw it you've got to have a nice, loose bend at the wrist as it spins down. The release point is the key. If you release the ball at your ear it's going to cross the plate waist-high. If you let it go at the chin, it's going to be a low one in the dirt. That's how fine you have to cut it."

Gooden went 19-4 that season in Lynchburg, and in 1984 made the huge jump to the major league club. His five-year totals through 1989 were a 100-39 record, an earned run average of 2.64 and 1,168 strikeouts. Of the top ten strikeout pitchers in history, only Bert Blyleven had more strikeouts by his twenty-fourth birthday. Gooden says the primary reason is his curveball, not his fastball.

Tim McCarver, who caught in the big leagues for twenty-one seasons, puts a spin on the pitch players call "Uncle Charlie" by dubbing Gooden's curve "Lord Charles." It is regal indeed. Gooden's has a tight spin and drops wickedly. A right-handed hitter has virtually no chance when the ball is delivered properly because it starts out in his face, only to dive into the strike zone as it approaches the plate. When thrown in concert with his fastball, the curve is even more dangerous because hitters have difficulty making the adjustment in the split second it takes to get to the plate. Gooden throws his good, tight curve at approximately seventy-six miles an hour and occasionally offers a slower version in the low seventies that features an enormous elegant break.

Sandy Koufax was another dominant pitcher who threw an equally potent mix of curveballs and fastballs. For six brief seasons, he was the greatest pitcher who

ever lived. Between 1961 and 1966, Koufax was 129-47 and produced five straight earned run titles. And then his left elbow succumbed to arthritis. Mordecai "Three-Finger" Brown, who played for nineteen seasons early in the twentieth century, built his reputation on a nasty curveball. The victim of a feed cutter accident as a youngster, Brown learned to pitch without parts of two fingers. He always maintained that the handicap enabled him to develop one of history's best curves. Camilo Pascual, born in Havana, Cuba, had a legendary curve. He led the American League in strikeouts for three consecutive years in the 1960s, relying on a bender that hitters of the time detested. Blyleven, who was born in Zeist, Holland, still has one of the most lethal curves in the business. When it snaps cleanly, most hitters in the American League can't stay with it. Through 1988, Blyleven had struck out 2,035 batters and thrown twenty-nine shutouts on the strength of his curveball.

Today, the curve still trails the fastball in popularity because it is more difficult to learn. Little Leaguers like Wes Gardner, now of the Boston Red Sox, are generally steered clear of the curve early on. "I didn't throw a curve in a game until I was in college," he says. "And they were cranked pretty good. So I put the curveball in my back pocket and left it there."

Years later, in 1989, Gardner started throwing it again with impressive results. "I don't know why he never threw one before," says Boston pitching coach Bill Fischer. "It's like having a six-shooter and only loading five shells. He needs a curve to show those big guys who are up there looking for heat. He has the slider, but that's only about five miles an hour slower than his fastball, so the good ones can sit on it. The curve will give them something to think about."

The Slider

Tim McCarver, the New York Mets broadcaster, seems quite comfortable behind the microphone, but you should have seen him behind the plate catching sliders. "And what a slider it was," McCarver says. "When Lefty was on, which was most of the time, guys would know it was coming, and they still couldn't hit it."

Steve Carlton, the left-hander in question, had one of the best sliders in modern history. That single pitch will almost certainly land him in the Hall of Fame in 1994, when he first becomes eligible for the shrine.

"The slider is really a hard curve," says McCarver, who caught Carlton for more than ten seasons in St. Louis and Philadelphia. "Or a fastball with a last-minute break. Coming in, it looks like a fastball, which is why it fools you. It might break only six inches, but that's enough if you're not looking for it."

The grip varies slightly from pitcher to pitcher, but most finger the seams of the baseball to produce the subtle break. Though most pitchers use it occasionally to keep hitters honest, others like Carlton have made a living with the slider. The other great slider of recent times belonged to Ron Guidry.

Known as "Louisiana Lightning" or "Gator," Guidry pitched for the New York Yankees from 1975 to 1989. At his peak, the slider he unleashed from the left side was virtually unhittable. Guidry's fastball, of no little consequence, complemented the slider wickedly. In 1978, Guidry's record was an astounding 25-3, a major league record for winning percentage (.893) for 20 wins or more. His nine shutouts were an American League record for a left-handed pitcher, and Guidry was the only choice for the Cy Young Award, becoming only the second unanimous choice in history. Seven years later, at the age of thirty-five, Guidry turned in a 22-6 record. His fastball wasn't what it used to be, but his slider had enough bite left in it to keep hitters off balance.

Opposite page: *No one threw the slider better, or more consistently, than Steve Carlton. In his prime with the Philadelphia Phillies, Carlton often led the league in games started and innings pitched.*
Below: *A better than passing fastball made Ron Guidry's slider even more unhittable.*

© J. Daniel/Allsport

The Split-Finger Fastball

The pitch of the 1980s and 1990s comes courtesy of Roger Craig (below), the San Francisco Giants manager. He looks innocent enough in the safety of his dugout, but the pitch, as hitters will tell you, can be horrifying. The split-finger fastball (demonstrated right) made Bruce Sutter (opposite page) one of history's great relief pitchers. He led the National League in saves four times and recorded twenty or more saves for nine consecutive seasons.

Between 1955 and 1966, Roger Craig produced a middling career record of 74-98 and an earned run average of 3.83. Craig, who pitched for six different teams in twelve seasons, exhibited good control, striking out 803 batters and walking only 522. He was 18-16 as a reliever and recorded nineteen saves. Serviceable numbers, to be sure, but hardly an indication that Craig would indirectly dominate a shift in pitching philosophy twenty years later.

Craig, now the manager of the San Francisco Giants, is the guru of the split-finger fastball, considered by most observers to be the pitch of the 1980s. "Call it anything you want," Craig says. "All I know is, it works."

The split-finger fastball is really a reincarnation of the old forkball. Craig has been teaching the pitch for years and though no accurate count exists, players estimate that between 20 and 30 percent of the major league's pitchers can regularly throw it for a strike. Here's how it works: The ball is grasped across the seams between the middle and index finger and thrown with the same motion and release as a conventional fastball. The action of the ball, however, is radically different than the fastball. As it approaches the plate, it begins to lose velocity and, at the last split-second, breaks sharply down.

Bruce Sutter learned how to throw the pitch in 1973 from a minor league instructor named Fred Martin. For nine consecutive seasons, from 1975 to 1984, Sutter recorded twenty or more saves. On four occasions, Sutter led the National League in saves, mostly on the strength of his split-finger fastball. Others followed Sutter's example. Jack Morris of the Detroit Tigers en-

joyed phenomenal success in the 1980s. He learned the pitch from Craig, who was then the Detroit pitching coach. "It's a great pitch," Morris says. "But it was better when they weren't expecting it. The more hitters see it, the easier it is to hit. I don't throw it as much as I used to because I learned a cut slider. I throw it enough to let hitters know I have it."

As the legion of split-finger fastball artists increases, hitters will adapt and learn how to handle the pitch. For now, it's the chic pitch of the moment.

The Changeup

The changeup is an innocent enough pitch; it floats in at seventy-five, eighty miles an hour, big as a beachball. The problem, of course, is that the hitter is usually primed for a fastball and has already committed his swing by the time the ball finally arrives. The changeup underlines the theory that changing speeds well is just as important (or perhaps more so) as raw speed itself. "The idea," explains the Cleveland Indians' Bobby Ojeda, "is to get them off balance. The changeup takes advantage of a batter's aggressiveness. It's one of the pitcher's best weapons because you're using a batter's strength against him."

Killing them softly is an Ojeda specialty. In fact, the junkballer used to act as something of a human changeup on the Mets' talented staff. After seeing Dwight Gooden, Sid Fernandez, and Ron Darling throwing peas, Ojeda's slow-motion offerings seem to pose problems for batters. In the tradition of Johnny Podres and Warren Spahn, the present-day master of the changeup is Frank Viola of the Boston Red Sox, who used the pitch to great effect in the 1987 World Series, while a member of the Minnesota Twins. Viola says he holds the ball in the back of his hand and uses the same motion as the fastball. Some pitchers use a circle change, forming a loop with the thumb and index finger. Upon release, the ball looks to be a fastball. In the split-second a batter takes to size up the pitch, the message from eyes to brain to wrists says fastball, dooming the batter if the pitcher has set him up correctly. A change-up is always a relative proposition; Nolan Ryan's changeup has been clocked at eighty-seven miles an hour, faster than many pitchers' fastballs.

"Fans often wonder why hitters get fooled so often by slow stuff," wrote Carl Yastrzemski with Al Hirshberg in his book on hitting. "This happens to the best of batters. A good pitcher always uses the same windup, if he uses one at all. Before he throws his slow pitch, he does everything exactly as he would if he were coming in with a fastball or a fast breaking ball. Watching him, the batter can't tell if the next pitch will be a change until it's halfway to the plate. By then, he may already have committed himself. From what I hear, Warren Spahn had the best change of any pitcher in the business. I faced Spahn a few times, in exhibition games down south, and by then he was beyond his peak. But he was still going, and his best pitch was that slow curve. He must have been one of the few pitchers in the game who used it in the clutch. It was so deceptive that when he put it where he wanted to, only luck or a miracle enabled a hitter to get a good piece of it."

It is only appropriate that the Human Changeup himself, Bobby Ojeda (below), is a master of killing them softly. Compared to the fire dished out by teammate Dwight Gooden, Ojeda's junkball offerings seem to stand still. **Opposite page:** *The speed of a baseball is relative. If set up properly, hitting even a modest fastball can be as effective as one that flies past at ninety-five miles an hour.*

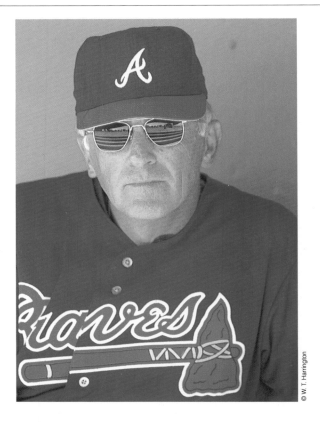

Phil Niekro (right) *can still throw a knuckleball that defies bats and explanations. The problem is, he doesn't know why it does what it does. Here, he demonstrates the grip* (below).

The Knuckleball

Perhaps because of its origins from deep within the nineteenth century, baseball has always been a sport closely associated with myth. And baseball's greatest mystery is the knuckleball. Ask Phil Niekro, who won 318 games with his elusive knuckler, how it works and he'll say:

"I don't know. I've been doing it all my life and I don't have the slightest idea why it does what it does. I've had all kinds of people test me, research groups from Columbia University and so on. I've thrown in wind tunnels so they could study the aerodynamic effects of the air on the ball, I've thrown balls with no seams, I've read all the books in the libraries. I'll tell you, all those physics phrases don't make any sense to me. In a strange way, I think it's kind of nice that no one is able to explain it."

A knuckleball (a misnomer actually) is a pitch thrown with the fingernails (not the knuckles) of the index and middle finger digging into the ball, with support from the thumb and remaining fingers. When released properly, a good knuckleball will experience almost no rotation. As it moves toward the plate, physicists tell us, the air currents work on the seams of the ball and cause it to dart and dip erratically. Niekro says his knuckleball velocity ranged from thirty-five to fifty-five miles an hour, depending on the wind conditions and the count on the hitter.

And though he didn't always know exactly where it was going, some internal sense told him when he had loosed a good one. Early in his career with the Atlanta Braves, his catchers noticed that occasionally after the release, Niekro would instinctively reach out with his glove. The pitcher himself wasn't aware of it, but the catchers soon discovered that every time it happened, the pitch was so perfect it was unhittable. Niekro subconsciously realized this when he let the pitch fly and was calling for the ball from the catcher, even before it arrived. In retrospect, Niekro says, "When it felt that way, even God couldn't hit it."

The knuckleball has always been part of the baseball landscape. Oddly enough, some of history's greatest knuckleball practitioners were not pitchers. "Mickey Mantle had a hellacious knuckleball," says Hall of Famer Whitey Ford. "When he had it going right, you couldn't catch it."

Pitchers had discovered the bizarre flight of the knuckleball early on, but very few had total command of the pitch. The reason is the narrow margin of error: When the release is off by just a few degrees, the ball spins and approaches the plate in the manner of a wounded duck. Early on, pitchers used the knuckleball as something of a changeup, a complement to their fastball and curve. Ted Lyons, who won 260 games for the Chicago White Sox from 1923 to 1946, was a thinking man's pitcher who used the knuckleball to save his arm and extend his career. That he completed nearly 75 percent of his starts was a tribute to his terrific control—with a little help from his knuckler.

Six years after Lyons retired, along came Hoyt Wilhelm, who appeared in more games than any pitcher in history. Naturally, his key to longevity was the knuckleball. He was a reliever by trade, long before it was fashionable, and in 1952 Wilhelm went 15-3 in relief as a rookie in New York. He used the same two-fingered pressure that Niekro describes, and it ultimately led to a record 123 victories from the bullpen and an incredible 227 saves. Successful knuckleballers have always enjoyed longevity, and managers like them because they take the pressure off the bullpen by going the distance so often. The drawback to the knuckleball is its unpredictability and the catcher's occasional inability to track it down. To combat this, most catchers use a special knuckleball mitt that approaches the size of Rhode Island.

Never a popular pitch because it is so difficult to master, the knuckleball is fading from the baseball scene. Charlie Hough was still in there pitching in 1993 for the Florida Marlins expansion team. He was forty-five years old, a tribute to the easy motion the knuckleball requires. Tom Candiotti is another present-day knuckleball artist.

Niekro learned the pitch from his father, who was an Ohio fastballer of some repute. When he blew out his arm and went to work in the coal mines, another miner taught him the pitch. Some of Niekro's fondest memories are of tossing the ball in his backyard. "That was his gift to me," Niekro says. "You know, the first thing that comes into your life, you kind of hang on to it. When you look back, it took me a long way. I just wish there had been times when I knew where it was going."

If Niekro didn't know where it was going, imagine how the hitters felt.

The venerable Charlie Hough was still throwing the low-stress knuckleball when the Florida Marlins were born in 1993.

THE HITTER

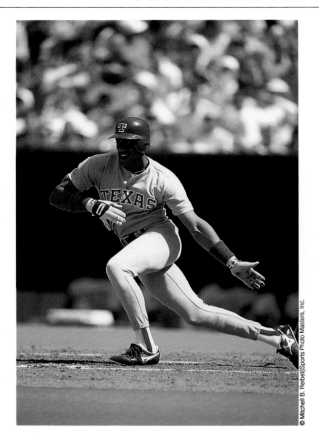

George Brett (below),
a lifetime .300 hitter,
flirted with the .400 mark
in 1980. Juan Gonzalez
(right) hit a major-league
high 43 home runs in 1992.
Gary Sheffield (opposite
page) made a mark as
the San Diego Padres
third baseman, hitting .330,
amassing 33 home runs,
and driving in 100 runners
in 1992. A year later,
he was producing
big numbers for the
expansion Florida Marlins.

ansas City's George Brett identifies the curve as it rolls out of the pitcher's hand, squints his eyes, tightens his left-handed grip on the bat, cocks his hips, moves his right foot forward, and begins his swing, shifting his weight fluidly from back to front. His hands stay back until the last possible second. In a place of pure poetry, he flicks the bat forward at the ball and sends it between the drawn-in first and second baseman for a run-scoring single to right field. The next time up, with two men in scoring position, he strikes out on that same curve, this one hopelessly out of reach in the dirt. At this moment, at least, Brett agrees that hitting a pitched baseball is indeed the most difficult feat in all of sport.

"When you're swinging good, it's the easiest thing in the world," he says later in the Royals' clubhouse. "When you're swinging bad, it's the hardest thing in the world. There are times when you go to the plate and just know you're going to get a hit. And then, there's nothing worse than going up and knowing that, no matter what you do, you're not going to hit the ball. That happens more than you think."

Then it would follow, wouldn't it, that hitting a baseball is a purely mental enterprise? "If you figure that

© Bob Rosato

Right: *Mike Schmidt, the former Philadelphia Phillies slugger, could also hit. The third baseman hit .293 as late as 1987.* **Below:** *Cincinnati Reds catcher Johnny Bench, discussing technique here with the Dodgers' Steve Yeager, knocked in 1,376 runs in seventeen seasons.*

TOP TEN CAREER HOME RUNS

1. Hank Aaron	755
2. Babe Ruth	714
3. Willie Mays	660
4. Frank Robinson	586
5. Harmon Killebrew	573
6. Reggie Jackson	563
7. Mike Schmidt	548
8. Mickey Mantle	536
9. Jimmie Foxx	534
10. Ted Williams	521
Willie McCovey	521

TOP TEN CAREER HOME RUN PERCENTAGE

1. Babe Ruth	8.5
2. Ralph Kiner	7.1
3. Harmon Killebrew	7.0
4. Ted Williams	6.8
5. Dave Kingman	6.6
Mickey Mantle	6.6
Jimmie Foxx	6.6
8. Mike Schmidt	6.56
9. Hank Greenberg	6.4
Willie McCovey	6.4

most guys in the majors have a certain level of talent," Brett says, "then, yes, it's 100-percent mental. Consistency is the thing. You have to stay focused."

For most of the 1980 season, Kansas City's third baseman was in one of history's rare concentration grooves. He was hurt for much of the first half, but after the All-Star break Brett flirted with the ethereal .400 mark, not achieved since Ted Williams hit .406 in 1941. Brett hit safely in sixty-three of his final seventy-two games for a .420 average, including a thirty-game hitting streak from July 18 to August 18. As the national media descended on Brett and the Royals, he remained relaxed at the plate and went above the .400 mark on August 17; nine days later he pushed his average to .407 with a 5-for-5 game at Milwaukee. As late as September 19, he hovered at or over the legendary number before finishing the season at .390.

"I was fortunate to keep my swing intact," says Brett, a .310 lifetime hitter. "Usually, it takes you a while to find the rhythm, get the swing going. That year, I had it almost every game."

Sounds scientific, doesn't it? "Not really," Brett says, laughing. "You just hope it's there when you get to the plate."

Baseball's line of demarcation is a .300 batting average, meaning that even the good hitter fails 70 percent of the time. Yes, hitting a ball that travels better than seventy-five miles an hour over the sixty-foot, six-inch distance from the rubber to the plate is that hard. Against a variety of wicked offerings like screwballs, forkballs, biting curves, and rising fastballs, a hitter has a margin of error that approaches one-quarter of an inch; that can be the difference between a towering fly ball out and a line drive home run.

Ty Cobb, who has the highest lifetime batting average in history at .367, hit .300 or better a staggering twenty-three times. Cap Anson, another nineteenth-century player, did it twenty times. Of course, Cobb and Anson did not hit for power, combining for only 209 home runs. Those rare hitters who hit for average and power do the most damage. Babe Ruth, for instance, has history's best slugging percentage (.690) because he hit 714 home runs and batted .342. Stan Musial (475 homers, .331 average) and Williams (521 homers and .344 average) were also among baseball's lethal hitters. And though Williams liked to talk about the weird science of hitting and knowing the strike zone, he was blessed with the attributes the great hitters share: exceptional eyesight, quick reflexes, and confidence. Williams, who flew planes for the Navy in World War II, had 20-10 vision, which is to say he saw the ball twice as well as a mere mortal. He was blessed with good stereoscopic vision: perception of depth and the ability to judge position in space. As the story goes, if Williams let a pitch go by, they figured it was a ball. Conversely, if he took a rare third strike, he often started walking away from the plate even before the umpire made the call.

"We were playing the Red Sox one time in Boston," says Luke Appling, the old Chicago White Sox player, "and there was a good ump behind the plate. Joe Haynes was on the mound for us, and with two out and the bases loaded Williams takes strike three. He starts going back to the dugout, but the ump called it a ball. He hit the next ball out of the park and beat us. After the game, I asked him where the pitch was. He laughed and said, 'Right down the middle, [waist] high.'"

Generally speaking, all great hitters share the gift of remarkable sight. Sportswriter John Kieran reported that Ruth once correctly read a license plate from so far away that the writer couldn't determine its color. Good

© Sportschrome East/West

TOP TEN CAREER SLUGGING PERCENTAGES (TOTAL BASES PER AT-BAT)	
1. Babe Ruth	.690
2. Ted Williams	.634
3. Lou Gehrig	.632
4. Jimmie Foxx	.609
5. Hank Greenberg	.605
6. Joe DiMaggio	.579
7. Rogers Hornsby	.577
8. Johnny Mize	.562
9. Stan Musial	.559
10. Willie Mays	.557
Mickey Mantle	.557

Above: *For years the standard at third base for the Boston Red Sox, Wade Boggs opted for the New York Yankees pinstripes in 1993.*

eyesight allows batters like Ruth and Williams, who worked pitchers for more walks than anyone else, better selectivity at the plate; Williams averaged 106 walks per season, while Ruth's career total of 2,056 is the highest in history. Since they watched more bad pitches go by, consequently they swung at better pitches. Boston's Wade Boggs, whose career batting average is .352 in eight seasons, has averaged 90 walks over that time. In 1988, Boggs became the first modern player to produce 200 hits or more for six straight seasons. He did it again in 1989. He did it, in part, because of his tenacity with two strikes. Boggs has the unnatural ability to pick out borderline pitches that are potential strikes but largely unhittable, and slap them foul. In 1988, he struck out only thirty-four times in 719 at-bats. "Hitting with a 2-1 or 3-0 count is pretty easy," Boggs says. "You're ahead and the pitcher has to come in with a strike. The good hitters get the job done when they're down in the count. Pitchers are basically trying to get you to hit their pitch, a pitch out of the strike zone. A good hitter hits the pitches he can handle, and you don't see too many of those."

Seeing the ball well isn't easy. "Sometimes you don't see it so much as feel it," Brett says. "The subconscious takes over and takes you through the swing. I've never really seen the ball hit the bat. After it leaves the bat, then you get it back in your vision."

Chicago White Sox hitting instructor Walt Hriniak teaches players to use their heads as a tool by putting it

Pete Rose made a career of keeping his eye on the ball. His overall batting average wasn't a thing of beauty, but no one has amassed more than his 4,256 hits.

out over the plate to better see the ball. That way, the head is on the same plane as the flight of the ball. This goes against Williams' precise mechanics, which stress fluid hip action.

"Everybody talks about watching the ball, but you've got to show them how to watch it," says Hriniak, a disciple of the legendary Charlie Lau. "We try to get them to do two things: Lower the head at contact and keep the head on the ball throughout, and finish the swing and get extension, releasing the top hand or keeping two hands on the bat and finishing high."

In his book on batting, Hall of Famer Carl Yastrzemski explained the delicate moment a hitter commits to a pitch. "The best time to swing," he wrote, "is the very last second. The best hitters are last-second hitters. One of the greatest who ever lived is Henry Aaron of the Braves. Old-time baseball men who have seen many more stars come and go than I have tell me Aaron has the fastest wrists the game has ever known. He can wait until the ball is almost on top of him before committing himself, then snap his bat so fast he literally takes the ball out of the catcher's hands.

"I keep my eye on the ball, picking it up as soon as possible after it leaves the pitcher's hand, but I don't decide whether or not to swing until it reaches a certain zone, a point roughly twenty-five feet in front of me. Remember, the ball is traveling so fast, I don't have all day to make up my mind. The longer I wait, the better off I am because the more I see. If I start swinging when the ball reaches my zone, I have to take it for granted I know where the ball will be when my bat reaches the point of contact. If I can wait, I don't have to take anything for granted."

Yastrzemski identified pitches in the following way: The fastball was coming if the ball was predominantly white as it left the pitcher's hand. The severe backspin rotation on the ball all but blurred the red seams. A curve and a slider have topspin, but the slider is much faster. Changeups rarely have much spin.

Aaron, who hit 755 home runs in his career, a baseball standard of excellence, credits his concentration more than his quick, supple wrists. "At the plate, you have these blinders on; you hear nothing, see nothing but the pitcher and his windup. That's the one-on-one challenge of hitting. I didn't usually react to the pitch as I guessed. I probably guessed ninety-five percent of the time. If the ball was in the right zone, I was ready for it."

Rod Carew was one of the purest hitters of all time. He led the American League in batting for seven of his first twelve seasons in Minnesota. His best mark was .388 in 1977, the season he also led the league in hits (239), runs (128), and triples (16). Carew explains, "I never, ever took my eyes off the ball. By watching the release point and how his hand moved in the follow-

© W. T. Harrington

TOP TEN CAREER HITS	
1. Pete Rose	4,256
2. Ty Cobb	4,191
3. Hank Aaron	3,771
4. Stan Musial	3,630
5. Tris Speaker	3,515
6. Honus Wagner	3,430
7. Carl Yastrzemski	3,419
8. Eddie Collins	3,311
9. Willie Mays	3,283
10. Nap Lajoie	3,251

© T. G. Higgins/Allsport

For Carl Yastrzemski of the Boston Red Sox, identifying the pitch early was the key. It worked for a Triple Crown (league-leading RBI's, home runs, and batting average) in 1967.

Above: *One of the best hitters in today's game is Minnesota's Kirby Puckett. After going 0-for-612 in home runs at the start of his major-league career, Puckett has learned to pick his pitches.*

TOP TEN LOWEST CAREER STRIKEOUT AVERAGES	
1. Joe Sewell	.016
2. Willie Keeler	.019
3. Lloyd Waner	.022
4. Nellie Fox	.023
5. Tommy Holmes	.024
6. Lave Cross	.028
Tris Speaker	.028
Stuffy McInnis	.028
9. Andy High	.030
Sam Rice	.030

through, I knew if the fastball or curve was coming. I rarely guessed."

And while great hitters are born and maximize their potential, even average players can make themselves into respectable hitters through experience. "It took me a long time to understand the whole picture," Brett says. "I have a better idea of what I'm supposed to do at the plate. I know the situations better, what pitchers will try to throw me at certain times. I also understand my limitations."

Brooks Robinson, the Baltimore Orioles' Hall of Fame third baseman, had one of the niftiest gloves in history. Even though he hit over .300 twice in his twenty-three seasons, Robinson's lifetime batting average was a pedestrian .267. "When I came up," he says, "I knew that Ted Williams was saying things like, 'The slider breaks fifty-nine-and-one-half feet from the mound . . .' and stuff like that. I was thinking to myself, 'Man, if hitting's going to be this tough, I don't know if I can do it.'"

After an outstanding minor league career, Gerald Perry finally delivered on his promise in 1988. He hit an even .300 for the Atlanta Braves—this after a .214 performance in 1985. "Gerald thought he could hit anything you threw," says his manager, Russ Nixon. "Now, he's got a lot better sense of what he can hit and what he hits best. He's one of those guys who's going to make contact every time he swings the bat. His average went way down when he was swinging at everything—but he'd hit the thing. He'd foul it off or hit it for an out."

Says former teammate Ted Simmons, the cerebral catcher, "The strike zone is usually the last refinement in an accomplished hitter. Gerald has the physical skills, he has the opportunity, and now he knows what is a strike and what isn't. When that time arrives, you're looking at a very dangerous offensive person."

Wade Boggs and San Diego's Tony Gwynn are examples of players who hit strictly for average. Kirby Puckett and Don Mattingly are two of today's best hitters for average and power. Both began as pure hitters and learned to pick their power spots as they matured.

The five-foot-eight, 210-pound Puckett was drafted by the Minnesota Twins in 1982. He led the Appalachian League that season with a .382 average and hit .314 the following year in Class A ball. Upon arriving in the major leagues for good in May 1984, Puckett went 612 at-bats without a home run. In fact, his first 1,248 at-bats produced only four home runs. In 1986, the Twins moved Puckett from the leadoff position to number three in the order. By keeping his weight on the back foot longer and waiting a little bit longer on the pitch, Puckett hit 83 home runs in three seasons and 220 runs batted in over the past two. Part of Puckett's success stems from his zeal. He is a classic free

TOP TEN CAREER RUNS BATTED IN	
1. Hank Aaron	2,297
2. Babe Ruth	2,211
3. Lou Gehrig	1,990
4. Ty Cobb	1,961
5. Stan Musial	1,951
6. Jimmie Foxx	1,921
7. Willie Mays	1,903
8. Mel Ott	1,860
9. Carl Yastrzemski	1,844
10. Ted Williams	1,839

swinger and walked only 23 times in 1988. "You don't ever want to take that aggressiveness away from him," says Twins' third base coach Rick Renick. "He's a bad-ball hitter. He'll hit a ball that's two inches off the ground for a double and hit a ball at eye-level for a home run. It's incredible to watch." In 1989, he obviously found some good balls to hit, winning the batting title with a .337 average.

Mattingly, the New York Yankees' first baseman, hit a total of 41 home runs in his first five years of organized baseball, but broke through for 137 the next five. His 1986 season was one for the books. He hit .352 with a league-high 238 hits, 53 doubles, 31 home runs, and 113 runs batted in. Like Puckett, Mattingly doesn't like to walk if he can help it; his highest season total is 56. "The difference," he says, "is I learned when I could and couldn't turn on the ball and pull it. It was in winter ball before the 1984 season. I never try to hit home runs . . . they just come from hitting line drives. As I've gotten older, I think I've gotten stronger and smarter, too. That's where the power comes from."

Don Baylor, who played in three consecutive World Series from 1986 to 1988, played with Mattingly, Boggs, and Carew, and is often asked to compare the three. "Those are the three best hitters I've ever seen, and I wouldn't know what order to put them in because they all do different things so well," Baylor wrote in his book, *Nothing but the Truth: A Player's Life*. "But of the three, Donnie is more of a damage guy than Boggs is or Rodney was. Donnie's more like Brett—a guy who will drive in the big run, collect the extra-base hit, and pull the ball over the right field wall. He doesn't possess the Boggs art of making contact. Nobody does. He is not as consistent as Carew. But as far as keeping the average up there and driving in runs, Mattingly is tops.

"He has great hand-eye coordination and does every single thing a hitter must do to hit .350. He locks out distractions as well as any player I've seen, a good attribute to have in New York."

Mattingly's Yankee teammate, Dave Winfield, is another power hitter with the ability to hit for average. On the final day of the 1984 season, Winfield lost a brilliant duel with Mattingly, finishing second in the American League by three points with a .340 batting average. "Hitting is about attitude," Winfield says. "It's in the swagger from the dugout. I go to the plate with the attitude that 'I'm going to beat you.' You try to intimidate the pitcher standing up there." That isn't difficult when you're built like a football tight end at six-foot-six, 220 pounds.

Johnny Bench, the great Hall of Fame catcher for the Cincinnati Reds, agrees that hitting is a matter of the mind. "It's inner conceit," Bench says, "It's knowing in your head that you can beat that pitcher. That is what hitting is: the power of positive thinking."

Some of today's hitters could use a little of Bench's optimism. They believe it's tougher to hit than it was five or ten years ago. Why? "Because every pitcher has added an extra pitch he can throw for a strike," says San Diego slugger Jack Clark. "Now, you have to be perfect to get a hit." Ryne Sandberg of the Chicago Cubs sees it the same way. "They're all coming up with new pitches. I see a lot of breaking pitches even when I'm ahead in the count. It used to be if you were ahead 2-0 or 3-0 or 3-1, you could expect the fastball. It doesn't work that way anymore."

Fortunately, some things never change. As Detroit Tigers manager Sparky Anderson says, "Hitting is always going to be the same thing: "It's a round ball, and a round bat, and you have to hit it square. Simple, huh?"

© Otto Greule Jr./Allsport

Above: *Reggie Jackson struck out four times for every home run, qualifying him as one of the game's most exciting sluggers.*

TOP TEN CAREER BATTING AVERAGE	
1. Ty Cobb	.367
2. Rogers Hornsby	.358
3. Joe Jackson	.356
4. Ed Delahanty	.345
Willie Keeler	.345
6. Ted Williams	.344
Tris Speaker	.344
Billy Hamilton	.344
9. Dan Brouthers	.343
Pete Browning	.343

CHAPTER 3

BEHIND THE PLATE

© W. T. Harrington

© W. T. Harrington

Unlike the outfielder, the catcher can never catch his breath squatting behind the plate. It's a nasty job back there, but someone has to do it. Rich Gedman (right), formerly of the Red Sox, is one of those few, proud men who makes his living in the dirt.

THE CATCHER

ormer Red Sox catcher Rich Gedman pulls off his spikes and winces. He's not sure which nagging injury hurts more—the foul ball he took off his right instep yesterday or the bouncing ball in the dirt that nicked his collarbone today. "Catching is a dirty job," says Gedman, explaining why most exuberant Little Leaguers (on the advice of their mothers) would rather play any other position. "There's a lot of things you go through, stuff you take for granted, that most people don't want to deal with. Nobody likes to get hit in the [nether regions] with a foul ball. Nobody likes to sit there in a crouch for nine innings. Nobody likes to block balls in the dirt. But you do it, because that's what you're supposed to do. I don't think catchers are mentally tougher than anyone else, they're just conditioned to not show pain. I mean, in April you take Roger Clemens' first fastball, even right in the pocket of the glove, and it's thirty degrees and you can't feel the ball at all for the whole first inning."

Gedman's not complaining, just stating the facts. Of all baseball's positions, catching is the least glamorous, which explains why a good catcher is hard to find. "It's a societal thing," says Montreal manager Buck Rodgers. "Mothers don't want their kids back there getting hit by foul tips and bats and being run over trying to block the plate. Fathers don't want the good athlete son catching, because he could get hurt. High

© W. T. Harrington

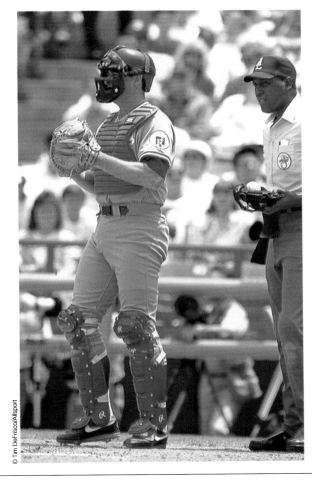

© Tim DeFrisco/Allsport

school and college coaches usually put their best athletes on the mound or at shortstop."

The career of Gedman is a case in point. A pitcher/ shortstop in Little League, he caught only one game while playing for St. Peter's of Worcester, Massachusetts, because his coach utilized him as a pitcher and first baseman. "I'd be dragging the day after pitching a game," Gedman says, "so they'd put me at first base. When I graduated, the scouts told me I was too slow to play the outfield and hit too good to be a pitcher. They were looking for a lot of home runs at third base, which wasn't me, they prolonged guys' careers at first, and my hands weren't quick enough to play second. So that left catching as a last resort."

Since most high school and college catchers are poorer athletes than their teammates, many of the better major league catchers are converted from other positions. Though Gary Carter was a shortstop and pitcher for Sunnyhills High School in Fullerton, California, Montreal was impressed with his arm, size, and leadership qualities. Bob Boone, who at age forty-one is still rated as the American League's best all-around catcher, was a third baseman in the Philadelphia Phillies farm system. Carlton Fisk was a shortstop and pitcher in high school, but in 1987 he caught his 1,807th game, setting an American League record. Because of the paucity of talent, any minor league catcher with prom-

Bob Boone (left) has defied tradition (and gravity) by remaining one of the game's great catchers past the age of forty. Truth is, there aren't any prospects down on the farms ready to replace him.

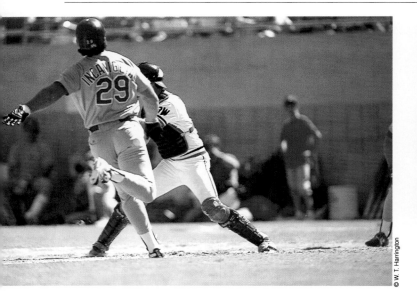

Above: *Pete Incaviglia of the Texas Rangers wheels around third base and heads for home. The ball beats him home and he's . . . he's. . . out. There are times when catchers must wish they had listened to their mothers.* **Opposite page:** *Carlton Fisk, hitter of a dramatic twelfth-inning home run in the 1975 World Series for the Boston Red Sox, carved a niche for himself with the White Sox in Chicago. Like Bob Boone, he is a future Hall of Famer who has thrived at an age when most player retire.*

ise gets rushed to the majors, leaving him with little time to develop. Catching remains the quickest way to the big leagues.

When former major leaguer Ozzie Virgil Sr., started grooming his son, Ozzie Jr., for the major leagues, he made him a catcher. "It was the fastest way to the majors," says Ozzie Jr. "For me, it was probably the only way."

And while the responsibility of calling all the pitches, flagging them down and keeping track of the base runners—all while carrying on regular duties as a hitter—can be daunting, it also makes the catcher the second most influential player on the field after the pitcher. "That's what I always liked about catching," says Johnny Bench, the 1989 Hall of Fame enshrinee. "There are so many ways to contribute to winning. You can call a good game, make a few throws to cut runners down on the bases, save a wild pitch, plus hit. A lot of guys dwell on the negatives and feel the pressure, but I always looked at it in a positive way."

Rick Cerone, a twelve-season veteran of six teams, uses a football metaphor to describe the catcher's job. "The catcher is sitting behind the plate looking at all the other positions," he says. "He's kind of like the quarterback. You're directing traffic, working with the pitcher, setting a tempo. I'll bet a lot of catchers were quarterbacks in high school. In a lot of ways, you're an extension of the manager out there, since he's not allowed on the field. You're carrying out his philosophy, sort of managing the game yourself."

Carter, an eleven-time All-Star and two-time High School All-America quarterback, says, "The emphasis is always on offensive statistics, but I think a catcher is more valuable for the other things he does. You have to

TOP TEN CAREER GAMES PLAYED AT CATCHER	
1. Bob Boone	2,187
2. Al Lopez	1,918
3. Jim Sundberg	1,926
4. Carlton Fisk	1,850
5. Rick Ferrell	1,805
6. Gabby Hartnett	1,790
7. Ted Simmons	1,762
8. Johnny Bench	1,744
9. Ray Schalk	1,726
10. Bill Dickey	1,712

The eternally enthusiastic Gary Carter was a terrific target for the New York Mets' young pitchers in the mid-1980s. A catcher's contribution behind the plate is as important as it is hard to quantify.

© W. T. Harrington

understand ten different egos out there on the mound, know their strengths and weaknesses. By matching a pitcher's strengths and what you know to be the hitter's weaknesses, you can win ball games. Catchers don't get enough credit for the mental work they do." Since the mid-1980s, Carter's former team, the Mets have boasted one of the finest pitching staffs in baseball. As blazers Dwight Gooden and Sid Fernandez, Yale University's Ron Darling, and junkball specialist Bobby Ojeda took the mound game after game, Carter was the one constant. And though he has hit 280 home runs as a catcher, fourth on the all-time list, Carter's enduring value to the Mets was his ability to get the most from his pitchers.

In baseball's early years, catchers, like shortstops, were prized for their defensive skills. Any kind of hitting was considered a bonus. Lately, there has been a trend toward offensive catchers. Johnny Bench, probably the greatest catcher in history, hit a major league record 327 home runs as a catcher and totaled 2,048 hits. At the same time, he revolutionized the catching game by catching the ball one-handed. By keeping the throwing hand behind him, the theory went, it would be protected from injury. This technique changed the way catchers approached balls in the dirt. Instead of blocking the ball in conventional down-and-dirty fashion, catchers attempted to stop the ball solely with the glove. Not only does this require more time to collect the ball and throw out a baserunner, but, as former catcher Tim McCarver points out, "It changes the way pitchers think. The basic purpose of a catcher never gets taught to most kids. If a catcher can't block a tough pitch in the dirt with a runner on third in a one-run game, the pitcher won't let his best curveball or split-finger fastball go for fear it'll end up at the screen. You'd be surprised how many times during the season a pitcher gets blamed for hanging a curveball or split-finger, and the reason he hung it is because he's afraid his catcher won't catch the tough one."

Since the minor leagues have failed to produce quality catchers lately, those few catchers of distinction last longer at the top, suggesting that catching may be more of a mental enterprise than people suspect. Boone, most recently of the Kansas City Royals, played the 1989 season at the age of forty-one, as did Fisk. Boone won three consecutive Gold Glove Awards from 1986 to 1988, on his way to the major league record for games caught, with 2,187. His 1988 Gold Glove, the sixth of his career, was based on a 38 percent success rate in throwing out baserunners (37 of 97), a league-high 66 assists among catchers, and just one passed ball. "Boone has elevated every team he has played on from that position," says Ron Swoboda, the former Mets outfielder. "Catching is an arcane science. There are very few people with the skill, the personality, and the intelligence to do it. If pitchers don't like the man they're throwing to, that can poison an entire staff. Boone can do the job as good as—no, better than—anybody. He knows how to handle any kind of pitcher. That's more important than what he can do with the bat. He's as bright as they come at that position."

Like Boone, Fisk has been hearing his age questioned for years.

"Since 1983, they've been telling me I'm too old to play," he says. "And whoever made the decision to replace me was trying to show everybody I was too old to play, or couldn't play. It's something I'll never forget. I've always worked hard; commitment knows no off-season. I've always believed the road to success is paved by hard work, not by somebody giving you something. And that was pretty evident in '86 and '87, when they tried to give my job to a couple of other players." The Chicago White Sox tried to put Fisk out to pasture in left field, but every season he wound up behind the plate. On August 19, 1988, the night he set the American League record for games caught, Fisk produced the first five-hit game of his career. "It means I've persevered against the odds," Fisk said that night. "I've had one career-threatening injury and I've missed three years with injuries because of positional play. I've also been confronted with a lot of organizational obstacles. This means perseverance beyond what is supposed to happen. It makes me feel good."

Like Fisk, Gedman is convinced that great catchers are made, not born. "When I broke into the Instructional League, I got my butt kicked around for two months," he says. "I took hundreds of balls off the chest protector, took a lot of grief. But, eventually, I got the hang of it. Catching is okay, since it's what I do. Still, in my heart I've always wondered if I could have been a big-league pitcher."

TOP TEN CAREER FIELDING PERCENTAGE AT CATCHER

1.	Bill Freehan	.993
2.	Elston Howard	.993
3.	Jim Sundberg	.992
4.	Sherm Lollar	.992
5.	Tom Haller	.992
6.	Johnny Edwards	.992
7.	Jerry Grote	.991
8.	Lance Parrish	.991
9.	Johnny Bench	.990
10.	Gary Carter	.990

Catcher Bo Diaz, looking more like Magic Johnson, follows the bouncing ball up the third base line in the 1983 World Series.

© John McDonough

The Greatest Catchers of All Time

There is more to catching than merely swinging a bat, which is all it essentially takes to play the outfield. Catching is a mental enterprise, which explains why the eleven receivers enshrined in the Hall of Fame collectively batted well under .300. It is difficult to judge a player's contribution behind the plate; only his pitcher and manager know the answer for sure.

Johnny Bench of the Cincinnati Reds was probably the greatest catcher to ever play the game. On July 23, 1989 he was inducted at Cooperstown and became only the nineteenth player in history to earn entry in his first year of eligibility. In fact, only Ty Cobb and Hank Aaron received a higher percentage of votes (96.4) than Bench did from the Baseball Writers Association of America.

Bench made his mark both with the glove and the bat. He revolutionized the way the position was played by catching with one hand, instead of using the classic two-hand approach. This enabled him to deftly stop balls in the dirt without losing his balance. This technique, coupled with a feared throwing arm, kept base runners in check. Bench's ability to handle the Reds' veteran pitching staff, even when he was in his early twenties, was another facet to his game. Ten consecutive Rawlings Gold Glove awards testify to his defensive greatness.

Bench's debut with the Reds in 1968 resulted in 15 home runs and 82 runs batted in. In a span of ten seasons, Bench drove in 1,032 runs, including three National League-leading totals. In 1970, Bench led the league with 45 home runs and 148 runs batted in on his way to the first of two Most Valuable Player awards. The second came two seasons later, when his totals of 40 homers and 125 runs batted in led the league again. Bench also won the 1976 World Series Most Valuable Player award. He finished his seventeen-year career with 389 home runs, 327 of them as a catcher—an all-time high when he retired in 1983.

Bob Boone, eighteen days younger than Bench, is still working the dirt behind the plate for the Kansas City Royals, while Bench is now a fixture behind the microphone for the Reds baseball network. That explains why Boone had already set a major league record for games caught (2,187), even before he opened the 1989 season behind the plate for Kansas City. At the age of forty-two, Boone's intelligence continued to make him one of the best catchers in the majors. He blocked balls well, exhibited a quick release, and called heady games that left several franchises hoping he would retire so he could pursue managing.

Boone had won six Gold Gloves with three different teams: the Philadelphia Phillies, the California Angels, and the Royals. In 1986 and 1987, he became the oldest nonpitcher to win the honor. In 1988, Boone had one of his best seasons ever. He led all

▲ **Johnny Bench**

© AP/Wide World Photos

▼ **Bill Dickey**

Baseball Hall of Fame

Baseball Hall of Fame

▲ Josh Gibson

American League catchers with 66 assists, allowed only one passed ball, and hit for the highest average—.296—of his seventeen-year career. Boone and his father, Ray, are only the second father and son combination in major league history to each produce 100 home runs, after Gus and Buddy Bell.

Yogi Berra could always turn a phrase; sometimes his fractured syntax tore a sentence in half. Berra, however, spoke most eloquently on the baseball diamond. The bare numbers do not tell the whole story: Berra's batting average was .285 for a nineteen-year career and he hit 358 home runs, though never more than 30 in a season. If you are looking for insight as to Berra's contribution to baseball, look in his safe deposit box, where ten world championship rings can be found—one for each finger. Now, some critics insist that Berra was lucky to find himself playing on a New York Yankees team with players like Whitey Ford, Mickey Mantle, Roger Maris, and Joe DiMaggio, but they, too, were fortunate.

Though, certainly, Berra was in the right place at the right time, he made the most of his opportunity. He played in a staggering fourteen World Series, compiling firsts for games (75), at-bats (259), hits (71), and doubles (10). Berra is second on the all-time list in runs (41) and runs batted in (39), and is third in home runs with 12. His best regular-season effort was in 1950, when the free swinger hit .322 with 28 home runs and 124 runs batted in. From 1953 to 1956, Berra drove in at least 105 runs. At the same time, he handled the Yankees' gifted pitching staff with aplomb. As a manager, Berra took the

Yankees and New York Mets to pennants in 1964 and 1973, respectively.

Bill Dickey, the Yankees' regular catcher from 1929 to 1941, taught Berra the finer points of catching. Dickey was one of the best catchers from the 1930s, a classic in build (six-foot-one, 185 pounds) and attitude. Dickey was a stoic player who was happy to let Babe Ruth, Lou Gehrig, and DiMaggio make most of the headlines. Still, only Bench, Boone, and Carlton Fisk produced a similar record of durability; Dickey caught 100 or more games for thirteen consecutive seasons. Like most catchers, he wasn't particularly fast, but Dickey was a career .313 hitter with 202 home runs.

Josh Gibson hit either 71 or 75 home runs for the Homestead Grays in 1931 (records for the time are sketchy), but because he was black he was never permitted to play in the major leagues. Gibson, six-foot-one and 215 pounds, was considered by some experts of the time to be a better catcher than Dickey. In his seventeen years of professional baseball, Gibson probably hit more than Ruth's record 714 home runs, but reliable records weren't kept.

Mickey Cochrane, another dominant catcher from the 1930s, was an all-around athlete at Boston University. The five-foot-ten, 180-pounder played halfback for the football team, found time for basketball and boxing and played five positions on the baseball team, including a brief stint at catcher. Cochrane, who hit well even in the minor leagues, gradually learned the art of catching under Philadelphia Athletics manager Connie Mack. Cochrane became a strong defensive player whose ability to block home plate on a throw from the outfield was unmatched in his day. Cochrane's lifetime batting average of .320 is the highest among the Hall of Fame's catchers.

Carlton Fisk, who ranked sixth on the all-time list for games caught, passed Berra as the American League catcher with the most home runs in 1989. Like Boone, he has shown no signs of retiring in the near future.

▼ Yogi Berra

Baseball Hall of Fame

THE UMPIRE

Above: *Even when the man in blue makes the proper call of out (Philadelphia's Chris James couldn't sneak past the New York Mets' Barry Lyons), he is never safe from detractors.*
Opposite page: *It's lonely being an umpire. Sometimes you need to lean on a friend with a steady hand. More often, however, the umpire goes it alone.*

Back in the rough-and-tumble days of baseball, umpires were very much as wild as the pitchers they sometimes judged. It was a more free-wheeling game then, and umpires went into the profession at their own risk—and they typically gave the players as much jawing as they received themselves.

As baseball matured, this history was largely forgotten; the umpire gradually was expected to be the model of decorum. In recent years, the umpire had performed his duty so exceedingly well that he was, except for rare and celebrated cases (hello, Don Denkinger and Larry Barnett), nearly invisible. Well, something less than an object of unadulterated hatred, anyway. They could go for days, even weeks, without anyone noticing.

That all changed in 1988, when umpires first found their faces on baseball trading cards. That not insignificant event coincided with one of the most visible seasons umpires have ever enjoyed (read endured). Dave Pallone stood up for umpires everywhere in May when he was pushed by Cincinnati Reds manager Pete Rose and dared to push back. Later that month, New York Yankees manager Billy Martin kicked, then heaped dirt on Dale Scott in an argument in Oakland. Scott did nothing to retaliate, but Major League Umpires' Association chief Richie Phillips threatened to deny Martin the privilege of arguing another call. Only the intervention of Commissioner Peter Ueberroth ended talk of arbitrary treatment and lawsuits. Umpires also drew the

scorn of managers for their new, hard-line interpretation of the balk rule and an expanded strike zone.

Observers wondered if the arrogance of Pallone and Phillips signaled a growing feeling among umpires that their authority was being threatened. "We took a position I felt we had to take [on Martin]," said Jim Evans, the president of the umpires' association. "I don't regret the position at all. It was a stand of principle. Something had to be done; we knew the consequences of the position we had taken. Our integrity is intact. We were just saying we were not going to tolerate maniacal behavior."

Ed Vargo, the National League supervisor of umpires, says things haven't changed much in the twenty-four seasons he officiated, from 1960 to 1983. "As soon as you put the uniform on, you're going to be in some sort of trouble with someone—but that's the way it's always been."

Others disagree. "You have a lot of problems, and the trouble is when an umpire walks toward a dugout instead of walking away," says Don Baylor, who played in three consecutive World Series from 1986 to 1988, with Boston, Minnesota, and Oakland. "And you can't ask an umpire anything anymore. I remember when a guy would say, 'Yeah, that ball may have been a little low.' Now they just say, 'I'm right, I'm always right. Don't question it.'"

Harry Wendelstedt, who was in his twenty-fourth season in the majors in 1989, refutes the charges of some players that umpires retaliate against those who speak ill of them. "It just goes to show you that even players don't understand the psyche of umpires," he says. "There are only sixty of us, sixty people under great scrutiny. Sixty who are the best at what they do

© W. T. Harrington

because they know if they don't do it well enough, they're gone. As far as retaliation, that's something you see in 'Rambo,' not a baseball field." Wendelstedt traces the deterioration of relations with players to society. "There's less respect for people in positions of authority," he says.

Adds Evans, an eighteen-year veteran of umpiring, "It's just a sign of the times. Ballplayers' salaries are greater, and the greater the salaries, the greater the pressure. It pushes us into the limelight more because the salaries are based so much on individual statistics."

Fortunately, for the umpire, he will never be confused with Pete Rose, Dwight Gooden, or Don Mattingly. "I'm not Robert Redford being recognized in a restaurant," says Ed Montague, a fourteen-year man. "I can still walk out of a ballpark after a big rhubarb and not be recognized."

The same does not go for Pam Postema. At the age of thirty-three, she was considered for a major league umpiring job in 1988 and again in 1989. Though she was returned to the AAA level, she was praised for her work, especially behind the plate. There is a good chance she'll be the first woman to make the bigs in the near future.

In the very early days of baseball, the lone umpire stood safely behind the pitcher, where he had an equally poor view of each base, including home plate. In 1888, John Gaffney moved behind the plate when the bases were empty. When a second official was added some years later, the umpire had a permanent home behind the plate.

Bill Klem, "The Old Arbitrator," came to the National League in 1905 and was immediately placed exclusively behind the plate, based on his keen eye and ability to make rational decisions under fire. He was a pioneer who devised arm signals to call balls and strikes. When Klem began his career, the umpire was an object of scorn for players and fans alike. When he left in 1940, the umpire was looked on by many as a figure of respect. Klem, one of five umpires enshrined at the Hall of Fame, was a chief reason.

Cal Hubbard, who made his mark on the gridiron (he is also honored at the Pro Football Hall of Fame in Canton, Ohio), labored as an umpire for eight years in the minor leagues before reaching the American League in 1936. He was a towering presence for fifteen seasons.

Jocko Conlan was playing the outfield for the Chicago White Sox in 1935 when umpire Red Ormsby succumbed to the heat. The man who hit .263 over two middling seasons in Chicago enjoyed the experience enough to take up umpiring full time the following season. Conlan, who had once been on the other side, hustled in a manner foreign to umpires of the time. His polka-dot tie and balloon chest protector became fixtures in the game for many years.

Tom Connolly was more familiar with cricket as a boy growing up in England, but he took to the American version when he started umpiring in the National League in 1898. Connolly umpired in the majors for thirty-four seasons and developed a reputation as a rules expert and a strict disciplinarian. Still, he once went ten years without ejecting a player.

Opposite page: *They are a rare breed, these sixty-something umpires. Through thick and thin, rainouts or shine, they must stick together.* **Above:** *The umpire, ever vigilant, leans in and makes the call. If he's wrong, the catcher or hitter is only too happy to explain what really happened.*

CHAPTER 4

THE REST OF THE FIELD

THE FIRST BASEMAN

There was a time, not long ago, when the first baseman was usually a good-hitting outfielder compelled by forces beyond his manager's control to play a sensitive infield position. Hitting was his primary task and fielding was left largely to his imagination, regardless of how limited it was. Dick Stuart, a.k.a. Dr. Strangeglove, the six-foot-four, 212-pound slugger who played with six teams in the 1950s and 1960s, serves as a gruesome example. Some of his teammates used to check his glove in the dugout because they were convinced it was made of steel or another alloy that continually repelled the baseball.

As Keith Hernandez sees it, first base has gotten a bad rap over the years. Outside of the pitcher and catcher, he maintains, the first baseman is in a position to win (or lose) more games than any other player. Gradually, this fact has dawned on major league baseball's decision makers, and lately the talent level at first base has improved dramatically.

"The day's of putting the aging veteran out there are gone," says Hernandez, who won eleven consecutive Rawlings Gold Glove awards through 1988. "You can lose the game so many ways with a butcher at first; he's too involved. There are so many skills you need to know to play it right: how to handle yourself around the bag, bunt plays, throws to the other bases, holding runners on base. It's not ever really dull out there at first."

Since the first baseman, according to the rules of the game, handles the ball more than any other infielder, he can help or hurt his ball club in ways that escape the box score. Making routine scoops in the dirt

Keith Hernandez (below) was one of the niftiest glove men at first base in the 1980s. Detroit's Cecil Fielder (opposite page) not only has power at the plate to equal his girth, but also a surprisingly deft touch around the first-base bag.

are a key part of saving games and can help the fielding percentage of shortstops and third basemen. Knowing when to field a ball hit to the right (and when not to) can make the difference between an infield hit and an out. The first baseman who can keep runners honest by holding them on the bag can give his catcher the split-second required to throw the would-be stealer out at second. The ability to spear line drives down the line can save dozens of runs over the course of a season.

The merits of a left-handed first baseman are obvious: Most throwing plays are to his right and, thus, left-handers don't have to turn awkwardly to make throws to second and third on grounders and bunts. Of the sixteen first basemen in the Hall of Fame, nine are left-handed. In the future, that percentage will increase. Both Hernandez and the New York Yankees' Don Mattingly, the game's most consistent first basemen of the 1970s and 1980s, are left-handed. Both of them cite the 3-6-3 double play as the toughest play to successfully complete. Both of them make it look easy.

"All of the elements of the positions are there," Mattingly says. "You have to make the play on the ground ball, get your feet into position to make the quick throw to second base, then get back to the bag and take the return throw. It might look easy, but I can't tell you how many times I've practiced that play. It took me a long time just to get comfortable around the bag, learn to know where it was all the time."

Even after a disappointing 1988 season (Mattingly only hit .311 with 18 home runs and 88 runs batted in), Mattingly is one of the major leagues' most well-rounded players. In four seasons, from 1985 through 1988, Mattingly averaged .337 with 30 home runs and 121 runs batted in. In 1989, he hit .303 and added 23 home runs and 113 runs batted in. "Mattingly's kind of

© W. T. Harrington

© W. T. Harrington

Kent Hrbek, seen here in the Minnesota Twins' Dugout, is a fine hitter with underrated fielding skills.

in a class by himself," says Clete Boyer, who played third base for the New York Yankees and Atlanta Braves and now manages in the Yankee system. "He can make every play, charging the ball and going to second, to third, back to first. If there's a fault, it's that he's not tall enough. Infielders like to throw to taller guys. But everything else, he's great, as good as anyone I've ever seen play."

Perhaps Mattingly's greatest asset is his ability to concentrate in pressure situations. "Mattingly can be 0-for-3 with three strikeouts, you might have your best pitcher on the mound with the game on the line, and he'll still find a way to beat you," says Milwaukee manager Tom Trebelhorn. "He can put the ball in play to center or left or pull it deep. He tunes in to a higher level when he comes up in clutch situations."

Cedric Tallis, former general manager for the Yankees and Kansas City Royals, prefers to discuss Mattingly's fielding skills, which have produced four consecutive Gold Glove awards. "He moves around well, and he's got soft hands," Tallis says. "He can short-hop the badly thrown balls, which is tremendously important. If you've got a first baseman who can't handle the low throws, the off-line throws, the fielders start aiming the ball, giving the runner an extra step. And they start throwing even worse."

Mattingly, who deflects such praise, likes to credit Keith Hernandez with bringing more talent to the position in the 1980s. "Keith had a lot to do with the position becoming more notable," he says. "He's brought an emphasis, helping establish its importance defensively. I don't get to watch him too often, but every time I see him I always ask him something about how to play there."

Growing up in Capuchino, California, Hernandez defied the typical mold of first baseman. He was the quar-

terback on the Capuchino High School football team and a guard on the basketball team. Hernandez produced a career .500 batting average there, a record for the Peninsula High School League. Though most major leaguers say mastering the field was more difficult than handling the bat, Hernandez begs to differ.

"If hitting was like fielding, I wouldn't have any gray hairs," says Hernandez, now thirty-seven. "Hitting, learning how to react to the ball, was a lot harder. For some reason, fielding always came naturally to me."

Still, it wasn't until his sixth year in the big leagues, 1981, that Hernandez felt completely comfortable around the bag. By that time, he already had won three Gold Glove awards playing for the St. Louis Cardinals. Hernandez learned the position from his father, John, who played first base in the Cardinals' minor league system. Another influence was Bill White, St. Louis' right-handed first baseman when Hernandez was in high school.

TOP TEN CAREER GAMES PLAYED AT FIRST BASE

1. Jake Beckley	2,377
2. Mickey Vernon	2,237
3. Lou Gehrig	2,136
4. Charlie Grimm	2,129
5. Joe Judge	2,084
6. Ed Konetchy	2,071
7. Steve Garvey	2,061
8. Cap Anson	2,058
9. Joe Kuhel	2,057
10. Willie McCovey	2,054

"My dad saw that I was left-handed and said, 'Well, your options are limited, Keith. We're going to put you at first base,'" Hernandez says. "I've worked hard to improve myself."

Not only does Hernandez have a lifetime .298 batting average, but his eleven Gold Gloves are surpassed only by third baseman Brooks Robinson and pitcher Jim Kaat (sixteen) and outfielders Roberto Clemente and Willie Mays (twelve).

Dwight Evans, who won eight Gold Gloves in right field for the Boston Red Sox, can attest to the skill that playing first base requires. For a brief, terrifying spell in 1988, Evans was asked to play first to open up a spot for the team's young, strong-hitting outfielders. Much to Evans' relief, the experiment failed.

"I started looking at those guys differently, that's for sure," Evans says. "Guys who play there and play well are great. Mentally, first base is very difficult. Physically, it wasn't as bad as the outfield. When I went back to the outfield I was out of shape. It took about a week-and-a-half to get my legs back."

As the sensitivity of the position has become more apparent, personnel men are steering gifted athletes to first base in increasing numbers. "I cannot remember first base ever being so rich with talent," says former Cincinnati Reds General Manager Murray Cook. "It's a cyclical thing. A couple of years ago, second base was the position filled with talent. Now it's first base."

Presently, there are enough good players to fill out an All-Star roster. Will Clark of the San Francisco Gi-ants, "Will the Thrill," promises to be one of the next great first basemen. Andres Galarraga, the Colorado Rockies' "Big Cat," is also blessed with the ability to hit for power and field with deftness. Mark McGwire of the Oakland A's and the California Angels' Wally Joyner are also young stars at first base.

"Last year I thought Clark was the best," says Hernandez, "but right now, I'd have to say the best young first baseman in baseball is Galarraga. He's a better fielder, too. He's a big guy who moves well. He's always leading the league in every category, and he's a good athlete."

At last, things are starting to look up at first.

TOP TEN CAREER FIELDING AVERAGE AT FIRST BASE	
1. Steve Garvey	.996
Wes Parker	.996
3. Dan Driessen	.995
Jim Spencer	.995
Frank McCormick	.995
6. Vic Power	.994
Carl Yastrzemski	.994
Joe Adcock	.994
Mike Jorgensen	.994
10. Keith Hernandez	.993

© W. T. Harrington

Fielding, in many cases, is merely a matter of concentration; nobody does it better than the Yankees' Don Mattingly.

The Greatest First Basemen of All Time

Lou Gehrig played in the shadow of Babe Ruth for most of his career with the New York Yankees. In 1927, the year Gehrig hit 47 home runs, Ruth set a record with 60. In the 1932 World Series against the Chicago Cubs, Ruth allegedly called his famous home run off Charlie Root. Whether or not he actually called it, Ruth's home run was the stuff of legend and rendered Gehrig's marvelous Series effort (three home runs, a .529 batting average, and eight runs batted in for four games) almost invisible. In his seventeen-year career, Gehrig hit 23 grand slams, while Ruth surprisingly managed only 16. This is one of the reasons Ruth generally hit third in the batting order and Gehrig followed him in

the cleanup spot. Ruth himself knew what Gehrig meant to the Yankees; his presence insured that the Bambino got good pitches to hit. Historians regard Gehrig as one of the game's finest first basemen—perhaps even the best.

Gehrig's greatest strength was his durability, a mark of his strong will, and sound six-foot, 200-pound body. Gehrig set an "Iron Man" standard for baseball that probably will never be equaled: Beginning in 1925, when he filled in for the ailing Wally Pipp, Gehrig played in 2,130 consecutive games. The standing record had belonged to shortstop L. Everett Scott, who had appeared in 1,307 straight games for the Red Sox and Yankees between 1914 and 1926.

Gehrig was born in New York City in 1903, attended Columbia University, and at the age of twenty played in his first few

games for the Yankees. Gehrig blossomed as a hitter in 1926, when he led the American League with twenty triples and batted .312. Even with Ruth as a teammate, Gehrig managed to lead the league in home runs three times and runs batted in on five occasions. His career batting and slugging averages in World Series play (.361 and .731, respectively) are among history's best standards. Though Jake Beckley and Mickey Vernon played more games at first base, no one ever made his games count more than Lou Gehrig.

Adrian Constantine Anson was probably the best player of the game's pre-modern era, where the line of demarcation is typically drawn at 1900. He was an enormous man by standards of the time, reported to be well over six-feet tall and more than 200 pounds. In 1870, Cap Anson, then eighteen, toured

▲ **Cap Anson**

Baseball Hall of Fame

▲ **Lou Gehrig**

Baseball Hall of Fame

Baseball Hall of Fame

▲ **Harmon Killebrew**

league six times and finished his career with 573 homers, fifth all-time. Only Babe Ruth and Pittsburgh outfielder Ralph Kiner hit home runs with more frequency than did Killebrew.

Willie McCovey, the six-foot-four, 198-pound slugger for the San Francisco Giants, is not far behind Killebrew on the home run list. He played twenty-two years and hit 521 home runs, equaling the total of Ted Williams. McCovey led the National League in homers three times and claimed two titles for runs batted in.

Jimmie Foxx was first spotted as a sixteen-year-old phenom in Maryland by Frank "Home Run" Baker. On Baker's recommendation, Philadelphia Athletics manager Connie Mack signed Foxx, who made the team at the age of eighteen. He was a stocky six-footer, weighing 195 pounds, and had the brute strength to jerk balls out of the park. He led the American League four times in home runs and finished his career with 534 homers, ninth on the all-time list.

© Bob Bartosz/Baseball Hall of Fame

▲ **Willie McCovey**

with a professional team from Rockford, Illinois, the Forest City Club. When Forest City joined with several other teams from Boston, New York, Philadelphia, and Chicago to form the National Association of Professional Baseball Players a year later, Anson helped usher in a new era of baseball as a third baseman. After jumping to Philadelphia in 1872 for an annual contract of $1,250, Anson signed in 1875 with the Chicago White Stockings, members of the National League as we know it today.

Anson managed the White Stockings from 1879 to 1898 and remained his team's best hitter. He hit from the right side with an open stance that left him nearly facing the pitcher. He eschewed the home run, opting instead to cleverly direct line drives between fielders. Anson led the league in hitting three times and maintained a career batting average of .334; he was the first hitter ever to reach the 3,000-hit mark.

Dan Brouthers was less celebrated, but his .343 career batting average ranks first among first basemen and ninth overall. He, too, was a hulking man, six-foot-two and 207 pounds. A muscular hitter, Brouthers hit 206 triples and 106 home runs over his career, sizeable numbers in his day. He played for eleven teams (Boston was affiliated with three different leagues in three consecutive seasons) in nineteen years and managed to hit .300 or better for sixteen of them.

Harmon Killebrew's first five seasons barely hinted of the power he possessed. From 1954 to 1958, the six-foot, 190-pound utility infielder from Payette, Idaho, hit a total of eleven home runs. Of course, he only reached the plate 254 times. Eventually, the Senators recognized his greatness. In Killebrew's first full season (his last before moving to first base), he led the American League with 42 home runs. He led the

THE SECOND BASEMAN

Below: *Ryne Sandberg of the Chicago Cubs is a regular Gold Glove Award winner. He is one of the best second basemen in the game today.* **Opposite page:** *Willie Randolph does all the little things that make a second baseman valuable. He makes all the plays, moves runners along, and provides leadership in the clubhouse.*

If it is anonymity you crave, play second base.

By nature, the position requires consistency and efficiency—hardly scintillating qualities that lift fans out of their seats. The shortstop has the flashy glove; the men at the corners are usually impressive power hitters; with their long runs and throws, the outfielders are more visible by far. Sometimes the umpire gets more attention than the second baseman.

Willie Randolph has played second base in the nation's two largest cities, for the New York Yankees and the Los Angeles Dodgers, yet there are times when, "I can walk down the street and no one knows me," he says. "Reggie Jackson couldn't go more than three steps without drawing a crowd."

Historically, second basemen have been an overlooked lot. The casual fan, who can cite dozens of Hall of Fame pitchers and outfielders, might have difficulty naming three of the nine second basemen enshrined at the Hall of Fame in Cooperstown. Rogers Hornsby, probably the best right-handed hitter in history, recorded the second-best career average ever, .358, behind Ty Cobb. He also played second base after experimenting at shortstop and third base, and maintained a respectable fielding average, leading the league in double plays several times. Jackie Robinson, the courageous Dodger who broke the race barrier in 1947, was a second baseman. So was Eddie Collins, a career .333 hitter over twenty-five seasons. Like so many of today's talented second basemen, Collins did all the little

things well. In addition to his consistent hitting, he had a good eye at the plate and averaged sixty walks a year. Four times he led the American League in stolen bases and finished with a total of 743, still fourth on the all-time list.

The second baseman must be flexible and adept at throwing the ball from all angles, since so many ground balls take him out of position in relation to first base. It is a subtle position; arm strength isn't nearly as important as accuracy. This premium on quickness and flexibility distinguishes second basemen from their fellow infielders. "It seems as though you're always moving to the ball," Randolph says. "You're backing up on a chopper, charging a dribbler off the end of the bat, running behind second and throwing back over your body. You go to first base over the top, sidearm, sometimes you just flip it underhand. It's a challenging position, because it seems like you rarely get a routine play."

Second basemen are generally judged on their ability to turn the double play. The good ones pivot and throw at the same time, something that isn't as easy as it sounds. A good working relationship with the shortstop is necessary; some double-play combinations seem to operate with telepathic precision. The tag play, a lost art, is another in the second baseman's bag of tricks.

Ryne Sandberg of the Chicago Cubs is presently the best second baseman in baseball. After playing third base as a rookie in 1982, Sandberg moved to second, where he won six consecutive Rawlings Gold Glove

© J. Daniel/Allsport

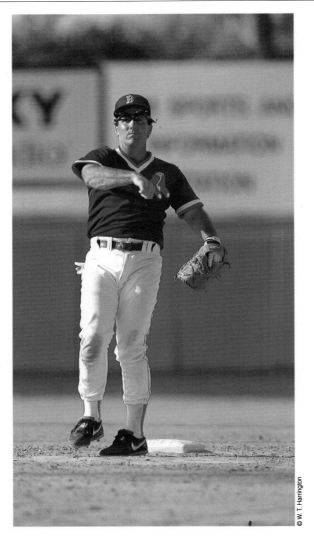

© W. T. Harrington

Right: *Boston's Marty Barrett was a nifty fielder and an above-average hitter with a surprising ability to hit in the clutch.* **Below:** *In this case, the second baseman is not at fault; the throw from the New York Yankees' catcher wasn't delivered in time to nail New York Mets baserunner Kevin Elster.*

Opposite page, above: *Tom Herr is a typical second baseman: overlooked and underappreciated.*

awards as the position's best fielder. In 1989, he passed the 1,000-game milestone, and so became the all-time fielding leader with a percentage of .989. For perspective, consider that before Sandberg qualified in the career category, five players were tied with a percentage of .984. In addition, Sandberg hits consistently in the .280s and steals an average of 34 bases a season. While most second basemen are cut from a typical five-foot-eleven, 190-pound mold, Sandberg, at six-foot-two and 180 pounds, is decidedly leaner.

For many years, Kansas City's Frank White was the standard at second base in the American League. In 1988, he committed just four errors, all of them throwing mistakes, and recorded the league's highest fielding percentage, .994. White was denied an unprecedented ninth Gold Glove losing to Seattle's Harold Reynolds, who committed eighteen errors. Along the way, White played seventy consecutive errorless games, a Royals' record. His total of eight Gold Gloves, six of them com-

TOP TEN CAREER GAMES PLAYED AT SECOND BASE	
1. Eddie Collins	2,650
2. Joe Morgan	2,527
3. Nellie Fox	2,295
4. Charlie Gehringer	2,206
5. Bid McPhee	2,125
6. Bill Mazeroski	2,094
7. Nap Lajoie	2,036
8. Bobby Doerr	1,852
9. Red Schoendienst	1,834
10. Billy Herman	1,829

© W. T. Harrington

© W. T. Harrington

TOP TEN CAREER FIELDING PERCENTAGE AT SECOND BASE	
1. Bobby Grich	.984
Jerry Lumpe	.984
Cookie Rojas	.984
Dave Cash	.984
Nellie Fox	.984
6. Tommy Helms	.983
Dick Green	.983
Red Schoendienst	.983
Lou Whitaker	.983
10. Frank White	.982

ing in consecutive seasons from 1976 to 1982, ties him with Bill Mazeroski for the all-time lead.

"I like to think I've been consistent," says White, whose 1989 season was his sixteenth in the major leagues. "I'm proud of my durability and longevity." Indeed, after White turned thirty-two, he averaged 145 games over seven seasons.

On most teams, Jose Oquendo would be the regular shortstop, but since he plays for the St. Louis Cardinals, who possess the amazing Ozzie Smith, Oquendo has become a second baseman. "Compared to shortstop, second base is a little trickier," he says. "At short, you're just going for the ball and you know pretty much where first base is, in front of you. At second, you're never really sure where first is. It took me a while to adjust there. The throws are a lot shorter, but they're harder. All things considered, I'd rather play short."

For now, Oquendo will have to accept second.

The Greatest Second Basemen of All Time

Rogers Hornsby was called "Rajah," a play on his first name and a back-handed reference to his regal, often pretentious bearing. Hornsby didn't play with the blazing passion of Ty Cobb, the only man to retire with a higher career batting average, but who did? "I don't fight with umpires and I'm not going to," he said. "I don't run wild on the base paths, spiking other players. If I had to play dirty baseball, I would rather not play at all."

Hornsby, the best second baseman ever to play the game, was gifted both physically and mentally; his analytical approach helped him to lead the National League in hitting for six consecutive seasons, including an astounding .424 average in 1924, the highest mark of the twentieth century. Like Cobb, he was an individualist who never went out of his way to endear himself to the fans—or the baseball establishment, for that matter. Hornsby invoked the wrath of Commissioner Kenesaw Mountain Landis for his habit of gambling. He played for five different teams and went on to manage another five. Hornsby's skill with the bat and his knowledge of the game were so appealing to major league owners that they were willing to endure his disruptive personality.

On the field, Hornsby had no equal at second base. In one ten-year stretch, he managed more than 200 hits seven times, including 250 for St. Louis in 1922. That was the torrid season he hit .401, 42 home runs, 46 doubles, drove in 152 runs, scored another 141, and fashioned a slugging percentage of .722. Hornsby's only weakness was a tendency to let his right fielder handle most pop flies over his head, a minor idiosyncrasy considering his offensive talents.

Jackie Robinson produced totals over his ten-year career that are hardly the stuff of legend. He led the National League in stolen bases twice and took the batting crown in 1949, with a .342 mark. His contributions in six World Series were modest enough, though a .234 batting average was balanced by seven doubles and 22 runs scored. No, Robinson's greatest contribution came in another arena—breaking down the barriers baseball had maintained for years to keep the black man out.

Branch Rickey had seen the change coming in America for some time when he dispatched Brooklyn Dodgers scout Clyde Sukeforth to sign the twenty-six-year-old shortstop of the Kansas City Monarchs. Rickey based his decision partly on Robinson's natural ability, but also on his intelligence and balanced personality. "Jack, I've been looking for a great colored ballplayer, but I need more than a great player. I need a man who will accept insults, take abuse . . . in a word, carry the flag for his race."

Rickey sent Robinson to Montreal to gain experience, then introduced him as the Dodgers' first baseman in 1947. Robinson was the victim of all the ugly words Rickey

▲ **Rogers Hornsby**

© AP/Wide World Photos

predicted, but responded with dignity—and a terrific season. The following year, the five-foot-eleven, 195-pound player was moved to second to better take advantage of his athletic ability. The Dodgers used the versatile Robinson at a number of positions. Over the course of his career, Robinson played 751 games at second, 256 at third, 197 at first, and 152 in the outfield. Robinson's courageous performance made it markedly easier for a new generation of black stars to contribute to the game.

Johnny Evers, the Chicago Cubs shortstop, was one-third of the greatest double play combination in the history of baseball: Tinker (shortstop) to Evers to Chance (first base). Evers, whose slight build of five-foot-nine and 125 pounds belied his intensity, was a terrific fielder with a brain to match.

His intellect was evident in one of history's great games—the 1908 regular-season finale between the Cubs and the New York Giants. The Cubs needed a victory to force a playoff game. The turning point came when the Giants' Fred Merkle missed second base on the way to third after a single by Al Bridwell. As umpire Billy Evans later pointed out, what Merkle did "would have been overlooked by ninety-nine out of one hundred players." Evers was that player. He called for the ball at second and Merkle was ruled out; a run was disallowed. The Cubs went on to win the playoff game and dismantled the Detroit Tigers in the World Series. Though Evers had a modest .270 career batting average, his nimble mind and glove carried him to the Hall of Fame.

Napoleon Lajoie produced the second-best career batting average by a second baseman, .339; Rogers Hornsby was the best. Lajoie was not built like a typical second baseman: At six-foot-one and 195 pounds, he looked more like an outfielder. Though he lacked speed, his grace in the field and control at the plate marked him early for the Hall of Fame. Lajoie, who played twenty-one seasons, can be found in the record book among the all-time top ten for put-outs, put-outs per game, assists, and chances, and thirteenth in double plays.

Edward Trowbridge Collins Sr. played more games (2,650) at second base than anyone, though Joe Morgan of the Cincinnati Reds came close with 2,527. Eddie Collins played 25 seasons for Philadelphia and Chicago of the American League and averaged .333 for his career. As a base runner, he led the league in runs scored three times. As a batter, he finished with 1,217 more bases on balls than strikeouts. Collins also stole 743 bases, leading his league four times, the last time at the age of thirty-seven. Collins is fourth on the all-time stolen base list.

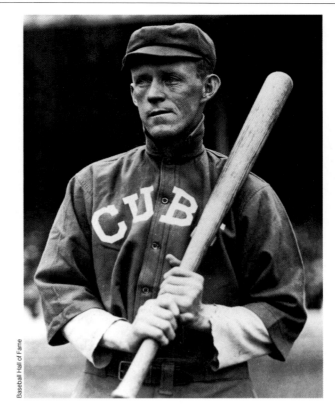

Baseball Hall of Fame

▲ **Johnny Evers**

▼ **Jackie Robinson**

Baseball Hall of Fame

© John McDonough

THE SHORTSTOP

Clearly, Ozzie Smith could have been a ballet dancer. Here, he pivots artfully after delivering the ball to first for another double play.

Osborne Earl Smith is one of those rare baseball players who consistently inspires awe among his peers.

"He was charging a bunt," says former St. Louis teammate Dan Quisenberry, "and he caught it and threw it in the same motion. I didn't see him release the ball; with most guys you can see the throwing motion. Ozzie didn't get the guy, but it was artistic. It belonged in a museum."

Former Cardinals manager Whitey Herzog smiles and says, "Every day. Every day I see him do something spectacular. After a while, you sort of get used to it."

Which is almost too bad. The "Wizard of Oz" is quick as a cat, exhibits incredible range, has a barely perceptible release, and moves like Mikhail Baryshnikov around the second base bag. He is considered the finest defensive shortstop of this or any era. Consider his achievements: He has won nine consecutive Rawlings Gold Glove Awards as the position's standard of excellence; his eight seasons with 500 assists are unequaled in major league history; and he shares the all-time record for most years leading the league in assists and total chances (eight).

Smith says he has succeeded because, with apologies to Frank Sinatra, he didn't succumb to generalizations. "People say, 'It's done this way, it's done that way,'" he says. "That was the protocol. I said. 'Wait a minute, I'll do it my way.'

"When I'm out at shortstop, I'm free to do whatever I want to. I don't put any blockades up, I don't limit myself; I'm free to be as creative as I can be. A big part of shortstop is being improvisational out there. It's almost an art form."

To see Smith gracefully slide behind second base, take the ball in his glove, and make the seemingly effortless toss to first base is indeed poetry. In truth, Smith has only an average arm, at best, after a troubling shoulder injury. His primary gifts are instinct and quickness. They allowed him to throw out more batters in a season (621 in 1980) than any shortstop in history. By the time he has run down the grounder and released it, the throw is usually academic. There have been times, notably game six of the 1987 World Series, when Smith actually both gloved the ball and made the throw while in mid-air.

"I think people take a lot for granted," Smith says. "They think things just happen, that you're born that way. That's not completely true. I practiced and practiced throwing the ball before I hit the ground. After a while, it became second nature. I would go into the hole [toward third base] and deliberately put myself in awkward positions; I'd trip or go down early or throw myself off balance. When you can make a throw after that, most plays don't seem that hard. When you do find yourself in that situation on a tough ball, you've already been there. You know what to do."

© Don Smith/Sports Photo Masters, Inc.

TOP TEN CAREER GAMES PLAYED AT SHORTSTOP

1. Luis Aparicio 2,581
2. Larry Bowa 2,222
3. Luke Appling 2,218
4. Dave Concepcion .2,165
5. Rabbit Maranville .2,154
6. Bill Dahlen 2,132
7. Bert Campaneris 2,097
8. Tommy Corcoran .2,073
9. Roy McMillan 2,028
10. Pee Wee Reese 2,014

Despite his flair for the dramatic, Smith believes that consistency is the quality that separates the good shortstops from the great ones. This is the prevailing wisdom in baseball that leads most managers to employ shortstops with the classic good-field, no-hit label. Because most hitters are right-handed and attempt to pull the ball toward left field, the shortstop generally gets more chances than any other infielder. Because he is appreciably farther from the first baseman, the shortstop must be able to track down ground balls and make a quicker throw than the second baseman, whose margin of error is greater because he is closer, giving more opportunities to make a mistake.

Turning the double play requires a deft touch and an almost telepathic understanding with the second base-

Even with the demands of a 162-game schedule, coast-to-coast travel, and numerous night games, Baltimore shortstop Cal Ripken comes to play ball every day.

© John McDonough

© John Iacono/Sports Illustrated

Above: *Cal Ripken Jr., of the Baltimore Orioles, is the ironman of contemporary shortstops. That could have something to do with his strapping six-foot-four, 225-pound frame.* **Right:** *Mark Belanger was a classic shortstop; he had the softest hands imaginable—and a batting average to match.*

man. Whether he starts the play with a soft, accurate toss or completes it with a pivot on the bag, a leap over an onrushing base runner, and the long throw to first, all of a shortstop's skills are required if two base runners are to be doubled up. And then there is the relay he must make from the center fielder when there is to be a play at the plate.

Consequently, shortstops are prized primarily for their gloves, not their bats. Mark Belanger, who played seventeen seasons for the Baltimore Orioles, was one of the finest defensive shortstops in history, but his career batting average was an anemic .228. "He could have hit .190 and I wouldn't have cared," says former Orioles Manager Earl Weaver. "As long as he could go get it in the hole."

Buck Rodgers, the Montreal Expos' manager, looks at his potent lineup that includes Tim Raines, Hubie Brooks, and Andres Galarraga and says, "Scoring runs isn't going to be a problem. If Spike Owen can hit over .240, it's a plus for us. I just want a guy who can play every day and catch the ball and throw it."

This is why shortstops usually hit eighth in the order, just ahead of the pitcher in the National League, and ninth in the American League. When a shortstop produces any kind of offense, it is considered a bonus. Smith, for instance, was paid $2.3 million to play in 1988—it was, at the time, the highest salary ever paid to a baseball player. Smith had his usual terrific season in the field, but he also batted .270, hit 27 doubles, scored 80 runs, drove in 51 runs, and stole 57 bases. Major league managers voted him the National League's best base runner in addition to the best defensive infielder. Smith, who hit .303 in 1987, struck out only once every 13.4 at-bats, third in the league.

Since hitting for power is usually the least of a shortstop's worries, they tend to run on the slow side. Smith, at five-foot-ten and 160 pounds, is the prototypical shortstop in every way. Pee Wee Reese, the legendary Brooklyn Dodgers' shortstop was precisely the same size. Luis Aparicio, who played more games at the position than anyone else (2,581), was the same weight and an inch shorter. Rabbit Maranville, the all-time leader in putouts (5,139), played at five-foot-five and 155 pounds. There are, however, those who succeed with something less than a diminutive build. Mickey Mantle, who went on to hit 536 home runs for the New York Yankees, started out as a shortstop. Belanger was a rangy six-foot-one and 170 pounds, and Cal Ripken of the present-day Orioles is an imposing six-foot-four and 225 pounds. Though he is noted for his homers and his durability, Ripken handles the leather as well as most shortstops. Of the sixteen shortstops enshrined in the Hall of Fame, Ernie Banks is the only one over six feet tall, though Honus Wagner and Luke Appling were a burly five-foot-eleven and 200 pounds.

Some shortstops are blessed with all-around skills. In a *St. Petersburg Times* survey of major league experts published before the 1989 season, Detroit's Alan Trammell won out over Ozzie Smith, based on his ability with the bat. "If I was picking someone primarily on defense, it would have to be Smith," explained Jim Kaat, the former hurler. "If I was looking primarily for offense, it would be Ripken. But my overall choice has to be Trammell. He's got the best combination of glove and bat. He's always good for the clutch RBI. He's not as good on defense as Ozzie—nobody is—but a .300-hitting shortstop is tough to beat."

Lawrence Robert Bowa grew up in Sacramento, California, and developed an intimate relationship with his garage door by the age of seven. His father wasn't exactly thrilled.

"He'd yell at me all the time because I kept chipping the paint off it," Bowa says. "I was out there three, four hours a day bouncing a tennis ball, catching and throwing it back. People say it's a God-given talent, but you have to practice and refine that ability. Baseball is a game of repetition.

"Guys told me I'd get worn out taking so many ground balls. Even my last year, they had to pull me off the field. It's like that with hitting, too. I'd hit baseballs until my hands bled, but I got my 2,000 hits (2,191)."

Bowa made himself into the best defensive shortstop in baseball history, if sheer numbers are your standard. His lifetime fielding percentage of .980 is history's best mark, though he avoided many of the bad hops old-timers suffered on grass by playing on Veterans Stadium's artificial turf in Philadelphia for eleven seasons.

At five-foot-ten and 160 pounds, Bowa was not blessed with a monstrous frame, but he had a lively arm and, more importantly, the work ethic that carried him past those with more pure ability. He studied players' hitting patterns, and with experience learned to position himself properly and save himself several steps in the process.

Not surprisingly, Bowa values consistency over flash and dash. "When I look for a shortstop, I look at arm strength and footwork," says Bowa, now the third base coach for the Phillies. "A lot of guys can make the flashy backhand play, but I look for a guy who can make the everyday play every time. You'll get fifty backhands over the course of the season, but then there's five hundred routine plays you have to make, too. More often than not, those are the ones that can cost you a ballgame."

© W. T. Harrington

TOP TEN CAREER FIELDING PERCENTAGE AT SHORTSTOP

1.	Larry Bowa	.980
2.	Ozzie Smith	.978
3.	Mark Belanger	.977
4.	Bucky Dent	.976
	Roger Metzger	.976
	Alan Trammell	.976
7.	Tim Foli	.973
	Dal Maxvill	.973
	Lou Boudreau	.973
10.	Eddie Miller	.972

Larry Bowa made himself into history's finest fielding shortstop. Remember that the next time your kids start bouncing tennis balls off the garage door.

The Greatest Shortstops of All Time

Shortstops are prized for their gloves, and through the years there have been some slick ones: Rabbitt Maranville, Pee Wee Reese, Phil Rizzuto, Luis Aparicio, Mark Belanger, Ozzie Smith.

John Peter Wagner did not fit the classic shortstop mold. At five-foot-eleven and 200 pounds, he had impressive upper-body strength, long arms, and enormous hands. Honus Wagner could throw the leather, and he could hit, too. Wagner drifted around the diamond for the National League's Louisville and Pittsburgh franchises, playing the outfield and first, second, and third base before coming to rest at shortstop in 1903. It was his true calling. He had the arm strength that froze base runners thinking about an extra base and the reflexes and quickness to make all the necessary plays. On occasion, he would knock down a line drive with his bare hand—whatever it took to record an out.

Wagner led the league in batting eight times, compiling 3,430 hits in his twenty-one seasons. He employed the curious batting grip favored by his American League rival, Ty Cobb, with the hands separated by a few inches. Wagner and the Pirates defeated Cobb's Detroit Tigers in the World Series of 1909. More than anything, Wagner was an all-around player. Not only did he field and bat well, he stole 722 bases in his career, good for sixth on the all-time list, including five league-leading totals. When he retired after the 1917 season, Wagner left totals that endure today as the best of the Hall of Fame's sixteen shortstops: a .329 career batting average, 1,732 runs batted in, 252 triples, and 1,740 runs scored.

Ernie Banks, the Hall of Famer who played with the Chicago Cubs from 1953 to 1971, was another double-edged threat at shortstop. In 1959, he led the National League with 143 runs batted in, and at the same time compiled the league's best fielding percentage for a shortstop, .985. A year later, he led the circuit with 41 home runs and won the fielding title again, with a percentage of .977.

Banks, a graceful six-foot-one and 180 pounds, arrived in the majors from the Kansas City Monarchs in 1953, but appeared in only ten games. Though he committed thirty-four errors in his first full season, Banks gradually grew accustomed to his role as chief defender. The Cubs never won a pennant in Banks' nineteen seasons with them; still, it was the beatific Banks who liked to say, "Let's play two," when the weather was right.

Luis Aparicio was playing across town for the Chicago White Sox from 1956 to 1962. Perhaps no city ever had such a simultaneous wealth of talent at one position. His final eleven seasons were shared with the Baltimore Orioles, the Boston Red Sox, and the White Sox, again. Aparicio, born in Maracaibo, Venezuela, learned the game from his father. Once in the major leagues, the five-foot-nine, 160-pound Aparicio produced some epic numbers.

He played in more games (2,581), compiled more assists (1,553), and turned more double plays (8,016) than any shortstop in history. Aparicio was a terrific fielder, with great range and a strong arm. Moreover, he supported his career batting average of .262 with nine consecutive stolen base titles, beginning with his rookie season. He won nine Rawlings Gold Glove awards, a record tied by the St. Louis Cardinals' Ozzie Smith in 1988.

▲ **Honus Wagner**

▲ **Ernie Banks**

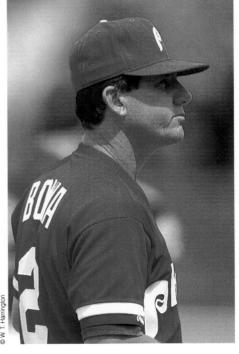

▲ Larry Bowa

The game has changed significantly, even since the days of Banks and Aparicio. Artificial turf has made for more consistent bounces and the fielding percentages of today's shortstops reflect that.

Larry Bowa heads the all-time list with a career fielding percentage of .980. He led the National League in fielding a record six times and produced the best single-season percentage in 1979, a dazzling mark of .991. That season, Bowa handled 677 chances and committed only six errors. Bowa's career average was an even .260, but he batted .375 in the Philadelphia Phillies' 1980 World Series victory over Kansas City and set a record by starting seven double plays.

The Cardinals' **Ozzie Smith** is right behind Bowa on the all-time fielding list. He may be history's most spectacular glove man at shortstop. Watching Smith play shortstop is to see an artist at work.

Seemingly effortlessly, Smith drifts behind second base, stabs the bouncer, and releases his deceptively soft throw to first base. Smith glides around the field, and his ability to catch and throw in one motion separates him from even the finest defensive shortstops. Not only has Smith won nine consecutive Gold Gloves, his range is so extraordinary that he holds the major-league record with eight 500-assist seasons. That's why they call him the "Wizard of Oz."

▲ Luke Appling

Luke Appling, who wore the White Sox uniform from 1930 to 1950, was similarly durable. Only Aparicio and Larry Bowa played in more than his 2,218 games. Appling was also able to maintain a .310 career average. He led the American League in batting twice, including a .388 season in 1936. After he turned forty, Appling hit .314, .314, and .301 before his final year at .234.

Lou Boudreau, who—along with Cleveland Indians teammate Ken Kelner—helped end Joe DiMaggio's famed fifty-six-game hitting streak on July 17, 1941 with several spectacular plays, was gifted with both the glove and bat. In 1948, he led the league's shortstops with a fielding percentage of .975 and managed to hit .355 with 116 runs scored and another 106 runs batted in. Boudreau finished his fifteen-year career with a batting average of .295.

▼ Luis Aparicio

© W. T. Harrington

THE THIRD BASEMAN

As a rule, the third baseman gets very little respect. He stands ninety feet from home plate, poised uneasily at the Hot Corner, the perfect target for a right-handed pull hitter. When the ball is smashed his way, he must spear it and make the long throw to first base, even if it means going far to his right and releasing the ball in foul territory. If the hitter accidentally tops the ball down the line with a check swing, the third baseman is expected to adjust by charging the ball and making the bare-handed play to first. The third baseman covers for the pitcher on fly balls, runs into the stands for foul pops, and starts the double play. Teammates, fans, and official scorers take little notice of the degree of difficulty third base requires. Look at the fielding percentages: They're historically the lowest of any position. This explains why there are fewer third basemen (seven) in the Hall of Fame than any other position.

Clearly, third basemen are made, not born. First of all, they are usually strong hitters, since their teammates at the sensitive positions of shortstop and second base are prized more for their gloves. Consequently, in the field the third baseman generally lacks the range, speed, and agility required at shortstop. Reflexes and an inclination to learn the art of fielding are two of the greatest attributes a third baseman can have, according to Eddie Mathews, one of those select Hall of Famers. "It's harder to play there than it looks," says Mathews, who still works with hitters in the Atlanta Braves organization. "Some guys are naturals,

mostly pitchers and outfielders. I wasn't that lucky. I could always hit, but fielding was a tough adjustment. It is harder to improve your hitting than it is your fielding. I think a lot of third basemen have been great hitters and made themselves into complete ballplayers."

Mathews hit 512 home runs (Brooks Robinson is a distant second on the Hall of Fame list at third with 268) in seventeen seasons, thirteen of those seasons with the Milwaukee Braves. Mathews led the National League in home run percentage three times and drove in more than 100 runs five times. He had a keen eye at the plate that allowed him to lead the league in walks on four occasions, something unusual for a home run hitter with a career batting average of .271.

"For the first few years, I took a lot of balls off the chest," Mathews says. "I had a good arm, but it took two, three years of extra ground balls, before and after practice, before I got comfortable. I just concentrated on getting in front of the ball, and pretty soon it became second nature. The hardest part about third base is knowing when to release the ball. You're running the ball down from so many different angles . . . try running full speed away from first base and then throw the ball all the way across your body. It isn't easy."

Playing third base, Mathews concedes, is all about finding confidence. Mike Schmidt, the future Hall of Famer who hit 548 home runs, seventh on the all-time list, and three-time National League Most Valuable Player, agrees. "In a lot of ways, third base is an unnatural position. Getting baseballs hit at you hard from that

An American League standard at third base for the 1980s was Kansas City's George Brett (opposite page and above). He demonstrated textbook good-field, good-hit talents at a position that requires unusual hand-eye coordination.

109

© W. T. Harrington

Right: *Time was when Wade Boggs was all hit and no field. These days, through patience and hard work, he holds his own without a bat in his hand.* **Below:** *Hitting home runs remains Mike Pagliarulo's chief talent.*

© W. T. Harrington

TOP TEN CAREER GAMES PLAYED AT THIRD BASE	
1. Brooks Robinson	2,870
2. Graig Nettles	2,400
3. Mike Schmidt	2,254
4. Eddie Mathews	2,181
5. Ron Santo	2,130
6. Buddy Bell	2,107
7. Eddie Yost	2,008
8. Ron Cey	1,989
9. Aurelio Rodriguez	1,983
10. Sal Bando	1,896

range is tough. You have to sort of train your body to stop flinching every time the bat is swung. Eventually, you relax a little."

Schmidt's lifetime fielding percentage of .955 doesn't rate in the all-time top ten, but he won ten Rawlings Gold Glove awards in his years with the Philadelphia Phillies. Schmidt retired in 1989, but almost certainly will be elected to the Hall of Fame when he is first eligible in 1994. No doubt Wade Boggs and George Brett will follow him there.

"If you're starting a franchise, you'd have to look long and hard to find someone better than Wade Boggs," says former Baltimore Orioles slugger Boog Powell. "And I don't think you would."

Boggs' exploits with the bat are well known. After his first seven seasons with the Boston Red Sox, Boggs had fashioned a career batting average of .356, the highest of any player in the last half-century, an average surpassed only by Ty Cobb, Rogers Hornsby, and Shoeless Joe Jackson. Boggs' string of six consecutive 200-hit seasons is the first by a major leaguer in the post-1900 modern era. "You simply can't ignore someone who hits .360 every year," says George Bamberger, the former manager of the Milwaukee Brewers and New York Mets. "And with all that hitting, something gets ignored. He's a better third baseman than people give him credit for."

Indeed, Boggs is regarded as a more than serviceable fielder these days. Like Mathews, however, Boggs struggled in the field for several years before he became merely proficient. Playing for Elmira, N.Y., Boggs led the New York-Pennsylvania League with sixteen errors in 1976, his first season of professional ball. In 1983, his second year with the Red Sox, Boggs hit .361 to win the American League batting title, but again led all third basemen with twenty-seven errors. Convinced that he had maximized his potential as a hitter, Boggs began to concentrate on the other side of his game. He often took an extra 200 ground balls each day and studied hitters' tendencies.

"I believe that hitting is a gift that you're given," Boggs says. "Sure, you can sharpen your skills, but really, you can either hit in the major leagues or you can't. Fielding is different. It's a reflex thing. By repetition, you learn what to do, how to play in a rhythm."

While Boggs led the league in hitting from 1985 to 1988, his error totals in the field declined, from 17 to 19 to 14 to 11. His 1988 total, which included five throwing errors, was his best as a regular in the majors. That placed him fourth in fielding percentage among the league's third basemen (.971) and first in put-outs with 122. In 1987, Boggs led the major leagues with 37 double plays.

Brett has an eerily similar dossier. "Yeah, I'm a real expert in fielding at third base," says the player who leads the Kansas City Royals in virtually every career

© W. T. Harrington

hitting statistic. "I've got more errors than any active player in the game."

This is, in part, due to Brett's longevity. The year that the eighteen-year-old Boggs was beginning his slow climb in the Boston franchise, Brett led the American League in hitting with an average of .333. As a rookie professional in 1971, Brett played shortstop at Billings, Montana, and was named to the All-Pioneer League team. Though he never hit .300 in the minors, Brett was eventually moved to third base because of his potent bat. He hit .308 in his first complete season in Kansas City, something of a miracle considering the state of his nerves when he played the field. Brett committed 26 errors in 1975, a total that led the league. In 1979, he again led all American League third basemen with 30 errors, before gaining control of his glove. And himself.

"I had a confidence problem," Brett says. "In the majors, you have to want to have the ball hit to you. But when I first came up, it was like 'Oh, damn, they hit the ball to me.' You're standing there saying, 'Please, please, don't hit down here.' I was like that for five or six years. That's how long it took to get my confidence in the field. By that time, I had seen every play so many times I knew what to do instinctively: when to cut the ball off from the shortstop going to my left, when to dive to the right, how to come up throwing off a bunt, stuff like that."

In 1985, with two batting titles under his belt, Brett won an honor that might have meant just as much: his first (and only) Rawlings Gold Glove award. Though he made the transition to first base/designated hitter in 1987, Brett is happy with the change of scenery. He smiles as he watches the Royals' present third baseman, Kevin Seitzer, field ground balls in batting practice. "After all those years down there, I deserve a break," Brett says. "Compared to third base, first base is like a vacation."

Mike Schmidt, winner of ten Rawlings Gold Glove Awards, worked hard at both defense and offense. He is a sure bet to be elected to the Hall of Fame once he is eligible.

TOP TEN CAREER FIELDING PERCENTAGE AT THIRD BASE

1. Brooks Robinson	.971
2. Ken Reitz	.970
3. George Kell	.969
4. Don Money	.968
Don Wert	.968
6. Willie Kamm	.967
Heinie Groh	.967
8. Clete Boyer	.965
Ken Keltner	.965
10. Carney Lansford	.962

The Greatest Third Basemen of All Time

Brooks Calbert Robinson was just a career .267 hitter. The record book indicates that he led the American League in a significant offensive category only once, in 1964, when he drove in 118 runs. Yet, the mind's eye refuses to release the image of Robinson: a lean six-foot-one with that businesslike lampblack under his eyes, diving to his right to backhand a would-be double over third base, regaining his balance in the elegant Baltimore Orioles uniform and releasing the throw that, impossibly, nips the runner at first base. That was Brooks Robinson.

He simply made all the plays. All of them. Remember the quick, chopping strides to his left and the spectacular diving snag of a Johnny Bench line drive in the 1970 World Series? Robinson was 7-for-12 in the American League Championship Series that year against the Minnesota Twins, a tidy .583 average. In addition to a handful of heart-stopping defensive plays in the World Series,

the third baseman was 9-for-21 at the plate (.429) with two home runs and six runs batted in as the Orioles whipped the Cincinnati Reds in five games. Robinson was voted the Most Valuable Player. A winner in the clutch situations, that was Brooks Robinson.

"I could always play the field," Robinson says today. "But hitting was a struggle all my life."

In his twenty-three big-league seasons, Robinson successfully handled 8,902 of 9,165 chances despite the rain, a myriad of bad bounces and an occasionally dimly lit field. Robinson, who many have judged to be the finest third baseman in history, won sixteen Rawlings Gold Glove awards as the best-fielding third baseman. His career games played (2,870), fielding percentage (.971), and total assists (6,205) are first on the all-time list. In truth, he was a pretty fair hitter, batting better than .300 twice and knocking in 100 runs or more twice.

When Robinson retired in 1977, the largest crowd ever to attend a Baltimore Orioles regular-season game stayed on its feet for

© W. T. Harrington

▲ **Mike Schmidt**

more than a quarter of an hour in tribute to the man who gave them so many thrills. "Never in my wildest dreams did I think I would be standing here twenty-three years later saying goodbye to so many people," he said. "For a guy who never wanted to do anything but put on a major league uniform, that goodbye comes tough. I would never want to change one day of my years here. It's been fantastic."

Mike Schmidt, the Philadelphia Phillies third baseman, retired in a similarly emotional moment on May 30, 1989, after seventeen glorious seasons. In the end, time and shoulder surgery rendered a thirty-nine-year-old body obsolete. A week earlier, Mike Marshall of the Los Angeles Dodgers hit a ball to Schmidt's left. "That should have been a fun play for me," Schmidt said, "I could show off a little, backhand the ball and throw him out. It was a play I've made many times. But the ball went [by me] into left field. They gave him a double. It was an error all the way. I left Dayton, Ohio, with a dream to become a major league player, and the dream came true."

Schmidt's election to the Hall of Fame, where only seven of history's third basemen are honored, is merely a formality. Small wonder, for Schmidt's 548 career home runs place him seventh on the all-time list. He played in 2,212 games at third base, third behind Robinson and Graig Nettles, and won ten Rawlings Gold Glove awards. Additionally, Schmidt, six-foot-two and 203 pounds, led the National League in home runs eight times and was named the league's Most Valuable Player three times.

From 1974 to 1977, Schmidt was nearly unconscious at the plate. He averaged 38 home runs and 105 runs batted in over that span, including four consecutive homers

▼ **Brooks Robinson**

Baseball Hall of Fame

▲ **Eddie Mathews**

▼ **Wade Boggs**

against the Chicago Cubs at Wrigley Field in 1976. In 1980, Schmidt's career-high 48 home runs led the Phillies to the World Series, where he batted .381 with two home runs and won another MVP award. Even after he announced his retirement, Schmidt was voted to a starting role in the All-Star Game by adoring fans. Though he was the first player so voted since the game's inception in 1933, Schmidt appropriately declined to play.

Harold "Pie" Traynor, a converted shortstop, was the next best Hall of Famer after Robinson. He hit .320 over seventeen seasons with the Pittsburgh Pirates and produced 1,273 runs batted in. Traynor was a daring fielder who played even with the bag, and his deft steps into the hole prompted some to label him as a second shortstop. His ability to glove line drives over third base, sometimes with his bare hand, was uncanny. Traynor explained his success this way: "Nobody taught me how to play third base. The way I learned was simply to tackle each situation as it arose and master it before going on to something else. I think I learned more about playing third base in the morning bull sessions in the hotel lobby than I did out on the field. The hardest thing in making the switch from short was learning to play that much closer to the hitter. A shortstop can always gamble a little because he can see the ball better and gets a better jump. When I

was young, I played in closer. As I grew older and found my reflexes slowing, I played back and relied more on positioning."

Eddie Mathews, the long-time Brave, is the other modern member of the Hall of Fame. He hit 512 home runs and drove home 1,453 in his seventeen-year career. Other Hall of Famers from an earlier era: Frank Baker (.307 career batting average), Jimmy Collins (.294), George Kell (.306), and Fred Lindstrom (.311).

Wade Boggs of the New York Yankees is likely to join them after his career is over. Not only did he carry a .352 lifetime average into the 1990 season, but he had produced many numbers of an historical nature. In 1988, he became the first player since Willie Keeler to produce 200 hits in six consecutive seasons. He did it again in 1989. Keeler did it eight times, from 1894 to 1901. Boggs may surpass that mark yet.

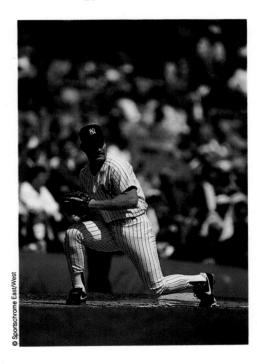

THE OUTFIELDER

Above: *Cleveland's Albert Belle is a typical power-hitting outfielder. While his fielding is credible, it is his bat that is the Indians' prize—in 1993, he amassed 38 home runs and a league-leading 129 RBIs.*

Opposite page: *Style points don't count for much in the outfield. The trick is to catch the ball any way you can.*

The outfielder has a serious public relations problem. It is very easy to get the impression that he views his time in the field as some sort of penance. Some outfielders admit they spend a great deal of time thinking about hitting, even when they are on the other side of a line drive. Listen to Ty Cobb, who played more games (2,943) in the outfield than any other major leaguer: "Playing out there is part of the job. You can't hit all the time." Ah, but the outfielder would if he could.

In his book, *Baseball for Everybody*, New York Yankees center fielder Joe DiMaggio wrote, "As an outfielder, I'm not going to defend our right to free admission or claim we're as busy as a catcher. The statistics show that outfielders average about three chances a game, which is slightly less than a third baseman's daily work. In some games, the fan sees an outfielder stand around for so many innings with nothing to do that they wonder why he doesn't take a chair out to the position with him."

While there have been some terrific defensive outfielders over the years (Paul Blair, Joe Rudi, and Jimmy Piersall come to mind), outfielders are basically marking time in the field until they are allowed to hit again. Most of the fifty-one outfielders you will find in the Hall of Fame were cleanup hitters for their teams. The ex-

ceptions, such as Lou Brock of the St. Louis Cardinals, brought another dimension to the position. Brock, for instance, is the all-time leader in stolen bases with 938.

In truth, outfielders don't work as hard as the six teammates in front of them. Still, their responsibilities are far from insignificant. A muff in the infield generally gives the other team an extra base. That same mistake in the outfield can lead to two or more bases and, frequently, a run scored. The well-rounded outfielder takes his defensive duties as seriously—well, almost as seriously—as his swings at the plate. In today's game, Pittsburgh's Andy Van Slyke fits that description.

A taut July 1988 game with the San Diego Padres best illustrates Van Slyke's emergence as a complete outfielder. The Pirates led the Padres 3-2 at Jack Murphy Stadium on the strength of Van Slyke's seventh-inning home run. Pittsburgh, involved in a battle with the New York Mets for the National League's Eastern Division title, had lost three straight games and desperately needed a victory. As Benito Santiago dug in at the plate to face pitcher Barry Jones in the bottom of the ninth with a man on second, Van Slyke thought to himself, "Okay, Benito. If you're going to do something, do it to me. If you're going to be a hero, be a hero toward me, because I'm going to try to be a bigger hero than you are."

TOP TEN CAREER GAMES PLAYED IN THE OUTFIELD

1. Ty Cobb 2,943
2. Willie Mays 2,843
3. Hank Aaron...........................2,760
4. Tris Speaker 2,700
5. Lou Brock............................2,507
6. Al Kaline 2,488
7. Max Carey 2,422
8. Vada Pinson 2,403
9. Roberto Clemente 2,370
10. Zack Wheat 2,350

TOP TEN CAREER FIELDING PERCENTAGE IN THE OUTFIELD	
1. Terry Puhl	.993
2. Pete Rose	.991
Amos Otis	.991
Joe Rudi	.991
Mickey Stanley	.991
6. Jimmy Piersall	.990
7. Jim Landis	.989
Ken Berry	.989
Tommy Holmes	.989
Gene Woodling	.989

Although Texas Ranger Juan Gonzalez is known best as a hitter—in 1992, he was the major league home run champ, with 43— he is also a surprisingly deft fielder.

© Brad Newton/Sports Photo Masters, Inc.

Sure enough, Santiago delivered a single up the middle, which sent John Kruk careening toward the plate with the potential tying run. Van Slyke charged the ball and loosed a throw with the arm many regard as one of baseball's finest. Pittsburgh catcher Junior Ortiz took the ball knee-high in the air and held on as Kruk ran him over. One out later, the Bucs had escaped with their precious win. Pirates manager Jim Leyland couldn't say enough about Van Slyke. "If Andy Van Slyke doesn't win the Gold Glove, they ought to throw away the award, because he's the best," Leyland said. "He's put on a clinic in center field for the last three weeks. The Pirates could make one separate highlight film of him playing center field this winter. Andy loves to play defense; he wants the ball hit to him. He charges the ball better than anybody in the league. He comes on like a maniac."

Van Slyke, who takes the game more seriously than his light-hearted manner suggests, says, "I don't want to just stand out there for nine innings and not have a say in the game. Anybody can do that. I want it to happen. I don't want to be unnoticed when I'm in the field." For the season, Van Slyke recorded twelve assists, nine at the plate. At the plate, he hit .288 with 25

home runs, 100 runs batted in, and 101 runs scored.

An aggressive attitude and unwavering concentration are nearly as important as physical ability in playing the outfield. "When you're talking about the major leagues, most players have a certain level of physical talent," says Dwight Evans, the right fielder of the Boston Red Sox, who has won a team-record eight Rawlings Gold Glove awards. "Some guys have better arms than others, but the real difference is the concentration level. If you keep your head in the game, you're going to make the plays. If you don't . . ."

No one produced more hits in major league history than Pete Rose, but most people don't realize he is one of history's most consistent defensive outfielders. Rose, Amos Otis, and Joe Rudi, all with a career fielding percentage of .991, are just behind the Houston Astros' Terry Puhl's all-time mark of .993. That is a tribute to Rose's hustling nature, his desire to play an important role on both sides of the ball.

Experience plays a key role in successful outfield play as well. Knowing the tricks of the home field helps enormously. Over the years Ted Williams, Carl Yastrzemski, Jim Rice, and Mike Greenwell all learned to deal with the idiosyncrasies of the Green Monster at

Boston's Fenway Park. A ball that in most parks would be a fly ball out can turn into a double or triple if the left fielder doesn't position himself far enough from the wall to receive the carom. Good outfielders also position themselves based on their knowledge of a specific hitter. Even before the ball is collected, a player should always know where he is going to throw it.

In his book, *Championship Baseball*, Hank Bauer, the fourteen-year outfielder for the New York Yankees and Kansas City, describes the thought process: "[An outfielder] won't know where to throw unless he is awake all the time to where the runners are, how many outs have already been made, what the score is, and what sort of runners are on base. An outfielder should always figure that the next ball is coming to him and he should have his mind made up as to what he will do with it: where to throw it if he catches it on the fly, where to throw it if he picks it up after it drops safely."

Center field is the toughest of the three outfield positions, since it overlaps the other two. The fleetest of players patrol this position since there is so much ground to cover. In addition, balls are more difficult for players to judge because they are coming on a direct line up the middle of the field.

"It took a long time to learn how to gauge the ball," says Willie McGee, the swift center fielder for the St. Louis Cardinals. "My speed always gave me a margin for error, but there are times when a false step means the ball is going to drop. The way the ball comes off the bat to center, you can't always judge the depth. Now, I can usually figure it out, depending on who's hitting and the sound the ball makes off the bat." McGee, the 1985 National League Most Valuable Player, is one of the most well-rounded center fielders in the game. He has a career batting average of .295 and remains a constant threat to steal a base.

The left fielder generally sees more action than the right fielder because of right-handed hitters' tendency to pull the ball. The right fielder must possess a strong throwing arm because he has a longer throw to third base when runners are trying to advance from first.

"That's what you're always hoping for," says Evans, who has played in more than 2,000 games in the outfield for Boston. "You want them to test your arm so you can show people what you can do. It's an ego thing, you against the runner. He's daring you to throw him out. That's what makes a good outfielder: a guy who wants to make the play."

Armed and dangerous: Pittsburgh's Andy Van Slyke has one of the game's most powerful guns.

The Greatest Outfielders of All Time

The greatest wealth of talent at the Hall of Fame in Cooperstown can be found among the careers of the fifty-one outfielders enshrined there. Eight of the top ten batters with the highest career average patrolled the outfield for their teams. Seven of the first ten players on the all-time home run list were outfielders by trade. The names are indeed formidable, even when narrowed to a specific position.

Who was the greatest centerfielder in history? Ty Cobb, with his all-time best career average of .367? The incomparable Willie Mays, with his 660 home runs? Joltin' Joe DiMaggio, who played center with unmatched grace? Mickey Mantle? Tris Speaker? Hack Wilson, who in 1930 hit 56 home runs and drove in an all-time high 190 runs for the Chicago Cubs?

The two leading home run hitters of all time played right field, Hank Aaron (755) and Babe Ruth (714). The elegant Roberto Clemente, powerful Frank Robinson (586 home runs), and Mel Ott are others worthy of consideration.

Left field boasts two of the best pure hitters for power the game has ever known: left-handers Ted Williams and Stan Musial. Ed Delahanty's career average of .345 is the fourth-best in history.

"Judging players is subjective at best," says Frank Robinson, now the manager of the Baltimore Orioles team he played on for six seasons. "Outfielders are really tough, there's so many good ones. With the different eras, it's hard to make an evaluation. Some players, though, would have been stars in any era."

A brief accounting:

George Herman Ruth could do it all. He was, according to those who saw the Babe play, the most compelling and dominating player to play the game of baseball. The Ruthian legend of his magnificent home runs and life off the field has done much to obscure his sheer athletic ability. At six-foot-two and 215 pounds, Ruth could hit, throw, field and run with the best who played the game. He achieved double figures in stolen bases five times during his glorious twenty-two year career, and rarely did he fail to go from first to third on a single. Oh, and he could pitch.

In 1914, when the Boston Red Sox purchased him from the bankrupt Baltimore Orioles for a paltry $2,900, Ruth had only reached the plate ten times in his first season. He was a left-handed pitcher by trade, and was a modest 2-1 before the Red Sox began to use him regularly in 1915. Ruth won eighteen games and lost only eight that season, and his hitting went largely ignored. The following year, Ruth was 23-12 on the mound with an American League-leading forty-one starts, nine shutouts, and an earned run average of 1.75. He beat the Brooklyn Dodgers in the World Series, and two years later defeated the Chicago Cubs twice in the Series. In the process, he strung together 29⅔ scoreless innings, a record that stood until Whitey Ford of the New York Yankees broke it in 1961. To this day, Ruth's perfect 3-0 mark in World Series play is a record in terms of winning percentage.

At the same time, Ruth's prowess with the bat was no longer a secret. He had ninety-five hits in 317 at-bats in 1918, good for a tidy .300 average. Ruth also led the league with eleven home runs. Thus, the man who won ninety-four games and lost

▲ **Ty Cobb**

only forty-six as a major-leaguer became a full-time outfielder. The next season, his last with the Red Sox, Ruth led the league in homers (29), runs batted in (114), runs scored (103), and slugging percentage (.657). None of this was lost on the Yankees, who made a pitch for Ruth when Boston owner Harry Frazee encountered a financial crisis. In exchange for $125,000 in cash and a $300,000 loan, Ruth was shipped to the Yankees, where he debuted in 1920 in spectacular fashion. Ruth hit fifty-four home runs in only 458 at-bats, a success percentage of 11.8, the best in history. Put another way, Ruth averaged a home run in less than every nine at-bats. There were also 137 runs batted in, 158 runs scored, and a slugging percentage of .847, another all-time mark.

Ruth is the all-time leader in slugging percentage (.690), the best indicator for quality power hitting. Twelve times, Ruth won the league's home run title, simultaneously redefining the art of the long ball.

Willie Mays, on the other hand, was recognized as the prototypical ballplayer. He was just over five-foot-ten and 170 pounds, and blessed with that rare combination of explosive speed and power. In his prime from the mid-1950s to mid-1960s, the "Say-Hey Kid" could do virtually anything the Giants required. He led the National League in home runs four different seasons, led the league in batting in 1954 with a .345 average, and was the stolen base champ for four years running. Beyond his marvelous batting touch, Mays consistently rendered spectacular plays in the outfield.

The one remembered best was the time he robbed Vic Wertz in the 1954 World Se-

▲ **Willie Mays**

ries. The New York Giants had come to the Series as heavy underdogs to the Cleveland Indians, but had defied the odds and were tied 2-2 in the eighth inning of the first game. With two men on base, Wertz drilled a Don Liddle pitch deep to center field, some 460 feet from the plate. Mays never hesitated as he tracked the ball down with his back to the rest of the field. The Giants survived the inning and went on to sweep the Indians in four games. Later, Mays would say his back-handed stab of a Wertz double in the tenth inning of that game was his toughest chance of the Series.

Ty Cobb, six-foot-one and 175 pounds, was a terrific runner who used his head to pick up additional bases. He stole 892 bases during his career, second on the all-time list behind Lou Brock. Cobb's daring on the base paths was legendary; thirty-five times he stole home plate. On defense, Cobb was underrated. He was usually among the league leaders in put-outs, assists, and double plays from his center field position. Overall, Cobb's consistency was frightening. In 1927, at the age of forty-one, he hit .357 for the Philadelphia Athletics, drove in 93 runs, and stole 22 bases.

In 1985 Pete Rose passed Ty Cobb as the man with the most hits in the major leagues, a dramatic moment that underlined the greatness of the former record holder. For when Rose stroked a slider from San Diego's Eric Show into left field, he had already been to the plate 2,300 times more than Cobb had required to produce his 4,191 hits. Cobb's career batting average is sixty-four points higher than Rose's, and he played in the dead-ball era when baseballs stayed in play practically until they unraveled.

Hank Aaron's ability to hit home runs was nothing short of amazing. His home run record is staggering enough, but consider that after hitting only thirteen homers in his rookie season with the Milwaukee Braves, Aaron averaged thirty-four home runs and nearly 100 runs batted in for each of the next twenty-two seasons. Those are career numbers for even the finest players. In addition, Aaron appeared in twenty-four All-Star games and averaged .305 for his career. He also holds major league records with 2,297 runs batted in, 6,856 total bases, and 1,477 extra-base hits.

The home run that people will talk about well into the next century was the one that propelled him past Ruth, his 715th. It came on April 8, 1974 at 9:07 p.m. Al Downing, who was the unfortunate pitcher on the mound for the Los Angeles Dodgers, had earlier walked Aaron on five pitches, but this time he came in with a 1-0 fastball. Aaron's first swing of the night took the ball over the fence in left field and into the glove of teammate Tom House in the Atlanta bullpen. The crowd of 53,775 at Atlanta Stadium stood to acknowledge the feat—the breaking of baseball's most cherished record.

"I saw him at home plate and he had tears hanging on his lids," House said later. "I

▲ Stan Musial

could hardly believe it, because he never got excited. 'Hammer, here it is,' I said. I put the ball in his hand. He said, 'Thanks, kid,' and touched me on the shoulder. I kept staring at him. And it was then that it was brought home to me what this home run meant—not only to him, but to all of us."

Ted Williams' greatest weapon was his eyesight. "The Splendid Splinter" had an uncanny eye at the plate; if he didn't offer at the pitch, umpires were inclined to call it a ball. Williams led the American League in bases on balls over a stretch of eight of nine seasons in which he played full time for the Boston Red Sox. Consequently, most of the pitches that appealed to him often wound up as base hits.

In his rookie season, 1939, Williams produced numbers of historical dimensions. He led the American League with 145 runs batted in (a record total for a rookie), finished second with forty-one doubles, and third in home runs (both the second-highest rookie totals ever), hit .327, and walked 107 times.

Though the Yankees' Joe DiMaggio was the focus of the baseball world in 1941 when he put together his record-setting fifty-six-game hitting streak, not many people knew that Williams outhit DiMaggio .412 to .408 over that stretch. At season's end, Williams had accumulated 185 hits in 456 official at bats, good for a .406 batting average. No player has hit over .400 since then, and when a player flirts with the celebrated mark, such as when George Brett of the Kansas City Royals hit .390 in 1980, it is treated as monumental news.

Stan Musial never hit higher than .376, but he was consistently brilliant enough to top the .335 mark eleven times and win seven National League batting titles. And it was the power he displayed along with the average that made the St. Louis Cardinals' left fielder so dangerous. Musial is second to Aaron in the important category of total bases (6,134) and is a fixture in baseball's top ten lists—from hits to runs batted in to runs scored.

▲ Ted Williams

CHAPTER 5

THE MANAGER AND HIS TOOLS

THE MANAGER/STRATEGY

*Oakland manager
Tony LaRusso (below),
a trained lawyer, has
one of the sharpest
minds in baseball.
Former Yankees
manager Dallas Green
(right) is somewhat
volatile, which could
explain why he was
fired after only one
season in New York.
Opposite page: You
can see the baseball
wisdom carved in the
lines on Sparky
Anderson's face. The
combination of
knowledge and
enthusiasm makes him
one of baseball's best
managers.*

allas Green, the former New York Yankees manager, pulls off his hat and smooths his silver hair, looking very much like John Wayne. He is a strapping six-foot-four and very much in command of the situation; confidence (some would call it cockiness) is his trademark. He was the manager of the 1980 World Series champion Philadelphia Phillies and the general manager of the Chicago Cubs' 1984 National League East division winner. Yet, somewhere beneath the blustery attitude developed late in his baseball life is the uncommon understanding of just what it takes to play in the major leagues. Green was 20-22 and allowed 647 hits in 562 innings over a stretch of eight seasons as a pitcher with the Phillies, Washington Senators, and New York Mets in the 1960s.

"You can't sit back and let the talent take over," he says. "Talent alone can't win. You need everyone to contribute, not a bunch of guys sitting on their cans and letting the stars do it all. We're in an era of guaranteed contracts. Some people think it's also the era of guaranteed jobs, and that's a lot of garbage. You never have to sell me on players who play hard, who hustle, because I was a very mediocre player and had to make sure I did the fundamental things just to survive. I had to get down the bunt or get to first in a hurry on an infield out or I'd be gone.

"I'm a ninety-foot guy. You get paid to run ninety feet. That's why I like [second baseman Steve] Sax. Those kind of guys find ways to beat guys with all the talent. Pete Rose is the best example I can think of. When you come down to it, he didn't do a lot of things very well, but he was a great hitter who worked hard on other phases of the game and always figured out a way to beat you."

And so it was natural that both Green and Rose have taken the logical step to managing after their playing days. And it followed that their relentless search for an edge usually elevated a team beyond its level of talent. That, after all, is what managing is all about. Generally speaking, most teams play to their ability. The manager, who usually doesn't swing a bat or field a ball, steps onto the field only to argue or change pitchers. Most baseball people concede that a good manager can make a difference in roughly ten games a season. Conversely, bad managers can exert the same influence. Thus, an 81-81 team can play to 91-71 or 71-91, a not-so-subtle swing of twenty games in the standings.

As Pete Rose said before he was banished from baseball in 1989, "Managing is a lot harder than playing. Just sitting there and watching can be a kind of helpless feeling. There are so many things you can't control. Basically, you send out the players every game and hope they're good enough to win."

In the days of Connie Mack, a manager tried to keep his veteran ballplayers out of trouble the night before a game and played the percentages: squeeze play, hit-and-run, intentional walk. That was fine around the turn of the century, but today managing a baseball team, like life itself, is a lot more complicated. A manager is the chief psychologist for twenty-five players. Those who fail to understand the self-absorbed stars of the "Me Generation" by running a ship taughter than a tightrope often fail to win. Gene Mauch, the acknowledged tactical genius of the most recent generation of managers, never reached the World Series.

"We all know L.A. had no business winning the championship [in 1988], but the Dodgers know how to spell t-e-a-m and took it to guys who didn't," Green says. "There are no dynasties anymore. Parity is where we are in town. So any team that gets it in gear can get a ring."

It was manager Tommy Lasorda who presided over the team that beat the heavily favored Oakland Athletics to win the 1988 World Series. Lasorda, who has won more than 1,000 games and six division titles since 1977, makes no attempt to blind people with his baseball knowledge. He's too busy entertaining the Hollywood crowd, and the entire baseball world, with his corny jokes.

"My philosophy," he says, "is to make every player feel important. A lot of times, people think all Tom does is give us B.S. about Dodger blue and the big Dodger in the sky. But it's not B.S. That's the point."

Lasorda, in fact, relies heavily on his ability to read people and motivate them. He also surrounds himself

Managerial style is a matter of choice. The Dodgers' Tommy Lasorda **(right)** *never stops chattering. The Mets' Davey Johnson* **(below)** *was more low-key.*

league career. Earl Weaver, the Baltimore Orioles' feisty manager from 1969 to 1982, nicknamed him "Dummy" for knowing it all. Johnson will never be confused with the rah-rah Lasorda; players say he is a man of too few words.

"I think I communicate well," Johnson says. "The loudest words you can say to a player are how you use them on the field. The biggest compliment you can give is letting them play. When people are attacking, you sure want an invisible shield to protect yourself. I'm more sensitive than people realize. I won't let them know, but sometimes I'm shocked at what they think."

Johnson won championships managing at the Double A and Triple A levels. As a rookie manager with the Mets in 1984, he created controversy by lifting his young pitchers early rather than late to build confidence. In retrospect, the stragegy that allowed Gooden, Ron Darling, and Sid Fernandez to develop slowly is viewed as brilliant. In 1986, Johnson demonstrated flexibility by relying on the emerging Len Dykstra and the aging Ray Knight when the Mets won the World Series. Still, his strict adherence to decisions often rubs his players the wrong way. Johnson doesn't much care. "If you don't want to make decisions," he says, "hold auditions every day."

In a sense, George Lee Anderson has played the managerial game from both sides. Sparky never hit a home run in his only season as a major leaguer, 1959, but he picked up knowledge a piece at a time in the minors. When he arrived in Cincinnati in 1970, he inherited a group of established stars led by Pete Rose, Johnny Bench, and Joe Morgan.

"When he was younger, he was almost like a general," says Ray Knight, who played for Anderson in Cincinnati and, later, in Detroit. "He was a very great demander. Not only of your work on the field, but he demanded that everything be the 'old school' way, from dress to being at the ballpark very early to extra workouts. He was almost a tyrant. It could be unpleasant for young players. He didn't say a whole lot to the younger guys. He didn't have much to do with us."

The formula worked, nonetheless, for 863 victories against 586 defeats in nine seasons. Under Anderson, dubbed "Captain Hook" for his itchy trigger finger with

with reliable baseball men, such as Bill Russell, Joe Amalfitano, and Joe Ferguson. When the Dodgers were labeled by many experts as one of the worst teams to ever reach the World Series, Lasorda used the tag as a powerful motivator. After Kirk Gibson's memorable pinch-hit home run won Game One, Lasorda had the only psychological edge he would need.

Tony LaRussa, the Oakland manager, has a much more analytical approach to the game. He was trained as a lawyer at Florida State University's School of Law and still gives dissertations on his chosen profession. Unlike many managers, LaRussa will share the reasoning behind a decision, no matter how convoluted it might be, with words curiously devoid of passion.

After his 43-home run season for the Atlanta Braves in 1973, Davey Johnson is probably best known for his use of computers. The former New York Mets' manager is foremost in the group of detached, new wave managers who lean heavily on statistics. In 1988, he became the first manager in National League history to win ninety or more games in each of his first five seasons. In the American League, Al Lopez managed the feat with the Cleveland Indians from 1951 to 1955.

Johnson has been blessed with a terrific organization, built and maintained by General Manager Frank Cashen and Joe McIlvaine, Vice President of Baseball Operations. Johnson's stable of stars, which included Dwight Gooden, Darryl Strawberry, Gary Carter, and Keith Hernandez, was the equal of any team in the mid-1980s. This gave rise to criticism that Johnson was merely an average manager—that he was, in effect, lucky to be there. At the very least, he is a detached, enigmatic man, even to his players.

"He's tied into statistics," says former Mets' center fielder Mookie Wilson. "Numbers are everything to Davey. I don't know if he ever goes by gut." Said Hernandez: "Davey plays hunches a lot more than anybody I've ever played for. He goes against the book."

Johnson has a mathematics degree from Trinity University in San Antonio, Texas, and took to studying computer printouts late in his thirteen-year major

© W. T. Harrington

starting pitchers, the Big Red Machine won four National League pennants and two World Series. Now, Anderson is the pilot of the Detroit Tigers and he's the only manager in history to have won more than 800 games with two different teams. How has he succeeded in Detroit with the new breed of ballplayer? "He's mellowed," Knight says. "I think he's come to the realization that you cannot change some things. You just give everything you have every day and accept the consequences."

Anderson admits he has undergone a conversion of sorts. "I used to think you had to be tough with players," Anderson says. "You don't have to be. Now, I understand how tough it is for them to go out for every game and perform. It's part of my job to show the players that I know they'll have ups and downs. Is there a perfect ballplayer? I try to adapt. I don't think the player has to understand the coach; the coach has to understand the player."

And what is the manager's role? "Staying out of the way," says Anderson, fifty-six, who says he would like to manage another thirty years. "The game we have no control over. We only have control over our attitudes. In any sporting event you should be able to write articles without ever mentioning the manager. All he does is represent the principals on the field."

When it comes to managers, style very often overshadows substance. Earl Weaver used to make headlines for challenging his players, then waiting for the home run ball. Former St. Louis Cardinals manager

Whitey Herzog, recognized as today's shrewdest manager, is a gifted personnel man who makes the most of what he has. Herzog, who won six division titles in his first twelve years of managing, fielded a team based on pitching, defense, and speed that succeeded on the artificial surface at St. Louis' Busch Stadium. Mostly, managing appears to be all about being in the right place at the right time. "What is the secret of managing?" asks former shortstop Larry Bowa, who appeared briefly as the manager of the San Diego Padres in 1987 and 1988. "Talent, talent, talent."

As his team's top administrator on the field, the manager's power to influence a game rests with the decision-making process. Perhaps his most important task is evaluating pitchers. The manager sets the rotation, taking into account the law of averages, an opposing team's lineup, a pitcher's fondness for his home field, or perhaps, a daytime setting. Beyond that, the manager must sense when his pitcher is no longer effective and select the proper replacement. Most managers tend to manage by the book, which is to say they play those percentages by using classic strategy, such as matching a right-handed pitcher against a right-handed batter.

"But," says Joe Morgan, the Red Sox's down-to-earth former manager, "there are times when you have to go against the book. Even though the percentages say the guy won't get him out, sometimes you just have to go with what your gut says. Of course, your gut can be wrong, too."

Pete Rose found the transition from player to manager difficult in Cincinnati. In 1989 his managing days ended when a gambling scandal rocked the baseball world.

baseman in the 1920s. "I used to walk out to talk to the pitcher with the ball in my right hand, in plain view of the runners, coaches, and everybody," Pinelli said. "I'd keep chunking the ball into my glove in that nervous way you've seen all infielders handle a ball during a time-out. I'd be doing this while I was talking to the pitcher. Then I'd take my bare hand, without the ball, and place it in the pitcher's glove, as though I were giving him the ball. I'd conceal the ball in my gloved hand by making a fist in my glove.

"The success of the play depended on the pitcher. It was up to him to keep his gloved hand close to his side as though he had the ball in it. Once, playing against Brooklyn, I picked a runner off second base with the hidden ball even though I was playing third at the time. Sammy Bohne was playing second and took my throw with the runner six feet off the bag. I whipped the ball to him and it landed in his glove with a snap like a rifle shot. The runner stopped in his tracks. The Brooklyn manager, Uncle Wilbert Robinson, yelled out, 'What happened out there?'

"I thought I was shot," the runner said.

Said Robinson, "You should have been."

Frank Robinson (above) and Cal Ripken (right) both managed to find time to guide the Baltimore Orioles. Opposite page: Dorrell Norman "Whitey" Herzog of the St. Louis Cardinals is probably the greatest manager in the game today.

Of course. Basic managing consists of deciding when to use the hit-and-run play. By starting the runner toward second base, a hole is created by the second baseman or shortstop running to the bag. If the hitter can push the ball through that spot, the team will have runners on first and third. Failure to make contact, on the other hand, can mean an out at second and the end of a promising rally. Managers make other lesser decisions, including when to issue intentional walks, where to play their fielders (based on their knowledge of opposing hitters), and when to attempt a stolen base.

Sometimes an individual can change the way a team formulates its strategy. Halfway through the 1946 season, the Cleveland Indians devised a way to stop slugger Ted Williams. They shifted shortstop Lou Boudreau behind second base to take advantage of the lefty's propensity to pull the ball toward right field. The St. Louis Cardinals employed the strategy in the World Series later that season and Williams struggled at the plate. Once, he pushed a bunt toward unprotected third base, but otherwise he failed to alter his swing.

There are times when strategy is merely a clever piece of deception. Babe Pinelli, later a National League umpire, used the "Hidden Ball Trick" as a regular part of his repertoire as a Cincinnati Reds third

MOST WINS BY A MANAGER

1.	Connie Mack	3,776
2.	John McGraw	2,840
3.	Bucky Harris	2,159
4.	Joe McCarthy	2,126
5.	Walter Alston	2,040
6.	Leo Durocher	2,010
7.	Casey Stengel	1,926
8.	Gene Mauch	1,901
9.	Bill McKechnie	1,898
10.	Sparky Anderson	1,753

The Greatest Managers of All Time

Connie Mack, a catcher for eleven seasons in the big leagues, pushed the rule book as far as it would go—anything to win a baseball game. Playing during a more innocent time, before the turn of the century, Mack perfected a devious technique of tapping the hitter's bat with the edge of his glove as he attempted to swing. This gave rise to the catcher's interference rule, which awarded the wronged batter first base. Later, Mack often removed his mask and pretended to adjust it in two-strike situations. As the hitter visibly relaxed, the pitcher quickly threw a strike. Soon baseball had some new statutes regarding quick pitches.

Mack wasn't much of a hitter, as his career batting average of .245 suggests, but he ran the bases well and rarely struck out. Like so many successful managers, he mastered the small details that win baseball games. It is hardly a coincidence that Mack, who was born Cornelius McGillicuddy in 1862, won more games (3,776) than any other major league manager. Mack's genius lay in his understanding of his players, which stemmed from his own experience in the field.

Unlike many managers of his time, Mack realized the baseball schedule was a marathon, not a sprint. Consequently, he worked them easier in spring training than most rivals. "There is no good in putting a team of ballplayers right on the edge for the opening of the season," he said. "The players should

be conditioned slowly. The race is so long that no matter how carefully the men are working, the players individually and collectively are certain to go stale at some stage of the campaign. For this reason, I do not believe in working players too hard down south."

Mack, known as "The Tall Tactician," managed for an amazing fifty-three years, and though he also appears first in the record book with 4,025 defeats, his Philadelphia Athletics didn't always field the most competitive teams; they finished last seventeen times. Along the way, there were eight World Series appearances and five World Series titles. Mack was also responsible for the development of numerous great players, including Lefty Grove, Jimmie Foxx, George Kell, and Mickey Cochrane.

John McGraw, like Mack, leaned toward Machiavellian tactics. As a third baseman for sixteen years in the majors, he liked to tug on the belts of opposing base runners as they passed. He earned the name of "Muggsy" from his teammates for his ceaseless arguments with umpires. At the same time, he was a keen student of the game. With teammate Wee Willie Keeler, he created the strategy that became known as the hit-and-run play. After three seasons in Baltimore, with two different teams, McGraw was hired to manage the New York Giants in 1902.

He held the job for thirty years and made some startling advances. McGraw was the first manager to delegate on-field duties to

his coaches, opting for the serenity of the dugout for his important decisions. McGraw was the first manager to hire a player exclusively for pinch-hitting situations, and he created the position of relief pitcher in an era when starters generally pitched all nine innings. McGraw's Giants finished last his first season, then second before taking back-to-back pennants. McGraw finished his managing career with a 2,840-1,984 record—a winning percentage of .589.

Bucky Harris, who won 2,159 games in eight different tours of duty (a major league record), is third on the all-time list, including three different turns with the Washington Senators. In fact, success came almost too quickly for Harris. At the age of twenty-seven, the Senators' second baseman was named manager by owner Clark Griffith in a move that drew boos from all quarters in 1924. Washington, a team that had finished 23½ games behind the New York Yankees, somehow managed to finish in first place that season, 2½ games ahead of the Yankees. Harris said there were only two things a manager needed to understand: how to get along with players and when to change pitchers. He mastered both over a twenty-nine-year career that included two World Series titles.

▲ Joe McCarthy

▲ Connie Mack

Joe McCarthy is fourth on the all-time list with 2,126 managing victories, and his winning percentage of .614 compiled over twenty-four seasons is unequaled. Certainly, McCarthy was blessed with some great players, particularly during his years with the New York Yankees when Babe Ruth, Lou Gehrig, and Joe DiMaggio were in uniform. Nonetheless, McCarthy was a shrewd psychologist and a stern disciplinarian. He believed in hustling, and squeezed nine pennants and seven World Series titles from his teams. Perhaps the greatest tribute to McCarthy is his remarkable consistency: No McCarthy team ever finished below .500 or lower than fourth place.

Walter Alston appeared in one major league game as a player and struck out in his only at-bat. He botched one of his two chances in the field. Fortunately, the lean, would-be first baseman eventually found employment with the Dodgers, first in Brooklyn, and later in Los Angeles. Alston won 2,040 games as a manager and collected four World Series titles in seven attempts. Patience was his chief virtue. "That's one of the important things," he says. "The other is keeping everyone together. I tried to understand my players, each and every one, tried to convince them to work together for the team."

Leo Durocher and **Casey Stengel**, two of baseball's most colorful managers, are next on the all time list, with 2,010 and 1,926 victories, respectively. "Leo the Lip" was a combative shortstop who took on revered players such as Ty Cobb and Babe Ruth. As a manager, he often pushed his players beyond their abilities. Stengel, "The Old Professor," appeared in ten World Series, all with the New York Yankees, and won seven. His total of 37 Series victories is a record.

Baseball Hall of Fame

▲ **Casey Stengel**

Baseball Hall of Fame

▲ **Leo Durocher**

The Designated Hitter

Below: Though Jim Rice was never a fan of the designated hitter, it certainly extended his fine career. Opposite page: While the outfielders were standing around shagging flies, Reggie Jackson was sitting in the clubhouse watching television.

Admittedly, the sight of a lanky, awkward pitcher at the plate swinging futilely at a medium-speed fastball is not baseball's best poetry. Still, it is strangely comforting, something vaguely related to the balance of power, or checks and balances.

In 1973, the powers atop the American League were not content to leave well enough alone. They fundamentally altered the structure of the game by introducing a hired gun for the pitcher. It was called the Designated Hitter Rule, and the theory was to increase offensive productivity and, therefore, attendance. "A hitter may be designated to bat for the starting pitcher and all subsequent pitchers in any game without otherwise affecting the status of the pitcher(s) in the game," the rule read. "A DH for the pitcher must be selected prior to the game and must be included in the lineup cards presented to the umpire-in-chief. It is not mandatory that a club designate a hitter for the pitcher, but failure to do so prior to the game precludes the use of a DH for that game."

Fat chance. Naturally, American League managers started salivating. Not only could they borrow on their depth by inserting another bat in the lineup, they could hide a player's liability in the field by allowing him only four or five at-bats per game. Since it was introduced, the DH has produced an approximate average of .270, roughly eighty points higher than the pitcher. Teams enjoy better run production, since most DHs hit in the middle of the lineup rather than in the number nine spot usually occupied by the pitcher. Additionally, a manager wasn't forced to make the difficult decisions over removing a pitcher in the late innings when his spot in the order came around. Players, on the other hand, are sharply divided on the issue of the DH.

"It stinks," said Boston slugger Jim Rice, when he was eased from his familiar position in left field in favor of the more defensive-minded Mike Greenwell. "Baseball is a two-way sport. You hit and you play the field. The DH takes away an important part of the game. What am I going to do with all that time?"

According to Reggie Jackson, whose career was extended by the DH rule, the DH will do a lot of walking around. "It's hard to blow off that nervous energy when you don't play the field," he says. "You walk around the clubhouse, watch the game on TV, ride the [stationary] bike. Anything to make the innings move a little faster. I kind of like the DH rule because it keeps more good hitters in the game."

Perhaps. A. Bartlett Giamatti, the former Commissioner of Baseball (before his death in 1989), admitted he hated the DH rule but said that until the American League capitulates, he would do nothing to reverse the decision. The National League, a bastion of baseball purity, steadfastly refuses to budge on the issue. Small wonder. Over the course of the 1988 season, the Texas Rangers used twenty-four different designated hitters and one couldn't help thinking that even Hoyt Wilhelm (lifetime batting average of .088, or thirty-eight hits in twenty-one years) could have done better at times.

© W. T. Harrington

THE DESIGNATED HITTER RULE

A hitter may be designated to bat for the pitcher in any spot in the batting order in any game without affecting the status of the pitcher. The designated hitter must be selected and be included on the lineup cards presented to the umpire-in-chief prior to the game. Failure to do so precludes the use of a designated hitter for that game.

The designated hitter is "locked" into the batting order but may be removed for a pinch hitter or pinch runner, who in turn becomes the designated hitter. The designated hitter, while still in the game, may be used defensively, but the pitcher then assumes the batting order of the replaced defensive player, thus terminating the designated hitter role.

© John McDonough

Above: *Vince Coleman, formerly of the St. Louis Cardinals, has blinding speed. When he ultimately masters the science of the bunt, he will be very difficult to the defense.*

Opposite page: *As New York Yankees announcer Phil Rizzuto suggests, the bunt is rapidly becoming a lost art. It is one of those small skills that makes baseball a subtle game of inches.*

The Bunt

Vince Coleman works alone in the hot sun, watched only by a batting practice pitcher and one Bunny Mick, who wears a Number 74 across his back. It is 9:30 a.m. at Al Lang Field, the St. Louis Cardinals' St. Petersburg facility. Coleman squares from his left-handed stance as the pitch comes in, slides his left hand down the barrel of the bat and a seventy-five-mile-an-hour fastball is transformed into a three-hop grounder that comes to rest ten feet down the third base line. Pfffft. "That's the idea," Mick says. "Keep the barrel level. Deaden that ball."

Mick knows more than a little about bunts and the subtle role they can play in a baseball game. A catcher in the New York Yankees chain, he never advanced to the major leagues. Still, from his vantage point behind the plate, Mick developed a head for the game. He once drew 183 bases on balls in a single season, an achievement he claims is a professional baseball record. Mick, a co-owner of the Tampa Tarpons of the Florida State League and a special bunting instructor for the Houston Astros, approached St. Louis manager Whitey Herzog during the 1988 off-season about improving Coleman's on-base percentage through bunting. When Coleman embraced the idea, Mick was dispatched to St. Petersburg. "Working with Bunny's got to help him." Herzog says. "Vince gets impatient at times. If he gets a little more selective, he'll reach base more often. The more Vince is on base, the better off we are."

Says Mick, "When Vince doesn't make contact, there's no chance for him to let his legs get him on base and into a position to score. I'd like to see him cut down to seventy strikeouts [from an average of more than 100 per season]. If he gets fourteen bunt hits out of those additional forty times he makes contact, that's fourteen more times he can make things happen on the base paths. Getting him to learn the strike zone and being more selective seem to be the keys. Get him to where he's stealing first base. A fellow has to learn his preferred strike zone. First, he visualizes a picture of it. Then he recognizes a pitch when it's there and he bunts it. If it's going to be close, he fouls it off with a half-swing and waits for the next one."

In Coleman's case, the goal is a .300 batting average. "If that happens, I can steal 140 bases," he says, somehow managing to avoid sounding arrogant. "I'd like to see that."

The bunt, one of baseball's best-kept secrets, generally is less of an offensive weapon. Most often it is used as a sacrifice to move a runner into scoring position, usually from first to second. Most swift runners learn the basics of bunting to take advantage of their speed more often. Teams that rely on speed rather than power, like Herzog's Cardinals, use the bunt as a regular part of their repertoire.

Many baseball men feel the bunt is a lost art. Former New York Yankees shortstop Phil Rizzuto sounds like the old-timer he is when he laments, "Kids coming up today don't take the time to learn to bunt. It's something you have to work at, and most guys don't want to bother. I've always thought it was a great play, if you could master it." Check back with Vince Coleman when he steals 140 bases.

© Otto Greule Jr/Allsport

© J. Daniel/Allsport

© Otto Greule Jr./Allsport

The Base Stealer

Willie Wilson grimaces as he talks of base-stealing and, perhaps unconsciously, rubs his left knee. "Speed is always an important thing," says the Kansas City outfielder. "But in the major leagues, there's more to stolen bases than raw speed. You have to be smart, have to study the pitchers and the situations. And there's another factor that people don't talk about: You have to want to do it. Sounds simple, but it isn't. The year Rickey Henderson stole all those bases, he was really beat up by the end of the season. You must have the desire, the willingness to throw yourself on the ground. It's like you're traveling in a car at twenty miles an hour. . . and, suddenly, you just jump out. Think about that."

Obviously, Wilson does. Through the 1988 season, Wilson, who at the time was a venerable thirty four years old, had thrown himself on the ground some 702 times. On 588 of those occasions he was called safe. Only Henderson of the Oakland Athletics has stolen more bases among active American Leaguers. Wilson may hve lost a half-step after twelve seasons, but he still managed to steal twenty-four bases in 1989. He was caught only seven times, a tribute to his wisdom on the base paths.

"Everything depends on the situation," Wilson says. "People try to make it more complicated than it is, but basically, you run when you need to get a run and when the pitcher has to throw a strike—say a 2-0 or 2-1 count. If they know you're running and can afford to pitch out, they'll do it. Sometimes you can beat it, but usually you don't. Of course, you'd like to go on a curveball, but usually you have to beat the fastball. The key is reading the pitcher to the plate and getting the good jump."

One of the lost arts in baseball is the ability of pitchers to hold runners on base. Slicing a step off a lead can make the difference between a catcher's success and failure in unloading the ball. If Wilson or any other base runner can get a four- or five-step lead off first base, even a good catcher will have difficulty throwing him out. Generally, it is easier to get a bigger lead off second because the shortstop has to cover his territory in the hole. Nobody is better at consistently pushing the envelope than Henderson, the leading base stealer in major league history.

"I guess you could call it arrogance," Henderson says. "It's believing that you can do something, even when everybody in the ballpark knows you're going to do it."

Through 1992, Henderson had stolen 1,042 bases, beating out Lou Brock (938) and Ty Cobb (892) for the all-time record. In 1989, Henderson surpassed fifty steals for the ninth time, an American League record. Incredibly, Brock cleared fifty steals twelve different times for the St. Louis Cardinals, the National League standard. Henderson, a deceptively powerful athlete at five-foot-ten and 195 pounds, was a blur in 1982, stealing a major league record 130 bases. In just over four seasons with the New York Yankees, Henderson set a team record with 326 stolen bases before a trade sent him back to Oakland. The value of a good base stealer is his ability to advance his team's cause by moving into scoring position. In 1985, his first season with the Yankees, Henderson scored a league-leading 146 runs batting ahead of Don Mattingly and Dave Winfield in the lineup. At the same time, Henderson is a terrific all-around athlete. Since stealing bases requires being on base, Henderson's career has benefitted from a batting average of approximately .290 and a discriminating eye at the plate; Henderson averages nearly ninety walks

There is more to stolen bases than mere speed of foot. Base stealers must judge the character of the pitcher, the pace of the game, and the arm strength of the catcher. A baserunner with the unmitigated gall of Oakland's Rickey Henderson (above and opposite page, above) can be a disruptive force for the team playing defense. In the 1989 World Series against San Francisco, Henderson demanded the constant attention of the pitcher.

W. T. Harrington

Knowing your limitations is the first rule of base stealing. The second? Don't get caught.

per season. No one has ever hit more home runs (35) from the lead-off position, and in 1981 Henderson was a Rawlings Gold Glove Award winner in the outfield.

The National League, generally more aggressive than its junior counterpart, has always enjoyed a grand tradition of base stealers. Willie Mays led the league for four consecutive years, from 1956-59, and was followed by the Dodgers' Maury Wills, who won six straight stolen base titles. Brock led the league eight times in nine years, from 1966 to 1974. Recently, Tim Raines and Vince Coleman have dominated the National League. Coleman, in fact, has a chance to set new standards.

In 1985, his first major league season, Coleman stole 110 bases, a rookie record. He led the National League each of the next three seasons as well, becoming the youngest player ever to reach 400 stolen bases. He began as a pure right-handed hitter, but the St. Louis organization converted him into a switch-hitter to take better advantage of his speed. In 1983, Coleman stole 145 bases in the South Atlantic League, a professional baseball record, despite missing thirty-one games with a hand injury. Though Coleman's stolen bases dipped slightly in recent years, he is merely becoming more selective. "Anyone's going to get the big numbers if they run enough," he says. "I'm trying to increase my odds by running in situations that favor

me, like against guys who throw junk and on better counts. Plus, I'm a lot smarter out there now that I've been around for awhile."

In 1989, Coleman's new approach to quality led to a remarkable piece of history. After he was thrown out by Damon Berryhill of the Chicago Cubs on September 11, 1988, Coleman stole an even fifty consecutive bases without getting caught. Montreal catcher Nelson Santovenia ended the streak more than ten months later with a strong throw that curiously reinforced how incredible Coleman's streak really was.

TOP TEN CAREER STOLEN BASES

1. Rickey Henderson	1,095
2. Lou Brock	938
3. Ty Cobb	892
4. Tim Raines	751
5. Eddie Collins	743
6. Max Carey	738
7. Honus Wagner	703
8. Joe Morgan	689
9. Willie Wilson	667
10. Vince Coleman	648

© W. T. Harrington

© W. T. Harrington

© W. T. Harrington

© W. T. Harrington

The Pinch Hitter

If hitting is largely a mental enterprise, then pinch-hitting is almost completely a cerebral affair. If hitting is the most difficult feat in all of professional sports, then pinch-hitting is even harder.

"You bet your butt—everything you've got—it's the toughest," says Rusty Staub, the former New York Mets and Montreal Expos star. "That's the reason you rarely find young players who can handle pinch-hitting. It takes a special kind of experience."

Manny Mota, now a coach for the Los Angeles Dodgers, leads all major leaguers with 150 career pinch-hits. He uses the words hard work instead of experience. "The pinch hitter has a tougher job because he's not always in the lineup," Mota says, "You have to work hard in the batting cage, and mentally, too, to keep your swing in a good rhythm." For the last eight years of his career, Mota was exclusively a pinch hitter. He required only 505 at-bats to reach the 150 mark, resulting in a .297 average, only seven points lower than his overall career average. Mota and Smoky Burgess, who is second on the all-time list with 145 pinch-hits, were basically singles hitters.

Some managers, notably Earl Weaver of the Baltimore Orioles, looked for home runs from his pinch hitters. Gates Brown, who played for the Detroit Tigers from 1963 to 1975, produced 107 pinch-hits, sixteen of them homers. Lee Lacy and Del Unser are both on record as having hit pinch-hit home runs in three consecutive game appearances. In 1957, the Cincinnati Reds set a major league record with twelve pinch-hit

home runs. The Mets equaled the mark in 1983, the same season Staub set a Mets record with twenty-four pinch-hits in a season, one short of the National League record of Jose Morales, who is third on the all-time list with 123 pinch-hits. Staub maximized his presence with twenty-five runs batted in, tying the league record set by Gerald Lynch in 1961.

"I think the hardest thing to deal with is the down time, that's rough," Staub says. "There are stretches where you can go 0-for-the-month. That means you have to have discipline and accept your role. It's your job to keep loose, keep ready, study pitchers, and get a feel for the way umpires are calling the game. Really, by the time you get to the plate, most of the work should be done. Then, all you have to do is get a hit."

Manny Mota, whose 150 pinch hits are a major-league record, says he sometimes used to swing at the first pitch and miss intentionally, just to loosen up.

TOP TEN CAREER PINCH-HITS

1. Manny Mota	150
2. Smoky Burgess	145
3. Jose Morales	123
Greg Gross	123
5. Jerry Lynch	116
6. Red Lucas	114
7. Steve Braun	113
8. Terry Crowley	108
9. Gates Brown	107
10. Mike Lum	103

© AP/Wide World Photos

© W. T. Harrington

For Rusty Staub, Le Grand Orange, experience and discipline were essential qualities for a good pinch hitter.

THE PINCH-HITTER RULE

A player shall be considered a pinch hitter only if he enters the game as a substitute batter, and then only on his first time at bat, which must be before he becomes a fielder (if the team bats around and a pinch hitter comes up a second time in the inning in which he first appeared, he will not be considered a pinch hitter during that second time up). A substitute hitter for the designated hitter is both a pinch hitter and a designated hitter on his first time at bat. On subsequent trips to the plate, he is a designated hitter only.

TOP TEN CAREER PINCH-HITTING AVERAGES

1.	Tommy Davis	.320
2.	Jerry Mumphrey	.318
3.	Frenchy Bordagaray	.312
4.	Frankie Baumholtz	.307
5.	Red Schoendienst	.303
6.	Bob Fothergill	.300
7.	Dave Philley	.299
8.	Manny Mota	.297
9.	Ted Easterly	.296
10.	Harvey Hendrick	.295

For several years, Mookie

Wilson (above) *and*

Len Dykstra (opposite

page) *were the New York*

Mets' two-headed center-

fielder. Together, their

contrasting styles helped

lead the Mets to the 1986

World Series title.

The Platoon

The Andre Dawsons, Corey Snyders, and Kevin Mitchells of the world sleep well at night. They know that, regardless of circumstance—left-handed pitcher, right-handed pitcher, home game, road game, night or day game—there is always a place for them in the lineup. The platoon player, however, never knows when the call will come.

"It's tough," says Mookie Wilson. "You're a baseball player, making a pretty good living, and you want to play every day. Sometimes it's just not that easy because you don't know for sure when you'll be playing. A lot of it is the way you're perceived. If I had played every day for the first three years, I'd be playing every day now. But I'm a realist; I understand what the Mets were trying to do. They had the joy of having two players who could play the position well. I'm not sure somebody was going to turn the center field job over to someone who's thirty-three years old."

Wilson would never acknowledge it, but the center field combination of Len Dykstra and himself—"Mook-Stra," as the New York tabloids called it—might have been better than the sum of its parts. Certainly it played a key role in the Mets' 1986 World Championship. Though they were opposites in many ways, Wilson and Dykstra were perfectly complementary. Dykstra, five-foot-ten and 170 pounds, gave the Mets power from the left side of the plate and a daring base runner. Wilson, a five-foot-ten, 174-pound switch hitter, was as smooth as Dykstra was hyperactive. Dykstra was seven years younger, a better defensive outfielder with a better arm and a penchant for swinging for the fences. Wilson was a better bet to steal a base under pressure and played a little more under control, though he was a free-swinger at the plate. Both players were swift, with career batting averages that hovered around .280.

"When Mookie [was] on fire and on the loose, then the Mets [got] hot," said Mets first baseman Keith Hernandez, thinking of 1988, when Wilson hit .385

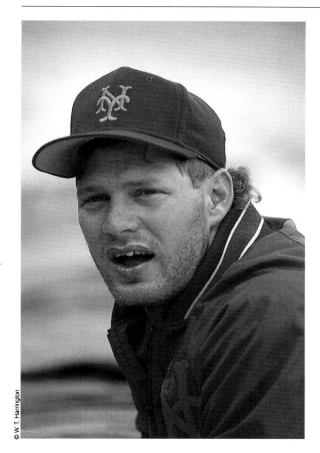

over a critical forty-six-game stretch on the way to the National League East title. "And 'Nails' [Dykstra's self-created nickname, as in 'as hard as nails'] gets us going, too. He's so aggressive."

Joe McIlvaine, the Mets' Vice President for Baseball Operations, described the two-headed center fielder this way before the 1989 season: "Although both players don't like to admit it, and won't admit it, they are a good tandem and have complemented each other well. Although we considered a lot of different possibilities involving both players in trades with other ballclubs, we've never really come up with a solution that would make us a better team."

Sniffed Dykstra, "That's great, for them. Not for us, though. It's frustrating. I wouldn't mind if some of those [trade rumors] came true, because this is definitely not easy to accept."

All parties were apparently satisfied in 1989 when Wilson and Dykstra parted company. The Mets found their everyday center fielder ninety minutes down the road in Philadelphia's Juan Samuel. They sent Dykstra and struggling reliever Roger McDowell to the Phillies in exchange for the twenty-eight-year-old athlete. Wilson was dispatched to Toronto as part of a deal for left-handed pitcher Jeff Musselman.

The platoon system has come into vogue in recent years as baseball has grown more specialized. The theory is to match a left-handed batter against a right-handed pitcher, and vice versa. This means the pitcher's curveball breaks into a hitter, making it substantially easier to hit. When two players are so close in ability that neither can win the starting job outright, a manager will use two players to fill the void.

"When I was a ballplayer, I wanted to be in there all the time," said Mets manager Davey Johnson. "I understand what guys go through. But I also know that platooning helps us win games. The more options you have, the better you're going to do. You get twenty-four guys and you have to get the most out of them, any way you can. That's why they call it a team."

CHAPTER 6

EXTRA INNINGS

For all his learning, A. Bartlett Giamatti, the seventh commissioner of baseball, was simply a Boston Red Sox fan at heart.

© J. Commentucci/Allsport

THE COMMISSIONER

Like Presidents of the United States, baseball's commissioners have always been judged by their performance in the crucible of crisis. Kenesaw Mountain Landis, the first commissioner, helped restore public confidence in the wake of the Black Sox scandal in the World Series of 1919. His successor, Happy Chandler, presided over a difficult time as well. When Dodgers general manager Branch Rickey wanted to break baseball's race barrier by signing Jackie Robinson to a minor league contract in October 1945, the other fifteen teams were against it. Chandler supported Rickey in his worthy enterprise and Robinson ultimately reached the major leagues in 1947. Bowie Kuhn, baseball's fifth commissioner, handled the position with firmness and insight when Curt Flood challenged the sport's reserve clause. Kuhn was the mediator between players and owners as a new free agency system was created.

Francis T. Vincent Jr., the most recent of eight commissioners, who assumed the responsibility upon the sudden death of A. Bartlett Giamatti in July 1989, acted with grace and compassion when an earthquake postponed Game Three of the 1989 World Series. In explaining a ten-day sabbatical, he told a large press gathering, "It is becoming very clear to all of us in Major League baseball that our concerns, despite this rather large gathering, our issue, is really a modest one in light of the great tragedy that hit this area. It is far better to wait here, recognizing that we support the community's effort." Though some people called for the cancellation of the series, Vincent found an historical precedent. "We can look to the British during the Second World War," he said. "Diversion was part of the healing process there. They continued to go to their movies even though London was being bombed. They affirmed life, and perhaps baseball can do the same."

Though organized baseball goes back to the 1850s, it wasn't until 1920 that the position of commissioner, as we know it today, was created. The power was finally centralized because a condition of general anarchy forced baseball's hand.

The first attempt at standardized rules came in 1857, when the Knickerbocker team of New York City brought together several neighboring clubs to agree on guidelines. The following season, the National Association of Baseball Players was formed, dedicated to keeping baseball a purely amateur sport. But inevitably, baseball evolved into a professional business. The Cincinnati Red Stockings, the first team to openly pay players, urged the formation of the National Association of Professional Baseball Players. Of course, with money came greed and, eventually, bribery and gambling found its way into baseball. As the organization of teams became the focus of the sport, rather than the association of players, the need for leadership became obvious. William A. Hulbert, the second president of the National League, expelled four players for "conduct in contravention of the objects of the league," when they were discovered in the company of gamblers discussing the throwing of games. Two years later, Hulbert tossed an entire team out of the leagues. Cincinnati was expelled for "selling malt or spiritous liquors on league grounds."

In 1903, when the National Agreement made peace between the American and National Leagues, the World Series was just one of the byproducts. Also created was a National Commission, a three-man panel that supervised the game and carried out the provisions of the National Agreement. Unfortunately, the three board members were all linked to various teams and routinely made self-serving decisions. Still, the position of commissioner might have been decades away if not for the scandal of the 1919 World Series. When it was revealed that eight White Sox players allegedly took bribes from gamblers to intentionally lose the Series to the Reds, the commission was slow to investigate. Perhaps August Hermann, the only chairman of the commission for eighteen years, didn't want to believe that his team hadn't won fairly or squarely.

In any case, the National League lobbied to replace the unwieldy commission with a single man of "unquestionable reputation and standing in fields other than baseball." Albert Lasker, a stockholder in the Chicago Cubs, authored the document that outlined the parameters of the job. Eventually, the American League saw the light and helped in the search for a man of uncompromising virtue. Kenesaw Mountain Landis, a United States District Judge appointed by President Theodore Roosevelt, was approached, but declined the offer. Later, he agreed on the condition that he could hold his court position and the new baseball job. Toward that end, Landis insisted that his baseball salary ($50,000) be adjusted by $7,500, the pay he received as a judge.

Under the Major League Agreement, signed in 1920, Landis was given full power over the league's teams. He took his responsibility seriously and banned the eight White Sox players involved in the World Series swindle. Landis banished Giants outfielder Benny Kauff for theft and receiving stolen property in 1921, as well as four others for improper conduct, including Philadelphia Phillies President William Cox for betting on games in 1943. When Landis died in 1944, the Major League Agreement was modified to reign the commissioner's power by giving clubs the right to challenge the commissioner's decisions in court.

Happy Chandler was the captain of his Corydon High School baseball and basketball teams in Kentucky and entered Transylvania College in Lexington in 1917. He served Kentucky as lieutenant governor, governor, and senator before baseball called. He defused the tension over the Jackie Robinson signing, suspended manager Leo Durocher for an entire season, and helped establish the first player pension fund with the $475,000 World Series radio rights contract.

Ford Frick, baseball's third commissioner, began as a sportswriter. He covered the Yankees for *New York Evening Journal* and became a ghost writer for Babe Ruth. In his fifteen years on the job, Frick saved at least three franchises from bankruptcy, shepherded over the expansion to four more teams, and helped secure lucrative television contracts.

General William Eckert earned the nickname "Spike" while playing football at the United States Military Academy, and was a darkhorse when Frick retired in 1965. Baseball's owners had a list of 156 candidates and Eckert was one name that never surfaced publicly. Nevertheless, he was unanimously elected baseball's fourth commissioner. Eckert served only three years before giving way to Bowie Kuhn, the right man for the troubled times which lay ahead. Kuhn was trained as a lawyer at the University of Virginia and spent nineteen years working on baseball's legal affairs for a New York law firm. One month after he was elected, Kuhn negotiated a delicate settlement between the players and owners. Conciliation was the benchmark of his fifteen-year tenure, the second longest among commissioners to Landis.

Recognizing the sport as big business, baseball's owners secured Peter Ueberroth as Kuhn's successor in 1984. He was highly visible as the president of the Los Angeles Olympic Organizing Committee that managed to net a $250 million profit. Clearly, baseball needed a quality control man. That's precisely what it got. When Ueberroth took office, twenty-one of twenty-six teams were losing money. When he left five years later, all of baseball's teams made money or broke even. By negotiating a landmark $1.1 billion, four-year television contract with CBS before he left, Ueberroth insured that baseball would be secure through the early 1990s.

Giamatti was the antithesis of Ueberroth. He was a scholar, a former president of Yale University. More than anything, he was a fan. In two years as National League president, Giamatti proved his love for the game by honoring its history and traditions. He was elected commissioner in September 1988, but died of a heart attack before serving his first full year. Fay Vincent, his hand-picked deputy commissioner, succeeded Giamatti. Judging from his early performance, Giamatti chose well.

BASEBALL'S COMMISSIONERS	
Kenesaw Mountain Landis	1921-44
Albert "Happy" Chandler	1945-51
Ford Christopher Frick	1951-65
General William "Spike" Eckert	1965-68
Bowie Kuhn	1969-84
Peter Victor Ueberroth	1984-89
A. Bartlett Giamatti	1989
Francis T. Vincent Jr.	1989-

© AP/Wide World Photos

Commissioners have come from all sectors of society: Kenesaw Mountain Landis **(below, left)** *was a United States district judge; Bowie Kuhn* **(left)** *was a lawyer; and Peter Ueberroth* **(below, right)** *was a marketing specialist.*

Baseball Hall of Fame

© V. J. Lovero/Allsport

THE WORLD SERIES

San Francisco's Terry Kennedy (below) up-ended Oakland shortstop Walt Weiss in the 1989 World Series, but the A's got the last laugh with a four-game sweep in the earthquake-interrupted classic. **Opposite page:** *Yes, Kirk, dreams do come true. In the 1988 World Series, the Dodger's hobbling outfielder caught up with a Dennis Eckersley slider and lifted it into the bleachers in right field. It gave the Dodgers the first game and set the tone for their Series upset.*

In 1986 and 1987, the Los Angeles Dodgers won a paltry seventy-three games per season, their lowest victory totals since 1967. Tommy Lasorda sat back at the Dodgers' spring training facility at Vero Beach, Florida, one morning in March 1988 and admitted, "The last two years have been tragic for me as a manager and as a part of this organization." Since Lasorda arrived in 1977, he had led the Dodgers to five division titles, four World Series, and one World Championship. Yet, in 1987, they were last in the majors in hitting (.252), runs scored (635), and on-base percentage (.309). Attendance at Dodger Stadium fell off nearly a half million over two seasons. "You can't win every year," said Dodgers owner Peter O'Malley, "but we haven't been in contention for two years. We're doing everything we can to get back into contention in 1988."

Even Lasorda and O'Malley couldn't have hoped for the kind of contention the 1988 season brought. Carried by pitching and timely hitting, the Dodgers won the National League's Western Division with a 94-67 record that was seven games better than Cincinnati's. And though they were heavy underdogs to the New York Mets in the League Championship Series, the Dodgers somehow escaped. With the Mets about to win their third game in four tries, Los Angeles catcher Mike Scioscia hit a two-run, game-tying home run in the ninth inning and Kirk Gibson won it in the twelfth with another homer. Eventually, the Dodgers prevailed in seven games to reach their fifth World Series under Lasorda.

According to the experts, this World Series would be no contest; the powerful Oakland Athletics, who romped through the regular season with a best-in-the-majors record of 104-58, would throttle the limping, gimping Dodgers. One commentator, NBC's Bob Costas, suggested that the Dodgers might be the worst team to reach the World Series in history. Lasorda shrugged and told his players the story of David and Goliath, saying, "That was the first time the underdog won." The first game seemed to support Costas' theory. With two outs in the bottom of the ninth inning, the A's had their relief ace, Dennis Eckersley, on the mound, holding a 4-3 lead. He walked Mike Davis, and when on-deck hitter Dave Anderson was called back to the dugout, the crowd of 55,983 at Dodger Stadium erupted as Kirk Gibson, the left fielder sidelined with a bruised right knee and a pulled left hamstring, emerged. Twenty minutes earlier, Gibson had been stretched out in the trainer's room minus his uniform top. He had heard television announcer Vin Scully say, "The man who is the spearhead of the Dodger offense throughout the year, who saved them in the League Championship Series, will not see any action tonight, for sure." Gibson jumped off the training table, crafted a choice reply [expletive deleted], grabbed some ice for his knee, and hobbled to the batting cage under the stands. He sent word through hitting coach Ben Hines that he expected to pinch-hit if Davis got on.

When Davis, a .196 hitter, walked, Lasorda turned toward the tunnel leading to the dugout and there was Gibson. He limped up the runway, then up the dugout

The pressure in the

World Series is immense.

Keith Hernandez (below),

a lifetime .300 hitter,

managed only a .245

average in two appear-

ances. He was 7-for-27 in

the 1982 World Series

when the Cardinals

played Milwaukee.

Opposite page, above: In

1976, Joe Morgan and the

Cincinnati Reds won a

second consecutive World

Series, this one over the

Yankees. Ten years later,

the Mets' Kevin Elster

sipped champagne with

his teammates after New

York edged Boston

(opposite page, below).

steps. Eckersely had pushed the count to 2-2, and Gibson then fouled off three straight pitches. The next pitch barely missed the plate; now the suspense was oppressive. Eckersley's next offering was a slider, low but over the plate. Gibson golfed at the ball and sent it five rows into the bleachers in right field. Gibson, dragging his right leg and stepping carefully on his left foot, circled the bases in agonizingly slow motion. The blow was a case of life imitating art, and the comparisons to Roy Hobbs and *The Natural* began immediately. Gibson's only at-bat of the Series might have legitimately earned him Most Valuable Player honors—if not for teammate Orel Hershiser.

Hershiser had gone 23-8 over the regular season with an earned run average of 2.26, and 15 complete games. He finished the 162-game schedule with a major league record fifty-nine consecutive scoreless innings that broke the standard set by former Dodger pitcher Don Drysdale. Hershiser won the deciding seventh game against the Mets in the League Championship Series, 6-0, with a five-hitter. In the second game of the World Series, Hershiser threw a brilliant three-hitter at the A's and distinguished himself with three hits of his own, including two doubles. Oakland came back to win Game Three, but lost the fourth by making two critical errors. Then Hershiser took the mound for Game Five and threw a four-hitter. Mickey Hatcher and Mike Davis each hit two-run home runs, and the Dodgers had their first World Championship in seven seasons. David had beaten Goliath again.

For Joe Amalfitano, the Dodgers' third base coach, lightning had struck at the World Series a second time. He was a twenty-year-old spare infielder for the New York Giants when they met the Cleveland Indians in the 1954 Series. The Indians had buried the favored New York Yankees over the regular season by winning 111

games. While most observers figured Cleveland would win easily, Willie Mays was not among them. Mays made his famous catch of Vic Wertz' smash to center in the eighth inning of a 2-2 game and, ultimately, the Giants prevailed in the tenth on Dusty Rhodes' pinch-hit home run. The Giants beat the Indians in four games—the first National League sweep in forty seasons.

Since the World Series began in 1903, when Boston beat Pittsburgh five games to three, it has grown into America's greatest sporting spectacle. Certainly, the Super Bowl annually draws better television ratings, but the World Series draws the nation's gaze for a week or more. Men and women devise ways to smuggle televisions into the workplace; children listen to transistor radios under the covers. Because it enjoys such a heightened atmosphere, events at the World Series are magnified and, quite often, memorable. A few choice examples:

On a pitching roster that featured Whitey Ford, Don Larsen didn't figure to become the 1956 World Series hero. He had led the American League with twenty-one losses only two seasons earlier and had played for three teams in four years. The six-foot-four right-hander lasted less than two innings in Game Two, when manager Casey Stengel worried that he might blow a 6-0 lead. Still, he started against the Brooklyn Dodgers on October 8, 1956, with the Series tied at two games apiece. Larsen threw the only perfect game in Series history, throwing 97 pitches to get 27 outs. Such was his control that Pee Wee Reese was the only batter to work the count to three balls.

In the seventh game of the 1926 World Series, October 9, 1926, the classic struggle of experience versus youth was personified in one critical matchup. St. Louis Cardinals pitcher Grover Cleveland Alexander, thirty-

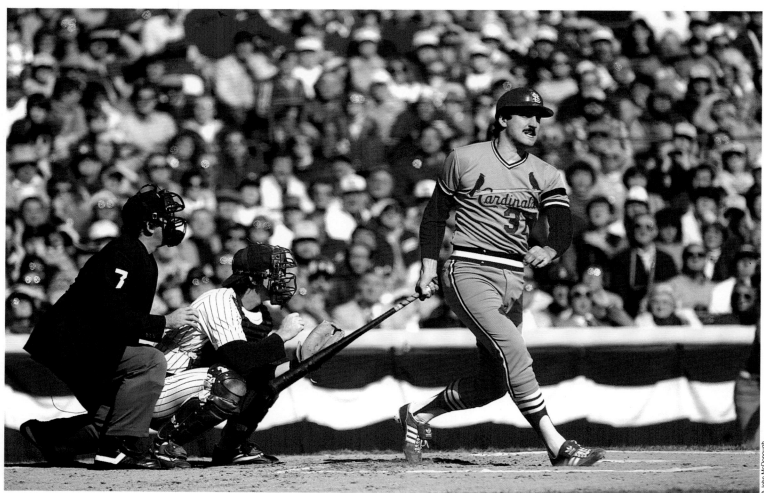

© John McDonough

nine, faced Tony Lazzeri, the New York Yankees' twenty-three-year-old rookie. The Cards led 3-2 in the seventh, but the Yankees had loaded the bases. Alexander, who had pitched St. Louis to victory in Game Six, was called into the tense game at Yankee Stadium by manager Rogers Hornsby to face Lazzeri, who had distinguished himself by leading the American League with 96 strikeouts during the regular season. This time, experience won out; a curve, followed by a fastball (stroked just foul down the left field line), and another curve turned Lazzeri into a statue. Alexander pitched the final innings and the Cards were champions.

For years, the Boston Red Sox have frustrated their New England fans by falling just short at the pinnacle. It happened in 1967, when the Cardinals prevailed in seven games; it happened in 1986, when the Red Sox were a strike away from eliminating the New York Mets and again failed. The results in 1975 were similar, but the glory of Game Six between Boston and the Cincinnati Reds far outshone the disappointment years later.

The Sox were down three games to two, but after a five-day rain delay, they ran out to a 3-0 lead in the first inning when Fred Lynn homered off Gary Nolan at Fenway Park. By the eighth inning, the Reds had taken a 6-3 lead and the Fenway fatalists were starting to wonder if it was all happening again. Then, in the bottom half of the inning, Red Sox hitter Bernie Carbo took a 3-2 fastball from Rawly Eastwick over the fence in center field. In the ninth, Boston's Denny Doyle was thrown out at the plate by George Foster. Dwight Evans' leaping catch of a Joe Morgan smash in the eleventh saved a home run and turned into a double play. Catcher Carlton Fisk came to the plate in the twelfth inning to face Pat Darcy, the Reds' eighth pitcher of the game. After laying off the first pitch, Fisk hoisted Darcy's next offering high down the left field line. Fisk knew it was high enough to clear the thirty-seven-foot wall known as the Green Monster, but would it be fair? Fisk used body language to wave the ball fair, jumped for joy when it landed inside the foul pole and circled the bases with delight. The Reds won 4-3 the next night on Morgan's two-out single in the ninth, but for one shining moment, the Red Sox and their fans were winners.

Even when the Oakland A's were winners in the fractured 1989 World Series, they couldn't bring themselves to celebrate with champagne. They dominated the outmanned San Francisco Giants in a four-game sweep by a total score of 32-14, tying them with the 1932 New York Yankees for the highest run differential in a four-game series. Still, the not-so-distant memory of the tragic earthquake left the A's players subdued, even as they reflected on the magnitude of their achievement and the events that preceded them.

Thirty minutes before the scheduled start of Game Three on October 17, 1989, an earthquake shook Candlestick Park in San Francisco. Though the epicenter was some fifty miles to the south, pieces of concrete broke loose and the players ran to the safety of the green grass. The quake registered 7.1 on the Richter scale, the largest to hit San Francisco since 1906.

Scores of people were left dead amid the fire and widespread destruction. Baseball acted wisely in suspending its games for ten days while the Bay Area recovered. The A's then dispatched the Giants with ease, running up an 8-0 score before hanging on to win 8-6 and then hammering San Francisco 9-6 in the finale. Understandably, the A's victory was anticlimactic.

"A natural disaster like that," said Oakland Manager Tony LaRussa, "kind of puts the game of baseball in perspective."

THE ALL-STAR GAME

The St. Louis Cardinals'
Ozzie Smith, demon-
strating some of the verve
the National League is
famous for, comes to
earth at second base.

The argument is as old as the All-Star Game itself, some fifty-six years: Should fans be given
the right to vote for the participants? Yes,
goes the company line, since the fans are pay-
ing all the bills. No, say the purists, who point out that
deserving players go unrewarded when All-Star balloting is essentially a popularity contest.

Sentiment has swung widely over the years. When
the game first began in 1933, it was a modest affair at
Comiskey Park in Chicago. Organizers of the city's
Century of Progress Exposition thought an exhibition
game between the American and National leagues was
a natural. Oddly enough, fans and managers picked
those first two teams. The *Chicago Tribune* sports editor Arch Ward developed an eighteen-player ballot and
urged some of the nation's great newspapers to print
it. Managers made their decisions based on the returns. When it was discovered that most of the ballots
came from the Chicago area, a panel of eight managers
from each league made the difficult choices.

After twelve seasons of selection by committee, the
vote was given to the fans in 1947. It wasn't until ten

years later that the fans, notably those in Cincinnati,
got carried away with their responsibility. More than a
half-million votes insured that virtually the entire Reds
lineup would represent the National League in St. Louis
that season. Commissioner Ford Frick, who clearly had
no sense of humor, took the vote from the fans. In
1970, the vote was returned to the fans by Commissioner Bowie Kuhn in one of his rare acts that met with
popular acclaim. For the sake of balance, fans chose
the starting lineups and the managers chose the rest of
the squad, based on the first half-season's performance. The debate continues, however.

"Of course the fans should decide which stars they
want to see," says former Commissioner Peter Ueberroth. "The bedrock of baseball is the fan."

"Are you kidding?" asks one player who shall re-
main nameless. "The fans are geeks. They don't know
who's hot and who's not. It's ridiculous when you look
at some of the guys they pick."

This is true. In 1989, for instance, the fans were so
enamored with the Oakland Athletics' Jose Canseco
that they voted him to a starting outfield berth for the

Left: *Bo knows All-Star games. Although Oakland's Jose Canseco was foolishly elected to play in the 1989 game (he was hurt the entire first half of the season), Kansas City's two-sport phenom proved he belonged there with a stout home run.* **Below:** *Canseco's team was well-represented nevertheless, with five members making the team that year.*

With all of those peers hanging on every pitch, players give the All-Star game their best shot. Here, Pedro Guerrero of St. Louis (right) takes a huge cut at a 1989 offering. **Opposite page, above:** *The All-Star game is a summit of sorts; a stage where Glenn Davis of the Houston Astros and the Yankees' Steve Sax can meet in the middle of a long baseball season. A place where San Francisco's Will Clark can display his sweet swing* **(opposite page, below).**

© Allsport

American League, along with Kansas City's Bo Jackson and Kirby Puckett of Minnesota. Canseco does cut a dashing figure, and yes, the previous season he became the first man to hit 40 home runs and steal 40 bases in a single season, but when he was named to the team he hadn't played in a single game that season because of a wrist injury. The National League starter at third base was one Mike Schmidt, who had retired from baseball earlier in the season. Canseco passed on the game, since he hadn't yet been activated to play for his own team, while Schmidt attended the game in street clothes.

Despite its political problems, the Midsummer Classic often results in a good game. Sometimes, the quality is exceptional. In recent years, the National League has taken the game more seriously than the American League. Look no farther than the Pete Rose-Ray Fosse incident in 1970. That year's game was played in Riverfront Stadium in Cincinnati, Rose's home field, and he was eager to please Reds' fans. It was 4-4 in the twelfth inning when Rose tried to score from second base on Jim Hickman's single to center. Rose beat the ball to the plate and crashed his shoulder into Fosse's heart. Both men were shaken by the collision, but the National League had prevailed, 5-4, for the eighth-straight time. The Americans ended the streak a year later on the strength of home runs by Reggie Jackson, Frank Robinson, and Harmon Killebrew. Jackson's effort, a monstrous 520-foot blast off a light tower in right field, helped the American League rally from a 3-0 deficit to win, 6-4.

The following year, however, the National League came back to win the first of eleven straight All-Star Games, from 1972 to 1982. The streak ended in 1983 at Comiskey Park, when the American League won 13-3, thanks largely to a grand slam by California's Fred Lynn. Fifty years earlier, the Americans had won the inaugural game at Comiskey, 4-2, on Babe Ruth's two-run homer. Ruth, who was thirty-eight at the time, also made a terrific catch in right field, robbing Chick Hafey of extra bases.

In 1934, Carl Hubbell made history by striking out Ruth, Gehrig, Jimmie Foxx, Al Simmons, and Joe Cronin in consecutive order. In 1941, Ted Williams won the All-Star game at Detroit's Briggs Stadium with two out in the ninth inning. Williams turned a 5-4 loss into a 7-5 victory when he touched Claude Passeau for a 450-foot home run with two men on. In 1946, after a one-year wartime sabbatical, Williams hit two home runs and drove in five runs in a 12-0 laugher for the American League. Johnny Callison rescued the National League in 1964 with a two-out, three-run home run in the ninth inning. They won the game 7-4 after trailing by a run.

The All-Star Game has always been billed as an exhibition, and though some players treat it as such by pulling out with minor injuries, most players consider it an honor and a duty to the game, and the fans, who have given them so much.

"The All-Star Game is something special," said Mike Schmidt, who played in twelve All-Star games. "It's a chance to talk baseball with the guys. The comradery is great; for one game, you're all on the same team. That's one of the things I'll miss most about baseball: wearing a Phillies uniform and pulling for the Mets and Dodgers."

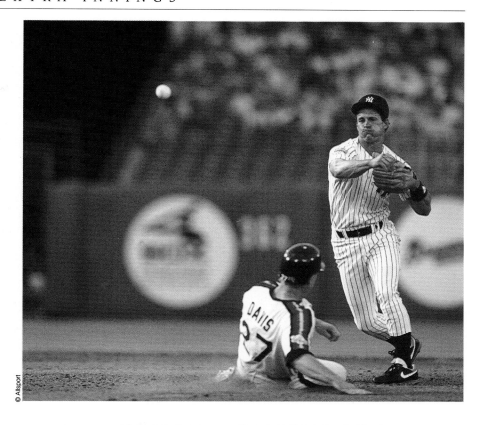

THE STADIUM

Quick, what is wrong with this picture? If you guessed that there are lights on at Wrigley Field, you're right. It happened in 1988, when progress finally caught up with the Cubs' park in Chicago.

There was a time in the past when ballparks were created with the fan in mind. Seats were nestled close to the action, not slammed into the middle of a parking lot somewhere high above right field. "All parks should be like Fenway," says Boston Red Sox left fielder Mike Greenwell, sweeping his hand in the general direction of the thirty-seven-foot Green Monster in left. "It's got a great atmosphere. This is what it must have been like in the old days."

Fenway Park, at 4 Yawkey Way, is nothing if not idiosyncratic. It is 420 feet to the corner in center field, but only 302 feet down the right field line. The scoreboard at the base of the wall in left field is run manually. One of the reasons the Red Sox are perenially one of the American League's best-hitting teams is the scarcity of foul territory; the seats seem to spill almost into fair territory. The park was opened in 1912 in the Fenway section of Boston and housed the Red Sox, a name owner John Taylor had changed from the Pilgrims in 1907. After a four-alarm, five-hour fire ruined refurbishing attempts in January 1934, three months of feverish work restored Fenway in time for the April 17 opener against the Washington Senators.

Over time, technology has subtly changed Fenway. The lights were installed in 1947, the same year that the advertisements on the left field wall ("Avoid 5 o'clock shadow with Gem Blades") were painted over. An electric message board was added in 1976, and in 1988 a total of 610 stadium club seats were added behind home plate above the grandstand. Still, Fenway is a charming monument to baseball's past. Only Chicago's Wrigley Field comes close to the feeling it imparts. Not coincidentally, Fenway and Wrigley, built in 1916, are the smallest parks in the major leagues. Wrigley's dimensions are more conventional, but where else is there a ground rule that reads: "When the ball sticks in vines on bleacher walls—two bases. If ball comes out—in play."

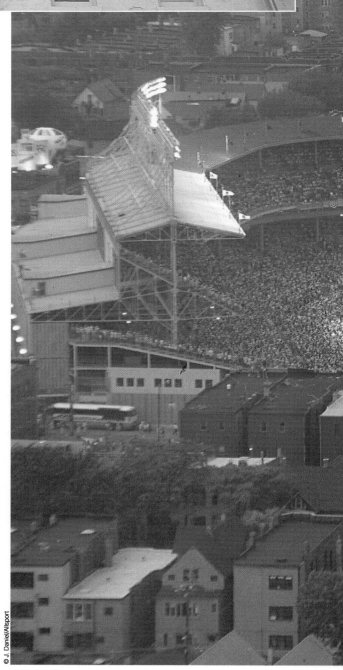

A few other stadiums have the old-time feel. Chicago's Comiskey Park, home of the White Sox, was the site of the first All-Star game in 1933. Tiger Stadium in Detroit is a hitter's park, despite the 440-foot distance to dead center field. Though Yankee Stadium's once-monstrous dimensions (402 feet to left, 461 feet to center, 344 feet to right) have been cut down drastically, the 1923 park remains a monument to the careers of Babe Ruth, Lou Gehrig, Mickey Mantle, Joe DiMaggio, and Whitey Ford, to name a few. Even Dodger Stadium, a relatively new temple built in 1962, is a gorgeous place to watch a baseball game.

And then there are the parks where the local environment sometimes makes the game nearly unbearable for fans and players alike. Cleveland Stadium (capacity 74,483) suffers from its proximity to Lake Erie. Some would argue that Cleveland isn't paradise to begin with, but sometimes April games are damp and chilly beyond belief. The same goes for San Francisco's Candlestick Park, where the wind-chill factor extends into July. The temperature at Texas' Arlington Stadium can rise above 100 degrees, which brings new meaning to high heat.

In the early 1960s, the bottom line came into play. Those cities with both a professional football and baseball team realized they could kill two birds with one albatross: a multi-versatile stadium, one size fits all. Atlanta was the first to cross the line with Atlanta Fulton County Stadium. The first ball was thrown out April 12, 1966, and the Braves and Falcons have coexisted ever since. The stadium is fine for football, a sport where fa-

There is nothing quite like Boston's Fenway Park if it's charm you seek. The "Green Monster" is a thirty-three-foot-high piece of work that changes the way hitters and pitchers view the game.

cial expressions are obscured by a helmet regardless of the distance of the seats. Baseball, however, suffers. The double-deck construction increases capacity as it decreases the immediacy vital to the game. Busch Stadium in St. Louis quickly followed, along with the interchangeable trio of the early 1970s, Riverfront Stadium in Cincinnati, Pittsburgh's Three Rivers Stadium, and Veterans Stadium in Philadelphia. All of these stadia were appropriately covered with artificial turf, thought to be the wave of the future at the time. The first turf had been installed at the Houston Astrodome in April 1965, proclaimed as the Eighth Wonder of the World. Eventually, domes appeared in Seattle (the Kingdome) and Minneapolis (the Hubert H. Humphrey Metrodome), where teams learned how to take advantage of the home field advantage by studying the air-conditioning patterns.

Now, there is a high-tech successor to these indoor venues: the indoor-outdoor stadiums north of the border in Montreal and Toronto. In June 1989, the Blue Jays and their fellow tenants, the Argonauts of the Canadian Football League, unveiled the $500 million Sky-Dome, which boasts a retractable roof that can open or close in twenty minutes. Unlike many of the newer ballparks, the Skydome was built to achieve intimacy—and the early reviews suggest architect Roderick Robbie succeeded. He pitched the upper deck seats steeply and used the major league minimum of foul territory. A month later, Montreal's Olympic Stadium introduced its retractable roof, a similar device that gives the home club a hedge against rain delays. Both stadiums, experts concede, could change the face of baseball forever.

"It's great," said Toronto pitcher Mike Flanagan on the eve of the Blue Jays' debut at the SkyDome. "But I was kind of hoping they'd have retractable fences."

At the opposite end of the spectrum from Fenway is the sparkling Toronto Sky-Dome, a stadium that lets in the sun or shuts out the rain in a matter of twenty minutes.

THE MINOR LEAGUES

Above: *Miracle pitcher Dave Alexander sends an offering to the plate.* **Above, right:** *A Vero Beach Dodger hitter dreams of reaching the big team in Los Angeles.*

After World War II, minor league baseball boomed. America hadn't yet discovered VCRs and television wasn't a factor yet; baseball was a natural. By 1949, there were fifty-nine different minor leagues and nearly forty-two million fans attending the games. Branch Rickey had conceived the idea while working in the St. Louis Cardinals' front office. It was easier to grow your own players, he reasoned, than to buy talent from other teams. Thus the farm system was born. Players could be nurtured as they worked their way up from rookie ball to Class A, and then to the more sophisticated levels of AA and AAA.

Those were the good times. Minor management was far from stable, but the cost of doing business was modest enough. As television proliferated and the major leagues expanded, however, the minors suffered. By 1962, there were fewer than twenty leagues in operation, and the total attendance hovered under ten million. That was the season the major league teams agreed to pay most of the escalating salaries for minor leaguers and maintain player-development contracts with at least three minor league teams. This allowed owners in the minors to concentrate on running their businesses. Today, the minors are anything but minor.

Miles Wolff, publisher of *Baseball America*, sits in his office situated among the bleacher seats along the third base line of the Durham Athletic Park, home of the Durham Bulls—yes, those Durham Bulls of *Bull Durham* fame. "The minor leagues are hot right now," he says. "They're drawing people and making money." It is hard to argue with him. He bought this North Carolina team for $2,500 in 1979, and now it is valued at over $2 million.

Wolff thinks the movie that was filmed at his ballpark during the fall of 1987 did a lot to bring minor league baseball into the public eye, not to mention bringing out the fans in North Carolina. The movie, which featured Kevin Costner and Susan Sarandon, was produced by Thom Mount, a Bulls shareholder, and written by Ron Shelton, a former minor leaguer who loved the atmosphere at the park. "Our souvenir sales went straight up," Wolff says, "I think it was good for minor league baseball, too. It made a lot of people really aware of it, and the fun. I think a lot of teams showed an increase because of it."

In 1988, minor league attendance that spanned nineteen leagues and 196 teams reached a thirty-six-year high. One of the great success stories came in Buffalo, where local businessmen had purchased the Wichita Bisons AAA franchise in 1984 for $1 million. Today, the team is worth an estimated $12 million. With attendance of 1.1 million, the Bisons outdrew three major league clubs in 1988 at Pilot Field, a new park with classic lines. Civic leaders tie the city's downtown renaissance to the emergence of the team. Harrisburg, Pennsylvania, brought in a Nashua, New Hampshire AA team in 1988 and experienced a similar rebirth.

Business aside, the minors are a necessary evil for the players themselves. They are all about dusty bus rides, bad lighting, too much beer, and not enough Susan Sarandons. A freshly signed player out of high school may wind up in the Appalachian League or the Gulf Coast League, the bottom rung for rookies, or land in one of the wide variety of A leagues: the New York-Penn, the South Atlantic, the Midwest, the Florida State, or the Carolina. As a player moves up the ladder, the working conditions and the pay improve. By the time a prospect reaches AA ball, a team has a pretty good idea if he can play or not. The level of play at AAA is just a notch under major league; consistency, not talent, is the deciding factor for those who are given the ultimate promotion.

Not too many players escape the long reach of the minor leagues, even in this day when colleges provide many of the services minor league teams used to. The California Angels' Jim Abbott, the one-handed lefty, is the most recent example. Most major league players speak fondly of their minor league days. "It's like college, I guess," says outfielder Dwight Evans of the Boston Red Sox. "It's fun while you're there, but it gets better in retrospect. There were a lot of long days and nights down there."

In many ways, the minor leagues are a buffer for young players, an opportunity to gain confidence and come up to speed with the very best the game has to offer. Evans' career is a case in point. He was drafted fifth by Boston in the 1969 June draft and dispatched to Jamestown, Virginia, where he hit .280 in thirty-four games. After one-season experiences at Greenville and Winston-Salem, Evans reached Louisville, then the Red Sox' AAA team. In 1972, Evans hit .300, added 17 home runs and 95 runs batted in and was named the International League's Most Valuable Player. When he was called up to Boston at season's end, Evans hit .263 with one home run in eighteen games. It took an entire year, when Evans weathered a .223 batting average in part-time duty, for the young right fielder to finally find himself.

Some players, despite the obvious evidence at hand, never give up. Shanie Dugas, the last player taken in the 1980 June draft, was still looking for his first big-league at-bat at the age of 31 in 1989. Dugas played 120 games with the Los Angeles Dodgers' AAA Albuquerque team in 1988, thirty each at second base, shortstop, third base, and designated hitter. "I think I could have a shot this year," he said at the Dodgers' Vero Beach, Florida, spring training base. "If the right things happen, I could get a look." Alas, when the season began, Dugas—a five-foot-ten, 155-pounder who had hit a total of 124 minor league home runs—still hadn't made the big club.

The Miracle, of the Florida State League, is evidence that the minor leagues are anything but minor as far as business is concerned.

SENIOR BASEBALL LEAGUE

Jim Morley was lying on a beach in Sydney, Australia, flipping through a newspaper and reading about a seniors golf tournament when the idea hit him. "Why not," he told his girlfriend, Annie Schmitt, "apply the idea to baseball?"

Morley, a thirty-two-year-old real estate developer from Colorado Springs, Colorado, lasted one season in the San Francisco Giants minor-league system, but his true mark in baseball proved to be in the research-and-development field. He quickly filled twenty pages with his notes on the subject. Soon the details began to emerge: There would be eight Florida teams, a seventy-two-game schedule, from November 1989 to January 1990. Players would be former major leaguers over the age of thirty-five. Catchers, because of the peculiar demands required behind the plate, could be thirty-two. Salaries would be relatively modest and range from a mere $5,000 to $15,000 a month. Soon, the Senior Professional Baseball Association would become a reality.

"I still have the notes," says Morley, who had never been to Florida before this venture. "Of the fifty things I wrote down, I've probably done forty of them exactly the way I planned. It hasn't changed much."

When the idea of a senior baseball league populated by late, great players attempting to recapture their youth in the Florida sunshine first surfaced, the joke was that the trainers would be the Most Valuable Players. One national columnist wondered if ambulances would be on hand for each game. On second thought, however, the whole thing made a great deal of sense. Why not let players (and perhaps more importantly, their fans) escape to the past? Professional golf had already created a tour for its over-fifty stars and the result was unprecedented interest, not to mention heady profits for all concerned.

And so it happened. More than five hundred former major leaguers expressed interest in the 176 roster spots available. Eight entrepreneurs came up with the $850,000 investment and the league was born. It was a phenomenal success.

"You can't really classify it," said former Baltimore Orioles manager Earl Weaver, who was reincarnated as the skipper of the Gold Coast Suns. "We knew it wasn't going to be as good as the major leagues. How could it be? But it wasn't going to be like Triple A, either. These guys have all been in the big leagues, and in many cases, they can still really bring it. No one's going to get rich playing in this league, but it'll pay the greens fees for the rest of my life."

With names like the St. Petersburg Pelicans, Orlando Juice, Winter Haven Super Sox, and West Palm

Below: *No, this isn't a Florida retirement home, it's the scintillating bullpen crew of the West Palm Beach Tropics of the Senior Baseball League. That's the distinguished Rollie Fingers, third from the right.*

© Bob Rosato/Allsport

© Scott Halleran/Allsport

The brains still work, it's just that the bats don't seem to get around as quickly and the pitches don't get to home plate quite as fast as they used to.

© Scott Halleran/Allsport

Beach Tropics, the league opened with a stellar roster of players and managers: Luis Tiant, Dick Williams, Al Oliver, Bill Lee, Ron LeFlore, Bernie Carbo, Hal McRae, Gates Brown, George Hendrick, Jose Cruz, Dennis Leonard, and Amos Otis among others.

Despite the cynicism in some quarters, the quality of play in the first season was surprisingly lush. "These aren't old cadavers waiting to have dirt thrown on them," said Commissioner Curt Flood. "These are serious baseball players, and they mean to play serious baseball. Just because they're over thirty-five doesn't mean they don't want to play hard."

Most players approached the league with a healthy sense of humor as well as purpose. "My theory of managing," said Bill "The Spaceman" Lee, who opened the season as manager of the Super Sox, "is the theory of Lao-tzu. He said the best form of leadership is no leadership at all. We only have one team rule: If you slide, get up."

And while the senior baseball league promises to keep fans thinking toward the fond memories of the past, clearly the same is true of the players. "Hell," said Graig Nettles, the former New York Yankees third baseman who played for the St. Lucie Legends, "if I can stay in baseball, I may never grow up."

© Scott Halleran/Allsport

STATISTICS

They are the very fabric of the game, the fascinating numbers that carry fans of all ages through those grim winter months when baseball is a game played in the mind's eye. "Statistics," says Mets pitcher Dwight Gooden, "are great if they say good things about you. If they don't, then, well, they're not so great. The problem with numbers is that you can make them say anything you want."

Of course, that is what makes statistics such subjective fun. Gooden has already compiled some of the best numbers in history. The Mets' public relations staff did some investigating and determined that among the top ten winningest pitchers of all time, only Kid Nichols had won more games than Gooden's 91 before his twenty-fourth birthday. The breakdown of the top ten winning pitchers and the numbers of games they won before their twenty-fourth birthdays are:

Kid Nichols	125
Dwight Gooden	91
Walter Johnson	82
Pud Galvin	57
Christy Mathewson	34
Steve Carlton	30
John Clarkson	11
Cy Young	9
Tim Keefe	6
Grover Alexander	0
Warren Spahn	0

Further, among history's top ten strikeout pitchers, only Bert Blyleven had recorded more than Gooden's 1,067 strikeouts by the age of twenty-four. "I guess," Gooden says, "that's good."

You want bad? The Texas Rangers' designated hitters combined for a batting average of .197 in 1988, just one point higher than the Mets' pitchers. Gooden himself had 16 hits, including a home run, and a .178 average.

More impressive is the batting average Kansas City's Pat Tabler has with the bases loaded. In ten years, Tabler, a career .290 hitter, has hit an incredible .507 (38-for-75) with 89 runs batted in and two grand slams with the bases loaded. "It's phenomenal," says Royals manager John Wathan. "It's one of the most amazing statistics in baseball. Nothing changes that's obvious to the naked eye. His wife asks him why he can't do it with no men on, and he tells her he doesn't know."

According to the Elias Sports Bureau, purveyors of numbers for the major leagues, Rudy Law (.469) is second on the career list of players with at least 15 bases-loaded hits. Tabler offers little insight into his peculiar ability. "I don't have any solid theory," he says. "I guess I just concentrate a little more. I've got the kind of swing where I just try to put the ball in play."

Statistics can magnify trends and instantly lend perspective to the moment. On June 8, 1989, shortstop Steve Jeltz of the Philadelphia Phillies hit two home runs in an amazing comeback over the Pittsburgh Pirates. The Phillies wiped out a 10-0 first-inning deficit and won 15-11 at Veterans Stadium. On the surface, Jeltz' feat was nothing extraordinary. Yet, in 1,451 previous at-bats over five seasons, Jeltz had hit a total of two home runs. Jeltz, a switch hitter, hit one from each side of the plate, becoming only the seventeenth National Leaguer to do it. Mickey Mantle was the champion, however, with ten such double blasts.

After that game, Jeltz had a .208 lifetime average, and in 1987 he had more errors (14) than he did runs batted in (12).

"The last time I did that was in college [Kansas] against Colorado," he said. "And the air is light out there. I was just up there trying to hit the ball hard somewhere, and thank God it went out of the ballpark."

Mickey Mantle may have hit 536 home runs in his celebrated career with the New York Yankees, but he had an Achilles heel named Dick Radatz, a journeyman right-handed pitcher who pitched for five teams in seven years. "They called him 'The Monster of the Beast,' but I had another name for him," says Mantle, who struck out 47 times in 63 career at-bats against Radatz.

Other statistics are more nebulous when framed against history. In 1989, Kansas City second baseman Frank White allowed a grounder by Minnesota's Dan Gladden to slip under his glove. It was the first fielding error for the eight-time Rawlings Gold Glove award winner in 198 games. It is not known if White set a major league record, since errors historically have not been categorized into fielding and throwing mistakes.

There are statistics for days (Tuesday historically has been kind to the New York Mets), months (the Cincinnati Reds posted a winning percentage of .889 in June 1981, when they were 8-1 in a strike-torn season), and even teams (the Philadelphia Phillies have had sixty-eight native Philadelphians on their roster). Some statistics extend far beyond the ballfield. For instance, under volatile owner George Steinbrenner, the New York Yankees have had seventeen managers over the last seventeen seasons, including Billy Martin five different times.

Some of baseball's more revered statistics are Opening Day numbers: Ted Williams of the Boston Red Sox hit .449 in fourteen openers; the Cleveland Indians' Bob Feller threw a no-hitter against the White Sox in 1940; the Dodgers' Don Drysdale was the only pitcher to hit two home runs on Opening Day; the aforementioned Billy Martin got his first two hits in his first two at-bats in the same inning (the eighth) in his 1950 major league debut; the Detroit Tigers' Gee Walker hit for the cycle in the 1937 opener, the only major leaguer to do so; Brooklyn's Jimmy Sheckard hit three triples in 1901, another Opening Day record; and in 1907 the Phillies were the first team to win a forfeit because a snowball fight among fans got out of control.

Statistics invariably rear their ugly head as the answers to trivia questions. Here's a tough one: Which pitcher has the second-best winning percentage against the New York Yankees? The answer, strangely enough, is George Herman Ruth, who was 17-5 (.773) for the Boston Red Sox against the Bronx Bombers, who was to be his future team.

TOP TEN CAREER GAMES PLAYED

1. Pete Rose	3,562
2. Carl Yastrzemski	3,308
3. Hank Aaron	3,298
4. Ty Cobb	3,034
5. Stan Musial	3,026
6. Willie Mays	2,992
7. Rusty Staub	2,951
8. Brooks Robinson	2,896
9. Al Kaline	2,834
10. Eddie Collins	2,826

TOP TEN CAREER RUNS SCORED

1. Ty Cobb 2,245
2. Babe Ruth. 2,174
   Hank Aaron. 2,174
4. Pete Rose 2,165
5. Willie Mays 2,062
6. Stan Musial. 1,949
7. Lou Gehrig 1,888
8. Tris Speaker 1,881
9. Mel Ott. 1,859
10. Frank Robinson .1,829

TOP TEN CAREER STRIKEOUTS PER NINE INNINGS

1. Nolan Ryan 9.55
2. Sandy Koufax 9.28
3. Sam McDowell 8.86
4. J.R. Richard 8.37
5. Bob Veale 7.96
6. Jim Maloney 7.81
7. Mario Soto 7.75
8. Goose Gossage 7.71
9. Sam Jones. 7.54
10. Fernando Valenzuela 6.90

TOP TEN CAREER EARNED RUN AVERAGES

1. Ed Walsh. 1.82
2. Addie Joss. 1.88
3. Three Finger Brown 2.06
4. Monte Ward 2.10
5. Christy Mathewson 2.13
6. Rube Waddell 2.16
7. Walter Johnson 2.17
8. Orval Overall. 2.24
9. Tommy Bond 2.25
10. Will White. 2.28

FIGURING BASEBALL STATISTICS

Batting Average: Divide the total number of safe hits by the total times at bat.

Slugging Percentage: Divide the total bases of all safe hits by the total times at bat.

Pitchers Earned Run Average: Multiply the total earned runs by nine, and divide the result by the total number of innings pitched.

Fielding Average: Divide the total put-outs and assists by the total put-outs, assists, and errors.

Won-Lost Percentage: Divide the number of games won by the total numbers of games won and lost.

On-Base Percentage: Divide the hits plus total bases on balls plus hit-by-pitcher by at-bats plus total bases on balls plus hit-by-pitcher and sacrifice flies.

THE RULES

In 1876, you had to have a pretty keen eye to wangle a base on balls. It took nine balls to cadge a free pass from the man on the mound. In 1880, baseball's early administrators decided eight balls was a more reasonable sum. As pitchers improved their craft, the rule still didn't seem quite right. Two years later, a base on balls was granted for those with the patience to wait for seven pitches outside of the strike zone. The total was reduced to six in 1884, then pushed back up to seven again in 1886. A season later it was five, and in 1889, the conventional four-ball walk was approved. One hundred years later, the number is still the same.

With a few notable exceptions, the rules of baseball have remained fairly static over the last century or so. The outlawing of the spitball (1920) and the advent of the designated hitter (1973) are some of the more radical changes the game has undergone. Generally, rule changes occurred early on. The distance of the pitcher from the plate is a good example. Before 1881, the hurler, who stationed himself in a four-foot by seven-foot box, was all of forty-five feet from the batter. The distance was then increased to fifty feet and the box further reduced to four by five-and-one-half. In 1893, the distance was finalized at sixty feet, six inches, and a twelve by four-inch rubber (now twenty-four by six) was introduced.

There was a time (1887) when a batter received four strikes instead of three, when a catcher received an error for a passed ball, when bats were allowed to have a flat side and when sacrifice flies counted as an at-bat. Lately, most of the rule changes have been on the technical side, such as the fine-tuning of those rules determining the winning pitcher, the batting champion, the Rookie of the Year, and relief pitching statistics.

Most fans know the basics: ground-rule doubles for balls that bounce into the stands and the infield fly rule, which automatically retires the batter when men are on base to discourage infielders who would intentionally drop the ball and try to double the runners up. Yet, the baseball rule book is full of fascinating minutiae that govern unlikely plays. For instance: What happens when a ball is scalded toward second base, deflects off the second baseman's mitt, hits the umpire, and is collected in mid-air by the shortstop? Even though the ball never touched the ground, Rule 5.09 says as long as the ball is in fair territory and deflected by either a runner or umpire, there is no catch and the batter is safe. Is it legal when the manager brings his outfielders in to play right behind the infielders with the bases loaded and nobody out in the ninth inning of a one-run game? Of course. Only the pitcher and catcher must play in a prescribed area. The long fly ball clearly is destined to be caught, but a fan reaches out and snags it before the left fielder can glove it. Does the runner score from third? If, in the judgment of the umpire, the ball would have been long enough to score the runner as a sacrifice, the runner scores, according to Rule 3.16. And is the batter within his rights when he steps over home plate to hack at a 3-0 pitch during an intentional walk? No. Rule 6.06 insists the batter keep both feet inside the batter's box. And you could look it up.

© W. T. Harrington

© W. T. Harrington

Time stands still when the Cactus and Grapefruit Leagues are in session. Nevertheless, the wave of the future is shiny new facilities like the Mets' complex in Port St. Lucie (above).

SPRING TRAINING

John Mayberry, the first real power hitter in Kansas City Royals history, tilts his head back to meet the sun here at Baseball City, Florida, and laughs. He is responding to the question: Does spring training still exhibit the charm it did in the early 1970s when you were breaking into the big leagues? "It's bigger now," he says, "more of a business. I mean, look at this place, it . . ."

He lets the sentence linger and points past third base, as a roller coaster clatters by and leaves a trail of shrieks in the morning air. "See?" he says, shaking his head. "It's different."

Baseball has always been big business, but the six weeks of spring training, in both the Grapefruit (Florida) and Cactus (Arizona) Leagues, always belonged to a time gone by. Since 1888, when the Washington Statesmen decided to get a head start on the regular season by training in Florida, baseball teams have been stretching their off-season muscles under the sun in Arizona and Florida. It was a low-key affair, with games played in quaint ballparks. For a long time, the major league clubs were just part of the scenery. Tickets were cheap and easy to come by. No more. One hundred years later, spring training has become a fixture in the local economies. Fans spend more than $300 million in Florida alone during the short season. Ticket prices rival the regular-season tariff; the schedule has been expanded to include thirty games, something the players grumble about. Many games are sold out. Baseball teams, even those with long-standing civic relationships, are selling themselves out to the highest bidder.

© W. T. Harrington

For nineteen years, the Royals trained in the pleasant west coast town of Fort Myers, Florida. And then, in 1988, Kansas City moved to Baseball City, south of Orlando. The Royals play in a high-tech, 7,000-seat stadium that is a miniature replica of Royals Stadium in Kansas City, with the same field dimensions. The only significant difference is the arresting combination of an artificial turf infield and a natural grass outfield. The line just behind second base where plastic meets grass serves as a convenient metaphor for the commercialism that recently has invaded these spring training sites.

The New York Mets left St. Petersburg, Florida, after 1986 to play in an $11 million complex in Port St. Lucie. The collection of fields is several miles from civilization, but soon an ambitious shopping mall will be completed. Home lots are moving briskly. More teams are expected to follow the Mets and Royals in the search to meet spring training expenses. The Chicago Cubs have expanded Ho Ho Kam Park in Mesa, Arizona, and now draw in excess of 125,000 fans for sixteen home dates. Even the Cubs are exploring the possibility of relocating to Florida if the offer is right.

Fortunately, there is still enough lyricism in spring training to make it hopelessly appealing. It remains a rich tableau of sweet and subtle moments. Some recent Grapefruit League snapshots:

Click! Here, wonder of wonders, is the great Sandy Koufax on the mound at Vero Beach. Koufax retired from the Los Angeles Dodgers in 1966 with a 165-87 career record and an aching, arthritic arm. A proud and reticent man, Koufax left baseball as one of two

pitchers to average more than nine strikeouts for every nine innings pitched. And now, at the age of fifty-four in 1989, here is the left-hander just smoking them in batting practice. The legendary curveball drops off the table as the Dodger batters swing in futility. The fastball crackles into the catcher's mitt. The radar gun says the last pitch was ninety miles an hour, faster than most major leaguers today. "Man," says Dodgers manager Tommy Lasorda, "if that doesn't give you goose bumps, nothing will."

Click! Joe Morgan, the terminally haggard manager of the Boston Red Sox, is musing about the team he hopes to bring north to defend the 1988 American League East title. Morgan doesn't get too excited; he spent sixteen years bouncing around the minors until he got a scouting job with the big club. After he replaced John McNamara at mid-season in 1988, Morgan's first chance to manage in the majors resulted in a 46-31 second half for the Red Sox. Now he is holding court with the expectant press the following March. "We've been a little inconsistent," he says, scratching his head. "We need some people to step up as starters. We need a backup catcher. [Randy] Kutcher, [Kevin] Romine, [Carlos] Quintana all have a chance to make it." Morgan is asked if shortstop Luis Rivera, an off-season acquisition from the Montreal Expos, will make the team. "Aw, I couldn't tell you," Morgan says. "I don't know what the hell is going on . . . yet. I'll let you know when we get to Boston."

Click! The St. Louis Cardinals, the team that didn't leave St. Petersburg, are spread out in a corner of left field at Al Lang Stadium. The players are stretching

Spring training is a time for autographs, photographs, laughter, and the light-hearted business of getting in shape under the warm sun.

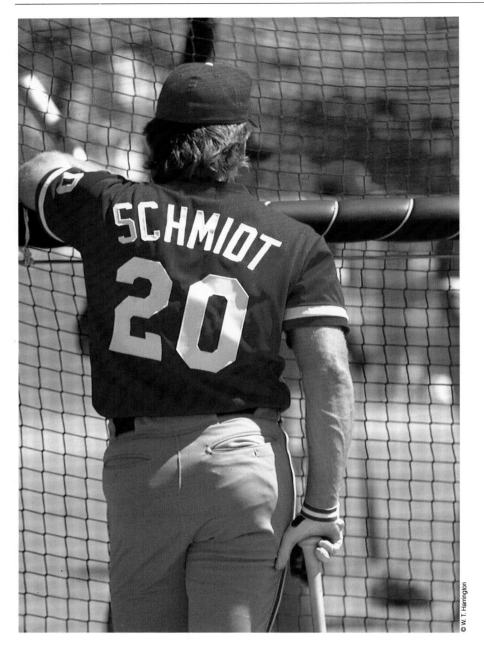

their expensive calf muscles when someone yells, "There it is." All the players jump to their feet and squint past the left field stands, up into the sky. It is the Space Shuttle taking off on another mission. Later, St. Louis manager Whitey Herzog labors over the lineup that will face the Houston Astros. He scratches the names in: Coleman, Smith, McGee, Guerrero, Brunansky, Oquendo, Peña, Jones, DeLeon. "There," he says to no one in particular. "If that sucker don't win today, I can't manage." The Cards proceed to obliterate the Astros, and yes, on this day at least, Herzog can manage.

Click! On the other coast, Dallas Green is settling in as the New York Yankees' eighteenth manager in seventeen seasons. Owner George Steinbrenner, generally regarded as a tyrant, has hired this strong-willed man to guide a team that cries for discipline. Green greets the veterans with a regimen that resembles basic training. The morning workouts sometimes last nearly three hours, and with the temperature approaching ninety degrees, the afternoon sessions are brutal. "They may not be able to pitch or hit," Green says coyly, "but at least they'll be in shape."

Click! The legends are everywhere this bright day in West Palm Beach. Inside Municipal Stadium, Eddie Mathews, the Hall of Fame third baseman for the Atlanta Braves, smokes a cigarette and pulls on his uniform. Two stools away sits Willie Stargell, who hit 475 home runs for the Pittsburgh Pirates. Not far away, Phil Niekro, a 318-game winner in the majors, contemplates a cup of coffee. Already outside is the amazing Luke Appling. Amazing, because at the age of eighty-two, Appling is still getting worked up over this grand game. The Hall of Fame shortstop, who batted .310 over twenty seasons in the majors, stands alone behind first base watching a rookie league game. "This kid can hit," Appling says of a blond outfielder in the Braves'

Spring training is about rebirth. Its familiar faces, from Schmidt to Appling to Mattingly to Anderson, are vaguely reassuring.

chain. "But he's too impatient up there. Look at him jerking those wrists. I've talked to him about it, but all the kids today want to hit home runs." Though Appling still carries a bat with him everywhere, it is less of an offensive weapon than a prop to lean on. Yet, when he swings it to demonstrate a finer point, his eyes light up. The swing looks good. "I could hit a little bit in my day," he says, smiling.

Click! Mike Schmidt finds himself in a familiar position in the Philadelphia Phillies dugout at Municipal Stadium: surrounded by the media.

The All-Star third baseman, now thirty-nine, is coming off the most disappointing season of his career, a campaign over which he batted .251 and hit but 12 home runs. The after-effects of arthroscopic shoulder surgery are telling. Schmidt doesn't make any strenuous throws in the field; he looks tentative at the plate. "I feel fine," he says with barely disguised disgust. "In time, the shoulder will come around. I've got a few more weeks to go. I've got arthritis in my knees, stiffness in my joints. I haven't hit live pitching in nine months, so of course I'm going to be a little rusty. Hey, spring training is tough for the older players. I saw Pete Rose go 0-for-30 during one spring training." Schmidt pauses for effect. "He hit something like .330 that year."

Schmidt's optimism is admirable. A few months later, one of the game's greatest home run hitters will decide to retire when his body doesn't respond as it used to.

Click! There is a weird sort of giddiness in the New York Mets' Port St. Lucie clubhouse today. The attendants are handing out green uniforms, caps, and shirts, in honor of St. Patrick's Day. "How do I look?" Darryl Strawberry asks teammate Tim Teufel. Teufel grimaces. "Green," he says.

Even the visiting Los Angeles Dodgers are sporting

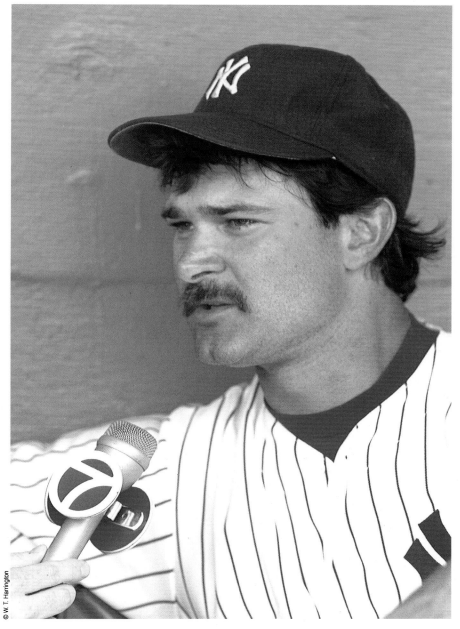

The speed of spring training is decidedly slow, which is saying something, considering baseball's generally leisurely pace.

green hats today, with the exception of starting pitcher Orel Hershiser, the World Series hero, who is wearing the old Dodger blue. He returns to the mound for the second inning with the appropriate green cap. Hershiser promptly records his first two strikeouts of the game, Strawberry and Teufel, both swinging.

After the game, a Dodgers blowout, Mets manager Davey Johnson sits in his office and ruminates about his up-and-down (mostly down) team. "My patience," he says, "is wearing a little thin. I don't feel we're going through the motions right now, but pretty soon the honeymoon down here will be over. We've had a lot of nagging injuries, but that's no excuse. We've been whipped in every category you can think of. We'll be ready one way or another, even if we have to stay out

there for eight hours a day."

Click! The thrills at Boardwalk and Baseball never seem to stop. Bo Jackson, the celebrated running back for the Los Angeles Raiders, is standing in for the Kansas City Royals against Dennis "Oil Can" Boyd of the Boston Red Sox. Jackson lashes at a Boyd offering and time seems to stand still as the ball arcs over the mammoth scoreboard in center field and comes to rest in a heap of sand some 518 feet away. "Did you see that shot?" asks veteran catcher Bob Boone after the game. "I'd pay to watch this guy play." By midseason, seemingly years since spring training began in February, Boyd is out of baseball with a reoccuring blood clot; Jackson has made his first All-Star game and hits a gigantic home run in his first at-bat.

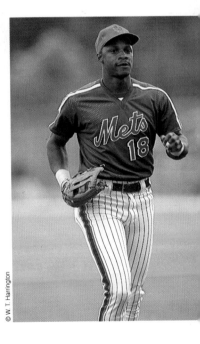

Superstars like Bo Jackson, Orel Hershiser, and Darryl Strawberry, have million dollar muscles that must be coaxed along slowly.

© W. T. Harrington

THE SCOREBOARD/SCORER

Scoreboards are like people: No two are alike. "I've seen some beauties in my time," says veteran scorer Red Foley. "Everybody has a different personality, and you can see them in the scorecards."

Most baseball fans keep score with the conventional numbering system: pitcher (1), catcher (2), first baseman (3), second baseman (4), third baseman (5), shortstop (6), left fielder (7), center fielder (8), and right fielder (9). Beside each batter's name on the scorecard are nine squares, one for each inning. Each square has a diamond in the middle, leaving a small triangle in each corner. A simple ground ball to second is noted as a 4-3, because the second baseman retires the batter by throwing to first. A fly ball to center is an F-8. A double play from shortstop to second to first is 6-4-3. Singles are a single dash in the bottom right triangle, doubles are two dashes, etc. Walks are W or B or BB, while strikeouts are K (swinging) or a reverse K for called third strikes. Errors are noted by position, such as E-6. Sacrifices are SAC-8 (a fly ball to center that drives in a run) and passed balls are PB. Runs are indicated by filling in the diamond. As the scorer becomes more sophisticated, he or she can add embellishments like L-7 for a line drive to left or P-3 for a pop fly to first.

The official scorers of baseball games are usually baseball writers. Foley, who worked for the *New York*

© Scott Smith/Sports File

Daily News for thirty-five years, scores eighty to ninety games each season for the Yankees and Mets. The biggest decisions concern the fine line between an error and a hit. Foley says scoring today is tougher than it used to be. "There is definitely more pressure being a scorer today because of all the big money tied to personal stats," he says, waving his trademark cigar. "I can't remember the last time I changed a call. My first judgment is usually the right one. I don't make incorrect calls, I make unpopular ones. They are judgment calls, and I don't have to explain judgment calls any more than an umpire does."

Scorers receive all of sixty dollars for their efforts, which include those delicate judgments and filling out involved forms that go to the Elias Sports Bureau in New York. It isn't worth the aggravation. Once in Anaheim, when the crowd lustily booed a decision, the scorer's wife stood up and yelled to the people surrounding her to shut up, that her husband was the scorer. Then they booed her. Decisions that aren't changed within twenty-four hours are final. Through the years, there have been some notable reversals. On the final day of the 1945 season, a New York scorer changed an error into a hit, allowing the Yankees' Snuffy Stirnweiss to edge Chicago's Tony Cuccinello for the American League batting title. A year later, an error was changed to a hit, giving Mickey Vernon the batting title by one point over Cleveland's Al Rosen.

"Players come crying to me that they should get a break at home," Foley says. "But I pride myself on being consistent. Being consistent is the key to good umpiring and scoring."

171

FOUL PLAY

Pine tar, applied here in conventional fashion (right), is only one of a multitude of icky, sticky substances that can get you in trouble on a baseball diamond.

Don Sutton is wandering around the Mets' spring training field in Port St. Lucie, Florida, talking with players from the Dodgers and Mets, waving to the fans in the stands. He will turn forty-four in a few days, but he looks great—all teeth and tan. Can this be the man who dominated the unofficial balloting as baseball's Public Enemy Number One during the 1970s?

"Listen," says Sutton, who still seems to relish his reputation as a pitcher who bent the rules—and his fastball—with regularity. "I never put a foreign substance on the ball . . . it was all made in the U.S.A."

He smiles and waits for the punch line to sink in. Sutton has always approached the game with a sense of humor as broad as his ability to make baseballs perform strangely with the aid of artificial means. It worked for 321 victories, eleventh on the all-time list, and frequently brought unwelcome guests to the mound in search of evidence.

"The umpires would come out and ask to see my glove or look in my pocket," Sutton says. "I'd have messages all over me. They said, 'Don't you really feel silly?' or 'You're getting closer, try the glove.' You try to turn it into an advantage, and it was almost like having another pitch because guys were thinking about it all the time. It affected their concentration. In the end, I was the most accused and the least convicted."

Though Sutton categorically denies using the usual tools of the trade—vaseline, KY-jelly, not to mention saliva supplemented by slippery elm lozenges—he does allow that there were times when a damaged ball came into his possession. "I could do a lot with a little," he says. "Common sense tells you that if the ball short-hops the infielder, or if it's thrown in the dirt, or fouled off, the blemish is going to change the flight of the ball.

I got into arguments with my first basemen, who would want to show those balls to the umpire. I'd say, 'Hey, just get me the ball, zip it to me before he has a chance to ask for it.' The fact is, any good player looks for an advantage, no matter how small. And, yeah, there's more speculation than actual cheating, but it happens every game in some way or other. I don't think that will ever change. Pitchers are always going to try doing something with the ball, and hitters are always going to try to get an edge."

The cold war has been going on since 1919, when the Chicago White Sox threw the World Series against the Cincinnati Reds, but it recently escalated to the point of absurdity. Dr. Bobby Brown and A. Bartlett Giamatti, the Presidents of the American and National Leagues, sent a memo to all teams in March 1988, explaining that anti-cheating rules 1.10 a-c and 6.06 d would be strictly enforced. In summary, they wrote, "The integrity of the game of baseball is at issue here and we will continue to count on your cooperation and personal sense of responsibility to maintain that integrity." A little dramatic, perhaps, but the game had suffered a few embarrassing moments in 1987.

When Houston Astros outfielder Billy Hatcher broke his bat, a cork center was revealed. Theoretically, cork lightens the bat head and allows the hitter to swing it more quickly through the strike zone, thus generating more distance. Hatcher, who claimed he borrowed the bat from a pitcher, was summarily suspended. Philadelphia Phillies pitcher Kevin Gross was suspended when a tack was discovered in his glove, and Minnesota Twins knuckleball pitcher Joe Niekro tried to ditch an emery board when umpires asked for an on-site inspection—Niekro said he liked to do his nails between innings. The New York Mets and most of the National League maintained that Houston Astros hurler Mike Scott scuffed baseballs, though nothing was ever proven. "I'd say corked bats and doctored balls are about even," said Royals second baseman Frank White at the height of the controversy. "As a matter of fact, I think they [pitchers] might even have an edge." Of course, White's a hitter.

The men with the bats were no doubt cheered when Jay Howell of the Los Angeles Dodgers was ejected from the 1988 National League Championship Series for using pine tar on his glove. The Dodgers' relief ace was suspended for three days when umpire chief Harry Wendelstedt discovered the foul substance on the mound in the eighth inning of Game Three. Howell claimed he was using the stuff to get a better grip on the ball in difficult weather conditions. No kidding.

The controversy was a wonderful echo of the famed Pine Tar Incident that unfolded on July 24, 1983. George Brett of the Kansas City Royals had just stroked what appeared to be a dramatic game-winning two-run home run with two out in the ninth inning off reliever Goose Gossage when the Yankees invoked a rarely used rule that insists no foreign substance may be used beyond eighteen inches from the bat handle. Brett, as a routine matter of practice, rubbed the brown, sticky ooze a good twenty inches along the bat. This was observed earlier in the season by Yankees Graig Nettles and Don Zimmer, who passed the information along to manager Billy Martin. And though it didn't affect the flight of the ball, the protest was upheld and the Yankees were declared 4-3 winners. "I don't know what to think," Nettles said later in the clubhouse. "I didn't feel like it was a victory, just an ugly win with an asterisk. The umpires said we won, but a guy had just gone one-on-one with our best reliever and beaten the Goose with his bat, only to lose his home run on a technicality. Say what you want about the rule, but pine tar did not help that ball out of the stadium. Brett did that all by himself."

Four days later, American League President Lee MacPhail reversed the umpires' decision and ordered the game resumed on August 18—with the Royals' 5-4 lead restored. To this day, Brett is mindful of how much pine tar he uses and admits, "When it's all over, people aren't going to remember ten seasons of hitting .500. They're going to remember the pine tar. Kind of funny, isn't it?"

Mets third baseman Howard Johnson, who was dogged by corking rumors in 1987 when he got off to a fast start, forced the league to write a new law allowing opposing managers to challenge one bat per game. Though various X-rays of Johnson's bat never revealed any tampering, his concentration and hitting were clearly affected. "It bothered him," says a teammate. "Even when [Manager Davey] Johnson would go to him and say, 'Hey, whose bat do you want me to impound?' he wasn't into it." For a brief time, managers employed their one bat challenge strategically, like a time-out.

Notorious cheaters deny the rumors while they're playing, then turn around and come clean in retirement, usually in book form. Pitchers Gaylord Perry and Whitey Ford admitted to spitballs and scuffballs. In Ford's case, New York Yankees catcher Elston Howard would cut the ball on a sharpened piece of his catching equipment. Norm Cash, the great Detroit Tigers first baseman, said he won the 1961 American League batting title using a corked bat all season long. That Cash hit .361, ninety points better than his career average, lends the admission some credence.

As the game evolved at the turn of the century, it didn't take the more innovative hurlers long to discover the wonder of saliva on a pitched ball. A little dab in the right place could cause the ball to sink and slide in a most unhittable manner. And though catchers weren't fond of the fallout, the spitball began a rise to prominence. Jack Chesbro was one of the first spitball artists. He reached the majors in 1899 with Pittsburgh before moving to the New York Highlanders in 1903. A season later, Chesbro started 51 games, finished 48 of them, and won a total of 41. Ed Walsh of the Chicago White Sox began his major league career in 1904. The right-hander won an amazing 40 games in 1908 and averaged 25 victories from 1907 to 1912. Walsh's career earned run average of 1.82 is the lowest in baseball history.

"The tough thing about the spitter is controlling it," says 300-game winner Phil Niekro. "So many people were getting hurt, they had to do something." In 1920, baseball finally was moved to outlaw the spitball. A special provision was made allowing each team to designate two spitball pitchers for the duration of the season. A year later, eight pitchers from the National League and nine from the American League were named spitball pitchers and allowed to continue the pitch through their careers. One of those was Burleigh Grimes, who as Ol' Stubblebeard was the first player to eschew shaving on game day. Grimes pitched for seven different teams through nineteen seasons and won 270 games, most of them on the strength of his spitball.

Some day soon, in a back-to-the-future stroke of genius, one of today's pitchers will eschew the variety of devious means available to alter the baseball and try a little saliva. After all, what goes around comes around.

Was the Mets' Howard Johnson doctoring his bat, or was he just hitting the heck out of the baseball? We may never know. One thing that is certain: A slight nick or blemish on the baseball can give a pitcher a huge advantage over a hitter.

© W. T. Harrington

THE BALLPARK PROMOTION

The Baltimore Orioles were horribly amazingly bad in the first month of the 1988 season. They were swept by the first two teams they played, and manager Cal Ripken Sr., was fired. The Orioles went on to break the all-time major league record for consecutive losses to open a season (thirteen) and kept right on losing. The nation couldn't help but watch in morbid fascination as the spectacle worsened. Finally, after twenty-one consecutive losses, the Orioles beat the Chicago White Sox 9-0 at Comiskey Park on April 29.

Though the Orioles struggled through a nightmarish season, they never lost their sense of humor. On the last home game of the season at Memorial Stadium on September 29, Baltimore hosted "Shirt Off Our Backs Night." David Cope of the Baltimore Orioles' marketing department explains: "We drew 1.7 million people that year, and if we hadn't led the majors in rainouts (seven), we might have had 1.8 million. We wanted to do something for the fans who stayed behind us all season long, but 'Fan Appreciation Night' never went over too well. We'd give away a lot of leftover promotional items and the people wouldn't really come out. So we came up with the shirt promotion. As the people came into the park they filled out applications, and at the end of the game we put them into the trunk of a car we were going to give away. The players went into the locker room and Frank [Robinson] gave them a final talk before they came back on the field. We played the stripper theme and all the players and coaches [thirty-five in all] took off their shirts. I think the players enjoyed it as much as the fans. We had 40,000 people that night, and more than 30,000 stuck around after the game to see who would win the shirts. And then we drew the names and gave them the shirts off our backs." It was the highlight of the evening, since—typically—the Orioles had lost earlier to New York.

Promotions—gimmicks to get people into the seats—have been around since baseball began, though they are usually more conventional than the Orioles' final 1988 effort. Bill Veeck, the father of the modern baseball promotion, had a particularly fertile mind. He once inserted a forty-three-inch midget, Eddie Gaedel, into the lineup to draw a predictable walk. Veeck also hired Satchel Paige, the forty-five-year-old pitcher, and set him up with a rocking chair in the bullpen.

Most major league teams offer more than a dozen specific promotions that include giveaways of bats, balls, and gloves—and sometimes stranger items. In 1989, the Cincinnati Reds offered, among other things, a travel mug, a Beach Boys concert, a batting helmet, a watch, Farmers Night, a pencil pouch, and a team picture. These were provided by the Reds and a number of sponsors, including Maxwell House, Gatorade, and Borden's.

Sometimes promotions backfire on a ballclub. Even Veeck was humbled on "Disco Sucks Night," when fans threw their most-hated 45-r.p.m. records onto the field. And then there was the infamous, "Nickel Beer Night" at Cleveland's Municipal Stadium, in which the Indians had to forfeit the game because there were some 35,000 slightly giddy patrons on the loose. Over the years, baseball has learned that, after all, nothing sells like excess.

Opposite page: *In a case study of how not to promote baseball, the Chicago White Sox put disco to bed on July 12, 1979.* **Below:** *In 1959, Chicago White Sox owner Bill Veeck unfurled this promotional gem. Four midgets dressed in spacesuits landed at Comiskey Park before a game with Cleveland. Not one of them appeared at the plate.*

Baseball Hall of Fame

THE TOBACCO CHEWER

While bubble gum represents the wave of the chewing future, there are still old-time practitioners of tobacco chewing like Minnesota Twins manager Tom Kelly and Philadelphia outfielder Len Dykstra (right).

Admittedly, baseball has its slow moments. As near as anyone can tell, this is why a lot of baseball folks chew tobacco; it helps kill time. "I don't know," says Len Dykstra of the Philadelphia Phillies, a man who stuffs prodigious amounts of tobacco into his cheek. "It's just something you do." Like most chewers, Dykstra's constant companion is a small styrofoam cup. Oh, make no mistake: He is only too happy to loose a stream of horrible brown juice in the outfield. It's just that even the clubhouse demands a modicum of etiquette.

Chewing tobacco is an "old school" thing. The numbers, according to the clubhouse men of the major leagues, are on the decline. "It's ridiculous," says one old-timer who dips into the snuff on occasion. "The kids today think it's dirty and unhealthy. I move a lot more gum than I used to." Nevertheless, there continues to be a market for long-leaf chewing tobacco (Beechnut or Red Man) and the more refined Skoal. Just a pinch between the cheek and gum, as they say, is all it takes to discover that smokeless tobacco pleasure.

Practitioners revel in their talents. Minnesota Twins manager Tom Kelly is a noted expert. Some of his free-form creations approach art. Chicago Cubs manager Don Zimmer, the quintessential baseball man, tells this story about himself from when he was managing the Boston Red Sox and arguing a call with umpire John Shulock: "During the argument, I took out my chaw and slammed it into the dirt, then Shulock slammed his chaw down. I took my pouch of tobacco out of my back pocket and slammed it down, so Shulock took out his pouch and slammed it down. But when I slammed my chaw down, my teeth had gone with it. I had to go down and get my teeth out of the chaw."

Even Zimmer, who sometimes resembled a gerbil when he chewed, quit the tobacco habit. He gave up tobacco because "it's healthier." It's also less embarrassing. Alas, in the heat of the 1989 pennant race, Zimmer went back to tobacco.

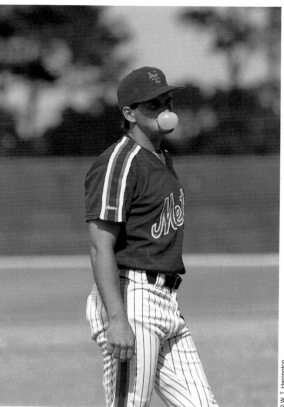

TOP TEN BASEBALL MOVIES

1. *The Natural*, 1984 (Starring Robert Redford)
2. *The Pride of the Yankees*, 1942 (Starring Gary Cooper)
3. *Eight Men Out*, 1988 (Starring Charlie Sheen)
4. *Take Me Out to the Ball Game*, 1949 (Starring Gene Kelly, Frank Sinatra, and Esther Williams)
5. *Field of Dreams*, 1989 (Starring Kevin Costner)
6. *The Jackie Robinson Story*, 1950 (Starring Jackie Robinson)
7. *Damn Yankees*, 1958 (Starring Gwen Verdon and Tab Hunter)
8. *The Babe Ruth Story*, 1948 (Starring William Bendix)
9. *The Winning Team*, 1952 (Starring Ronald Reagan and Doris Day)
10. *Fear Strikes Out*, 1957 (Starring Anthony Perkins)

TOP FIFTEEN BASEBALL BOOKS

1. *The Summer Game*, Roger Angell
2. *The Great American Novel*, Philip Roth
3. *The Boys of Summer*, Roger Kahn
4. *The Baseball Encyclopedia*, Joseph Reichler
5. *Babe*, Robert Creamer
6. *Ball Four*, Jim Bouton
7. *Bang the Drum Slowly*, Michael Harris
8. *Baseball America*, Donald Honig
9. *The Way It Is*, Curt Flood
10. *Late Innings*, Roger Angell
11. *Baseball: An Informal History*, Douglass Wallop
12. *Destiny's Darlings*, Martin Ralbovsky
13. *Fathers Playing Catch With Sons*, Donald Hall
14. *Five Seasons*, Roger Angell
15. *Baseball Anecdotes*, Daniel Okrent and Steve Wulf

TOP TEN BEST HALL OF FAME NAMES

1. Eppa Rixey
2. Rabbit Maranville
3. Zack Wheat
4. Enos Slaughter
5. Dizzy Dean
6. Dazzy Vance
7. Nap Lajoie
8. Pee Wee Reese
9. Hack Wilson
10. Elmer Flick

© AP/Wide World Photos

EPILOGUE

Above: *In a game that has remained largely unchanged since its inception, a notable exception was the introduction of lights at Wrigley Field in 1988. Another notable change that was a long time in coming are minority managers, such as Cito Gaston (opposite page), manager of the Toronto Blue Jays, who guided his team to a 1989 playoff berth against the Oakland Athletics.*

If someone had asked the professional baseball players of the 1890s what the next century held for baseball, they might have talked about bigger and better gloves, a more tightly wound ball, and higher salaries. Chances are, they couldn't have seen the designated hitter, artificial turf, or the lights at Wrigley Field coming.

Yes, even the jewel of Chicago was not immune to technology and the pursuit of the dollar. On August 8, 1988, the Cubs played their first game at home under a $5 million set of new lights. Chicago led 3-1, but in the fourth inning thundershowers forced the game to be cancelled. "It looked like the good Lord said, 'I'm going to show you why Wrigley Field has always been in daylight,'" said pitcher Rick Sutcliffe. "He was pretty upset about this. He's telling us he'll determine when the first night game is." That turned out to be one night later, when the Cubs dispatched the New York Mets 6-4.

While the last one hundred years of baseball have brought dozens of advances, the game has remained fundamentally unchanged. The designated hitter, a gimmick created by the American League in 1973 to increase scoring, has taken the pitcher's bat out of the game, allowing managers to go with starters longer. Most of the changes have involved the irresistible trend toward more sophisticated equipment. Gloves are as big as peach baskets now, uniforms are sleek and

streamlined, wooden bats are gradually giving way to the more cost-effective aluminum bats. As in all sports, specialization has become the new byword. There are relief specialists now, even sub-divisions of that category, such as long relievers, middle-inning set-up men, and closers. Managers sometimes platoon right- and left-handed players, depending on who takes the mound for the opposition.

What will be the state of the game as we move into the twenty-first century? "That," says St. Louis shortstop Ozzie Smith, "is hard to figure. I just hope I'm comfortable, drawing a good pension."

Tony Kubek, the former New York Yankees shortstop and currently an astute television analyst, is worried about the state of the game he loves so much. He ties a recent downturn to the state of the nation. "American kids just don't play that much anymore," he says. "They play golf, and fish, and have so many other things to do. Where would we be without the players from the Dominican Republic, Puerto Rico, and Venezuela?" As Kubek points out, many of the stars of the 1950s and 1960s came from poor environments and played the game seemingly around the clock. "In Detroit last year, a fellow told me they went door to door recruiting kids to play baseball, but drugs were too prevalent," Kubek says. "It's probably that way in most cities."

The late Bartlett A. Giamatti (right) was a man of integrity who loved the game of baseball. As a tribute to his principles, Giamatti's hand-picked deputy commissioner, Fay Vincent, was unanimously chosen as his successor.

Don Baylor (opposite page), who was hit by more pitches than any player in the history of baseball, was named manager of the expansion Colorado Rockies before the 1993 season.

Kubek believes that major league rosters suffer on two important levels: "The older players are hanging on for the money, and the younger guys are rushed up too soon. In the middle are the players in their prime, but there are not enough of them on the roster. Last year, one of the players said there must have been some bad players in the old days, too. I told him, 'Sure, but they played for losing teams. Now they play for every team.'"

Certainly, expansion has diluted the quality of baseball. In 1903, the first year of the World Series, there were sixteen major league teams, eight in the National League and eight in the American League. Today, there are twenty-eight teams, including the recently added expansion teams: the Colorado Rockies and the Florida Marlins. The minor leagues are creaking under the strain of producing all that talent. In recent years, colleges and universities have become more and more involved in the finishing process. Today's prospects often weigh a signing bonus ranging from $50,000 to $100,000 and a college education that can run from $80,000 to $100,000.

"It was to my advantage to go to college," says Baltimore Orioles pitcher Jeff Ballard. "For one thing, my education is done. I have my degree and I don't have to worry about it if something happens in baseball. For another, the level of competition in college is pretty high in baseball, especially in the Pac-10. I had to learn how to pitch before I ever got to the minor leagues."

Not surprisingly, Mark Marques, who was instrumental in elevating Stanford University's baseball team to national prominence, has a strong belief in the future of the college system. "We're better than we were fifteen years ago," he says. "You'll get some arguments. A lot of people say we've got to get them out of high school because those college coaches screw them all up. But we're doing a good job of training, even though the majority of our players won't be professional players.

"The minor leagues, in most cases, are losing money, and I think over the long haul we're helping them. If you're a scout, it's much easier to evaluate a twenty-year-old and project what he will do down the road than it is with an eighteen-year-old. We have the

same problem in recruiting each year. There's a lot of luck involved for both of us. You never know. My point is, we're training them as well as the low minor leagues. If your eighteen-year-old son is considering college, and he has the grades and background to get into schools like this one, he's going to college. That's just the thing to do. The risky thing is to sign, not get your degree, and not make it. The big advantage for us is the power of the degree. The baseball takes care of itself."

In general, baseball has always taken care of itself, although there have been scandals. The Chicago White Sox threw the 1919 World Series to the Cincinnati Reds. Pete Rose of those same Reds was himself snared on gambling charges in 1989, when baseball officials accused him of betting on the team he managed. By the end of the season, he had been banned from baseball for life. Recently, baseball has suffered a number of bad hops.

"In the last ten or fifteen years, baseball has had to go through a series of dislocations, new elements with no niche, no fit," said A. Bartlett Giamatti, baseball's former commissioner. "Free agency has been an economic dislocation that baseball has had to learn to handle. In fact, there are a whole new set of forces to which baseball must come to some sense of balance, some sense of poise and equilibrium. My priorities? Well, I'm not going to sit here and decide if equal opportunity is more important than [fighting] drugs. You can't sit here and make neat categories about social forces that must be managed so that people don't die or have a chance to fulfill themselves. All institutions go through these changes."

Expansion, Giamatti reported, is inevitable. "There are other more immediate issues, but in time there will be expansion. At first, there will be no more than two new teams in the National league. There will be labor questions if there is going to be expansion. There has to be a view that would look to the redesign of the major league player contract. There has to be a whole set of intelligent strategies on the part of the commissioner's office and the two leagues in regard to amateur baseball. We can all argue how long the player pool will be diluted by expansion, but we can't argue that it isn't."

With the proliferation of cable television, could there be a time in the foreseeable future when the World Series might be presented by an entity other than the major networks? "Pay-per-view in the playoffs or World Series? Not in my view," Giamatti said. "As far as I'm concerned, that will not happen unless the market changes dramatically. I'm told that overall, the numbers of people watching the network have gone down. If in fact there is a tipping point where perhaps more people do see it on cable all year, then I suppose you take the market into consideration."

Under Peter Ueberroth, who served as commissioner of baseball from 1984 through 1988, baseball began to offer more management opportunities to minorities, and this trend continued under Bartlett Giamatti. "In baseball, you're not dealing with entities that take federal funds," he said. "Therefore, you are not dealing with entities that are obliged by law to do it [integrate] voluntarily. Baseball is doing as it must and should. That is, after all, how baseball—ahead of most American institutions, including the Army, the public schools, or anything else—integrated itself in 1947. Voluntarily.

"That decision [to sign Jackie Robinson] was a massive promise made to this country: that people would play on a level field and that the history of racism in baseball was over. Well, it had better be over. It

shouldn't be just for players, but for anyone who believes he or she has a skill or talent that ought to compete with others. It doesn't mandate this person or that person. I'm not going to sit here and say who should be hired. But I will sit here and expunge any vestige [of small-mindedness] that says some group defined by sex or race is going to have a better purchase on getting a job than others. That's just not the way I want it to work."

The designated hitter may always be a part of baseball. Then again . . . "I know the designated hitter is something I don't like," Giamatti admitted. "I never said that I did. I'm not going to do anything about it. It does not rise as an issue to engage the commissioner's 'best interest of baseball' powers. It's the best non-life-threatening controversy in baseball. I would rather have it resolved by the same mechanism that put it in place. That is to say, if the league that adopted it would like to think it through again, I would be delighted. Because the league that didn't adopt it is not about to.

"If you ask me what I would get rid of, artificial surfaces or the DH, I'd get rid of the artificial surfaces, and I'd do it for the players; the player who can't tell if the ball is going to bounce three inches or seven inches from one surface to another, or who has to go from grass to the other. My interest in fundamental places is to provide an environment where a player can finally perform at his best."

APPENDICES

MOST VALUABLE PLAYER AWARD WINNERS

AS VOTED BY THE BASEBALL WRITERS' ASSOCIATION

NATIONAL LEAGUE

1931 Frank Frisch, St. Louis	1953 Roy Campanella, Brooklyn	1975 Joe Morgan, Cincinnati
1932 Charles Klein, Philadelphia	1954 Willie Mays, New York	1976 Joe Morgan, Cincinnati
1933 Carl Hubbell, New York	1955 Roy Campanella, Brooklyn	1977 George Foster, Cincinnati
1934 Dizzy Dean, St. Louis	1956 Don Newcombe, Brooklyn	1978 Dave Parker, Pittsburgh
1935 Gabby Hartnett, Chicago	1957 Henry Aaron, Milwaukee	1979 (tie) Willie Stargell, Pittsburgh
1936 Carl Hubbell, New York	1958 Ernie Banks, Chicago	Keith Hernandez, St. Louis
1937 Joe Medwick, St. Louis	1959 Ernie Banks, Chicago	1980 Mike Schmidt, Philadelphia
1938 Ernie Lombardi, Cincinnati	1960 Dick Groat, Pittsburgh	1981 Mike Schmidt, Philadelphia
1939 Bucky Walters, Cincinnati	1961 Frank Robinson, Cincinnati	1982 Dale Murphy, Atlanta
1940 Frank McCormick, Cincinnati	1962 Maury Wills, Los Angeles	1983 Dale Murphy, Atlanta
1941 Dolph Camilli, Brooklyn	1963 Sandy Koufax, Los Angeles	1984 Ryne Sandberg, Chicago
1942 Mort Cooper, St. Louis	1964 Ken Boyer, St. Louis	1985 Willie McGee, St. Louis
1943 Stan Musial, St. Louis	1965 Willie Mays, San Francisco	1986 Mike Schmidt, Philadelphia
1944 Martin Marion, St. Louis	1966 Roberto Clemente, Pittsburgh	1987 Andre Dawson, Chicago
1945 Phil Cavarretta, Chicago	1967 Orlando Cepeda, St. Louis	1988 Kirk Gibson, Los Angeles
1946 Stan Musial, St. Louis	1968 Bob Gibson, St. Louis	1989 Kevin Mitchell, San Francisco
1947 Bob Elliott, Boston	1969 Willie McCovey, San Francisco	1990 Barry Bonds, Pittsburgh
1948 Stan Musial, St. Louis	1970 Johnny Bench, Cincinnati	1991 Terry Pendleton, Atlanta
1949 Jackie Robinson, Brooklyn	1971 Joe Torre, St. Louis	1992 Barry Bonds, Pittsburgh
1950 Jim Konstanty, Philadelphia	1972 Johnny Bench, Cincinnati	1993 Barry Bonds, San Francisco
1951 Roy Campanella, Brooklyn	1973 Pete Rose, Cincinnati	
1952 Hank Sauer, Chicago	1974 Steve Garvey, Los Angeles	

AMERICAN LEAGUE

1931 Lefty Grove, Philadelphia	1952 Bobby Shantz, Philadelphia	1973 Reggie Jackson, Oakland
1932 Jimmy Foxx, Philadelphia	1953 Al Rosen, Cleveland	1974 Jeff Burroughs, Texas
1933 Jimmy Foxx, Philadelphia	1954 Yogi Berra, New York	1975 Fred Lynn, Boston
1934 Mickey Cochrane, Detroit	1955 Yogi Berra, New York	1976 Thurman Munson, New York
1935 Henry Greenberg, Detroit	1956 Mickey Mantle, New York	1977 Rod Carew, Minnesota
1936 Lou Gehrig, New York	1957 Mickey Mantle, New York	1978 Jim Rice, Boston
1937 Charles Gehringer, Detroit	1958 Jackie Jensen, Boston	1979 Don Baylor, California
1938 Jimmy Foxx, Boston	1959 Nellie Fox, Chicago	1980 George Brett, Kansas City
1939 Joe DiMaggio, New York	1960 Roger Maris, New York	1981 Rollie Fingers, Milwaukee
1940 Hank Greenberg, Detroit	1961 Roger Maris, New York	1982 Robin Yount, Milwaukee
1941 Joe DiMaggio, New York	1962 Mickey Mantle, New York	1983 Cal Ripken Jr., Baltimore
1942 Joe Gordon, New York	1963 Elston Howard, New York	1984 Willie Hernandez, Detroit
1943 Spurgeon Chandler, New York	1964 Brooks Robinson, Baltimore	1985 Don Mattingly, New York
1944 Hal Newhouser, Detroit	1965 Zoila Versailles, Minnesota	1986 Rober Clemens, Boston
1945 Hal Newhouser, Detroit	1966 Frank Robinson, Baltimore	1987 George Bell, Toronto
1946 Ted Williams, Boston	1967 Carl Yastrzemski, Boston	1988 Jose Canseco, Oakland
1947 Joe DiMaggio, New York	1968 Denny McLain, Detroit	1989 Robin Yount, Milwaukee
1948 Lou Boudreau, Cleveland	1969 Harmon Killebrew, Minnesota	1990 Rickey Henderson, Oakland
1949 Ted Williams, Boston	1970 John (Boog) Powell, Baltimore	1991 Cal Ripken, Baltimore
1950 Phil Rizzuto, New York	1971 Vida Blue, Oakland	1992 Dennis Eckersley, Oakland
1951 Yogi Berra, New York	1972 Dick Allen, Chicago	1993 Frank Thomas, Chicago

WORLD SERIES RESULTS

1903 Boston AL 5, Pittsburgh NL 3	1934 St. Louis NL 4, Detroit AL 3	1965 Los Angeles NL 4, Minnesota AL 3
1904 No series	1935 Detroit AL 4, Chicago NL 2	1966 Baltimore AL 4, Los Angeles NL 0
1905 New York NL 4, Philadelphia AL 1	1936 New York AL 4, New York NL 2	1967 St. Louis NL 4, Boston Al 3
1906 Chicago AL 4, Chicago NL 2	1937 New York AL 4, New York NL 2	1968 Detroit AL 4, St. Louis NL 3
1907 Chicago NL 4, Detroit AL 0, 1 tie	1938 New York AL 4, Chicago NL 0	1969 New York NL 4, Baltimore AL 1
1908 Chicago NL 4, Detroit AL 1	1939 New York AL 4, Cincinnati NL 0	1970 Baltimore AL 4, Cincinnati NL 1
1909 Pittsburgh NL 4, Detroit AL 3	1940 Cincinnati NL 4, Detroit AL 3	1971 Pittsburgh NL 4, Baltimore AL 3
1910 Philadelphia AL 4, Chicago NL 1	1941 New York AL 4, St. Louis NL 1	1972 Oakland AL 4, Cincinnati NL 3
1911 Philadelphia AL 4, New York NL 2	1942 St. Louis NL 4, New York AL 1	1973 Oakland AL 4, New York NL 3
1912 Boston AL 4, New York NL 3, 1 tie	1943 New York AL 4, St. Louis NL 1	1974 Oakland AL 4, Los Angeles NL 1
1913 Philadelphia AL 4, New York NL 1	1944 St. Louis NL 4, St. Louis AL 2	1975 Cincinnati NL 4, Boston AL 3
1914 Boston NL 4, Philadelphia AL 0	1945 Detroit AL 4, Chicago NL 3	1976 Cincinnati NL 4, New York AL 0
1915 Boston AL 4, Philadelphia NL 1	1946 St. Louis NL 4, Boston AL 3	1977 New York AL 4, Los Angeles NL 2
1916 Boston AL 4, Brooklyn NL 1	1947 New York AL 4, Brooklyn NL 3	1978 New York AL 4, Los Angeles NL 2
1917 Chicago AL 4, New York NL 2	1948 Cleveland AL 4, Boston NL 2	1979 Pittsburgh NL 4, Baltimore AL 3
1918 Boston AL 4, Chicago NL 2	1949 New York AL 4, Brooklyn NL 1	1980 Philadelphia NL 4, Kansas City AL 2
1919 Cincinnati NL 5, Chicago AL 3	1950 New York AL 4, Philadelphia NL 0	1981 Los Angeles NL 4, New York AL 2
1920 Cleveland AL 5, Brooklyn NL 2	1951 New York AL 4, New York NL 2	1982 St. Louis NL 4, Milwaukee AL 3
1921 New York NL 5, New York AL 3	1952 New York AL 4, Brooklyn NL 3	1983 Baltimore AL 4, Philadelphia NL 1
1922 New York NL 4, New York AL 0, 1 tie	1953 New York AL 4, Brooklyn NL 2	1984 Detroit AL 4, San Diego NL 1
1923 New York AL 4, New York NL 2	1954 New York NL 4, Cleveland AL 0	1985 Kansas City AL 4, St. Louis NL 3
1924 Washington AL 4, New York NL 3	1955 Brooklyn NL 4, New York AL 3	1986 New York NL 4, Boston AL 3
1925 Pittsburgh NL 4, Washington AL 3	1956 New York AL 4, Brooklyn NL 3	1987 Minnesota AL 4, St. Louis NL 3
1926 St. Louis NL 4, New York AL 3	1957 Milwaukee NL 4, New York AL 3	1988 Los Angeles NL 4, Oakland AL 1
1927 New York AL 4, Pittsburgh NL 0	1958 New York AL 4, Milwaukee NL 3	1989 Oakland AL 4, San Francisco NL 0
1928 New York AL 4, St. Louis NL 0	1959 Los Angeles NL 4, Chicago AL 2	1990 Cincinnati NL 4, Oakland AL 0
1929 Philadelphia AL 4, Chicago NL 1	1960 Pittsburgh NL 4, New York AL 3	1991 Minnesota AL 4, Atlanta NL 3
1930 Philadelphia AL 4, St. Louis NL 3	1961 New York AL 4, Cincinnati NL 1	1992 Toronto AL 4, Atlanta NL 2
1931 St. Louis NL 4, Philadelphia AL 3	1962 New York AL 4, San Francisco NL 3	1993 Toronto AL 4, Philadelphia NL 2
1932 New York AL 4, Chicago NL 0	1963 Los Angeles NL 4, New York AL 0	
1933 New York NL 4, Washington AL 1	1964 St. Louis NL 4, New York AL 3	

© AP/Wide World Photos

© AP/Wide World Photos

PENNANT WINNERS –National League

Year	Winner	Won	Lost	Pct	Year	Winner	Won	Lost	Pct
1901	Pittsburgh	90	49	.647	1935	Chicago	100	54	.649
1902	Pittsburgh	103	36	.741	1936	New York	91	62	.597
1903	Pittsburgh	91	49	.650	1937	New York	95	57	.625
1904	New York	106	47	.693	1938	Chicago	89	63	.586
1905	New York	105	48	.686	1939	Cincinnati	97	57	.630
1906	Chicago	116	36	.763	1940	Cincinnati	100	53	.654
1907	Chicago	107	45	.704	1941	Brooklyn	100	54	.649
1908	Chicago	99	55	.643	1942	St. Louis	106	48	.688
1909	Pittsburgh	110	42	.724	1943	St. Louis	105	49	.682
1910	Chicago	104	50	.675	1944	St. Louis	105	49	.682
1911	New York	99	54	.647	1945	Chicago	98	56	.636
1912	New York	103	48	.682	1946	St. Louis	98	58	.628
1913	New York	101	51	.664	1947	Brooklyn	94	60	.610
1914	Boston	94	59	.614	1948	Boston	91	62	.595
1915	Philadelphia	90	62	.592	1949	Brooklyn	97	57	.630
1916	Brooklyn	94	60	.610	1950	Philadelphia	91	63	.591
1917	New York	98	56	.636	1951	New York	98	59	.624
1918	Chicago	84	45	.651	1952	Brooklyn	96	57	.627
1919	Cincinnati	96	44	.606	1953	Brooklyn	105	49	.682
1920	Brooklyn	93	60	.604	1954	New York	97	57	.630
1921	New York	94	56	.614	1955	Brooklyn	98	55	.641
1922	New York	93	61	.604	1956	Brooklyn	93	61	.604
1923	New York	95	58	.621	1957	Milwaukee	95	59	.617
1924	New York	93	60	.608	1958	Milwaukee	92	62	.597
1925	Pittsburgh	95	58	.621	1959	Los Angeles	88	68	.564
1926	St. Louis	89	65	.578	1960	Pittsburgh	95	59	.617
1927	Pittsburgh	94	60	.610	1961	Cincinnati	93	61	.604
1928	St. Louis	95	59	.617	1962	San Francisco	103	62	.624
1929	Chicago	98	54	.645	1963	Los Angeles	99	63	.611
1930	St. Louis	92	62	.597	1964	St. Louis	93	69	.574
1931	St. Louis	101	53	.656	1965	Los Angeles	97	65	.599
1932	Chicago	90	64	.584	1966	Los Angeles	95	67	.586
1933	New York	91	61	.599	1967	St. Louis	101	60	.627
1934	St. Louis	95	58	.621	1968	St. Louis	97	65	.599

East Year	Winner	W	L	Pct	West Winner	W	L	Pct	Playoff Winner
1969	N.Y. Mets	100	62	.617	Atlanta	93	69	.574	N.Y. Mets
1970	Pittsburgh	89	73	.549	Cincinnati	102	60	.630	Cincinnati
1971	Pittsburgh	97	65	.599	San Francisco	90	72	.556	Pittsburgh
1972	Pittsburgh	96	59	.619	Cincinnati	95	59	.617	Cincinnati
1973	N.Y. Mets	82	79	.509	Cincinnati	99	63	.611	N.Y. Mets
1974	Pittsburgh	88	74	.543	Los Angeles	102	60	.630	Los Angeles
1975	Pittsburgh	92	69	.571	Cincinnati	108	54	.667	Cincinnati
1976	Philadelphia	101	61	.623	Cincinnati	102	60	.630	Cincinnati
1977	Philadelphia	101	61	.623	Los Angeles	98	64	.605	Los Angeles
1978	Philadelphia	90	72	.556	Los Angeles	95	67	.586	Los Angeles
1979	Pittsburgh	98	64	.605	Cincinnati	90	71	.559	Pittsburgh
1980	Philadelphia	91	71	.562	Houston	93	70	.571	Philadelphia
1981	Philadelphia	34	21	.618	Los Angeles	36	21	.632	Los Angeles
1981	Montreal	30	23	.566	Houston	33	20	.623	Montreal
1982	St. Louis	92	70	.588	Atlanta	89	73	.549	St. Louis
1983	Philadelphia	90	72	.556	Los Angeles	91	71	.562	Philadelphia
1984	Chicago	96	65	.596	San Diego	92	70	.568	San Diego
1985	St. Louis	101	61	.623	Los Angeles	95	67	.586	St. Louis
1986	N.Y. Mets	108	54	.667	Houston	96	66	.593	N.Y. Mets
1987	St. Louis	95	67	.586	San Francisco	90	72	.556	St. Louis
1988	N.Y. Mets	100	60	.625	Los Angeles	94	67	.584	Los Angeles
1989	Chicago	93	69	.571	San Francisco	92	70	.568	San Francisco
1990	Pittsburgh	95	67	.586	Cincinnati	91	71	.562	Cincinnati
1991	Pittsburgh	98	64	.605	Atlanta	94	68	.580	Atlanta
1992	Pittsburgh	96	66	.593	Atlanta	98	64	.605	Atlanta
1993	Philadelphia	97	65	.599	Atlanta	104	58	.642	Philadelphia

*Due to the 1981 players' strike, there were four divisional winners (instead of two), and two pennant winners (instead of one) in each league.

PENNANT WINNERS –American League

Year	Winner	Won	Lost	Pct	Year	Winner	Won	Lost	Pct
1901	Chicago	83	53	.610	1935	Detroit	93	58	.616
1902	Philadelphia	83	53	.610	1936	New York	102	51	.667
1903	Boston	91	47	.659	1937	New York	102	52	.662
1904	Boston	95	59	.617	1938	New York	99	53	.651
1905	Philadelphia	92	56	.622	1939	New York	106	45	.702
1906	Chicago	93	58	.616	1940	Detroit	90	64	.584
1907	Detroit	92	58	.613	1941	New York	101	53	.656
1908	Detroit	90	63	.588	1942	New York	103	51	.669
1909	Detroit	98	54	.645	1943	New York	98	56	.636
1910	Philadelphia	102	48	.680	1944	St. Louis	89	65	.578
1911	Philadelphia	101	50	.669	1945	Detroit	88	65	.575
1912	Boston	105	47	.691	1946	Boston	104	50	.675
1913	Philadelphia	96	57	.627	1947	New York	97	57	.630
1914	Philadelphia	99	53	.651	1948	Cleveland	97	58	.626
1915	Boston	101	50	.669	1949	New York	97	57	.630
1916	Boston	91	63	.591	1950	New York	98	56	.636
1917	Chicago	100	54	.649	1951	New York	98	56	.636
1918	Boston	75	51	.595	1952	New York	95	59	.617
1919	Chicago	88	52	.629	1953	New York	99	52	.656
1920	Cleveland	98	56	.636	1954	Cleveland	111	43	.721
1921	New York	98	55	.641	1955	New York	96	58	.623
1922	New York	94	60	.610	1956	New York	97	57	.630
1923	New York	98	54	.645	1957	New York	98	56	.636
1924	Washington	92	62	.597	1958	New York	92	62	.597
1925	Washington	96	55	.636	1959	Chicago	94	60	.610
1926	New York	91	63	.591	1960	New York	97	57	.630
1927	New York	110	44	.714	1961	New York	109	53	.673
1928	New York	101	53	.656	1962	New York	96	66	.593
1929	Philadelphia	104	46	.693	1963	New York	104	57	.646
1930	Philadelphia	102	52	.662	1964	New York	99	63	.611
1931	Philadelphia	107	45	.704	1965	Minnesota	102	60	.630
1932	New York	107	47	.695	1966	Baltimore	97	63	.606
1933	Washington	99	53	.651	1967	Boston	92	70	.568
1934	Detroit	101	53	.656	1968	Detroit	103	59	.636

East					West				
Year	Winner	W	L	Pct	Winner	W	L	Pct	Playoff Winner
1969	Baltimore	109	53	.673	Minnesota	97	65	.599	Baltimore
1970	Baltimore	108	54	.667	Minnesota	98	64	.605	Baltimore
1971	Baltimore	101	57	.639	Oakland	101	60	.627	Baltimore
1972	Detroit	86	70	.551	Oakland	93	62	.600	Oakland
1973	Baltimore	97	65	.599	Oakland	94	68	.580	Oakland
1974	Baltimore	91	71	.562	Oakland	90	72	.556	Oakland
1975	Boston	95	65	.594	Oakland	98	64	.605	Boston
1976	N.Y. Yankees	97	62	.610	Kansas City	90	72	.556	N.Y. Yankees
1977	N.Y. Yankees	100	62	.617	Kansas City	102	60	.630	N.Y. Yankees
1978	N.Y. Yankees	100	63	.613	Kansas City	92	70	.568	N.Y. Yankees
1979	Baltimore	102	57	.642	California	88	74	.543	Baltimore
1980	N.Y. Yankees	103	59	.636	Kansas City	97	65	.599	Kansas City
1981	N.Y. Yankees	34	22	.607	Oakland	37	23	.617	N.Y. Yankees
1981	Milwaukee	31	22	.585	Kansas City	30	23	.566	Kansas City
1982	Milwaukee	95	67	.586	California	93	69	.574	Milwaukee
1983	Baltimore	98	64	.605	Chicago	99	63	.611	Baltimore
1984	Detroit	104	58	.642	Kansas City	84	78	.519	Detroit
1985	Toronto	99	62	.615	Kansas City	91	71	.562	Kansas City
1986	Boston	95	66	.590	California	92	70	.568	Boston
1987	Detroit	98	64	.605	Minnesota	85	77	.525	Minnesota
1988	Boston	89	73	.549	Oakland	104	58	.642	Oakland
1989	Toronto	89	73	.549	Oakland	99	63	.611	Oakland
1990	Boston	88	74	.543	Oakland	103	59	.636	Oakland
1991	Toronto	91	71	.562	Minnesota	95	57	.586	Minnesota
1992	Toronto	96	66	.593	Oakland	96	66	.593	Toronto
1993	Toronto	95	67	.586	Chicago	94	68	.580	Toronto

*Due to the 1981 players' strike, there were four divisional winners (instead of two), and two pennant winners (instead of one) in each league.

HALL OF FAME MEMBERS

PITCHERS IN THE HALL OF FAME

Grover Alexander
Chief Bender
Mordecai Brown
Jack Chesbro
John Clarkson
Stan Coveleski
Dizzy Dean
Don Drysdale
Red Faber
Bob Feller
Rollie Fingers
Whitey Ford
Pud Galvin
Bob Gibson
Lefty Gomez
Burleigh Grimes
Lefty Grove
Jess Haines
Waite Hoyt
Carl Hubbell
Catfish Hunter
Ferguson Jenkins
Walter Johnson
Addie Joss
Tim Keete

Sandy Koufax
Bob Lemon
Ted Lyons
Juan Marichal
Rube Marquard
Christy Mathewson
Joe McGinnity
Kid Nichols
Jim Palmer
Herb Pennock
Gaylord Perry
Eddie Plank
Old Hoss Radbourne
Eppa Rixey
Robin Roberts
Red Ruffing
Amos Rusie
Tom Seaver
Warren Spahn
Dazzy Vance
Rube Waddell
Ed Walsh
Mickey Welch
Hoyt Wilhelm
Early Wynn
Cy Young

CATCHERS IN THE HALL OF FAME

Johnny Bench
Yogi Berra
Roger Bresnahan
Roy Campanella
Mickey Cochrane
Bill Dickey

Buck Ewing
Rick Ferrell
Gabby Hartnett
Ernie Lombardi
Ray Schalk

FIRST BASEMEN IN THE HALL OF FAME

Cap Anson
Jake Beckley
Jim Bottomley
Dan Brouthers
Rod Carew
Frank Chance
Roger Connor
Jimmie Foxx
Lou Gehrig

Hank Greenberg
George Kelly
Harmon Killebrew
Willie McCovey
Johnny Mize
George Sisler
Willie Stargell
Bill Terry

SECOND BASEMEN IN THE HALL OF FAME

Eddie Collins
Bobby Doerr
Johnny Evers
Frankie Frisch
Charlie Gehringer

Billy Herman
Rogers Hornsby
Nap Lajoie
Joe Morgan
Jackie Robinson

SHORTSTOPS IN THE HALL OF FAME

Luis Aparicio
Luke Appling
Dave Bancroft
Ernie Banks
Lou Boudreau
Joe Cronin
Travis Jackson
Hugh Jennings

Rabbit Maranville
Pee Wee Reese
Joe Sewell
Joe Tinker
Arky Vaughan
Honus Wagner
Bobby Wallace
Monte Ward

THIRD BASEMEN IN THE HALL OF FAME

Frank Baker
Jimmy Collins
George Kell
Fred Lindstrom

Eddie Mathews
Brooks Robinson
Pie Traynor

LEFT FIELDERS IN THE HALL OF FAME

Lou Brock
Jesse Burkett
Fred Clarke
Ed Delahanty
Goose Goslin
Chick Hafey
Joe Kelley
Ralph Kiner
Heinie Manush

Joe Medwick
Stan Musial
Jim O'Rourke
Al Simmons
Zack Wheat
Billy Williams
Ted Williams
Carl Yastrzemski

CENTER FIELDERS IN THE HALL OF FAME

Earl Averill
Max Carey
Ty Cobb
Earle Combs
Joe DiMaggio
Hugh Duffy
Billy Hamilton

Mickey Mantle
Willie Mays
Edd Roush
Duke Snider
Tris Speaker
Lloyd Waner
Hack Wilson

RIGHT FIELDERS IN THE HALL OF FAME

Hank Aaron	Chuck Klein
Roberto Clemente	Tommy McCarthy
Sam Crawford	Mel Ott
Kiki Cuyler	Sam Rice
Elmer Flick	Frank Robinson
Harry Heilmann	Babe Ruth
Harry Hooper	Enos Slaughter
Reggie Jackson	Sam Thompson
Al Kaline	Paul Waner
Willie Keeler	Ross Youngs
King Kelly	

PIONEERS AND EXECUTIVES IN THE HALL OF FAME

Ed Barrow	Will Harridge
Morgan Buckeley	Ben Johnson
Alexander Cartwright	Kenesaw Mountain Landis
Henry Chadwick	Larry McPhail
Albert Chandler	Branch Rickey
Charles Comiskey	Al Spalding
Candy Cummings	George Weiss
Ford Frick	George Wright
Warren Giles	Harry Wright
Clark Griffith	Tom Yawkey

MEMBERS IN THE HALL OF FAME FROM THE NEGRO LEAGUES

Cool Papa Bell	Monte Irvin
Oscar Charleston	Judy Johnson
Ray Dandridge	Buck Leonard
Martin Dihigo	John Lloyd
Rube Foster	Satchel Paige
Josh Gibson	

MANAGERS IN THE HALL OF FAME

Walter Alston	Joe McCarthy
Bucky Harris	John McGraw
Miller Huggins	Bill McKechnie
Al Lopez	Wilbert Robinson
Connie Mack	Casey Stengel

UMPIRES IN THE HALL OF FAME

Jocko Conlan	Cal Hubbard
Tom Connolly	Bill Klem
Billy Evans	

USEFUL ADDRESSES

AMERICAN LEAGUE

American League Office
350 Park Ave.
New York, NY 10022

Baltimore Orioles
Memorial Stadium
Baltimore, MD 21218

Boston Red Sox
24 Yawkey Way
Boston, MA 02215

California Angels
Anaheim Stadium
Anaheim, CA 92806

Chicago White Sox
324 W. 35th St.
Chicago, IL 60616

Cleveland Indians
Cleveland Stadium
Cleveland, OH 44114

Detroit Tigers
Tiger Stadium
Detroit, MI 48216

Kansas City Royals
Harry S. Truman Sports Complex
Kansas City, MO 64141

Milwaukee Brewers
Milwaukee County Stadium
Milwaukee, WI 53214

Minnesota Twins
501 Chicago Ave. South
Minneapolis, MN 55415

New York Yankees
Yankee Stadium
Bronx, NY 10451

Oakland A's
Oakland Coliseum
Oakland, CA 94621

Seattle Mariners
100 S. King St.
Seattle, WA 98104

Texas Rangers
1200 Copeland Rd.
Arlington, TX 76011

Toronto Blue Jays
Box 7777
Adelaide St. PO
Toronto, Ont. M5C 2K7

NATIONAL LEAGUE

National League Office
350 Park Ave.
New York, NY 10022

Atlanta Braves
PO Box 4064
Atlanta, GA 30302

Chicago Cubs
Wrigley Field
Chicago, IL 60613

Cincinnati Reds
100 Riverfront Stadium
Cincinnati, OH 45202

Colorado Rockies
1700 Broadway
Denver, CO 80290

Florida Marlins
100 NE Third Ave.
Ft. Lauderdale, FL 33301

Houston Astros
Astrodome
Houston, TX 77001

Los Angeles Dodgers
Dodger Stadium
Los Angeles, CA 90012

Montreal Expos
PO Box 500, Station M
Montreal, Que. H1V 3P2

New York Mets
Shea Stadium
Flushing, NY 11368

Philadelphia Phillies
PO Box 7575
Philadelphia, PA 19101

Pittsburgh Pirates
Three Rivers Stadium
Pittsburgh, PA 15212

St. Louis Cardinals
Busch Stadium
St. Louis, MO 63102

San Diego Padres
PO Box 2000
San Diego, CA 92120

San Francisco Giants
Candlestick Park
San Francisco, CA 94124

Baseball Commissioner's Office
350 Park Ave.
New York, NY 10022

INDEX

Page numbers in italics refer to captions, illustrations, and sidebars.